"Your 'Tor-tell-ah's' Upside Down!"

"Your 'Tor-tell-ah's' Upside Down!"

Spiritual Evolution on the Flip Side

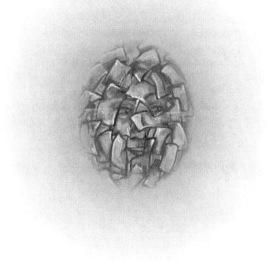

Cynthia Boulton

Copyright © 2012 by Cynthia Boulton.

Cover art by Richard Mazzola
www.mazzolagallery.com

Library of Congress Control Number:		2012906569
ISBN:	Hardcover	978-1-4691-9732-6
	Softcover	978-1-4691-9731-9
	Ebook	978-1-4691-9733-3

All rights reserved. No part of this book may be reproduced or transmitted in any form or by any means, electronic or mechanical, including photocopying, recording, or by any information storage and retrieval system, without permission in writing from the copyright owner.

This book was printed in the United States of America.

To order additional copies of this book, contact:
Xlibris Corporation
1-888-795-4274
www.Xlibris.com
Orders@Xlibris.com

"Out beyond ideas of wrongdoing and rightdoing there is a field. I'll meet you there."

—Rumi

AUTHOR'S NOTE

The spiritual journey is a bit like stepping onto a glass field of brightly colored marbles. By the time the quick step is over, you find yourself in places never imagined.

In this time of unprecedented shifts, we find ourselves scrambling for ballast. Our hopes and fears are laid before us daily as we make choices out of the chaos of new creation. I am inviting you to share in my odyssey which ultimately calls us all to face our darkest secrets, our deepest truths, and our divine co-creative dance.

May this book challenge you to step beyond duality and "safe territories" to a path uniquely your own, judgments be damned! For after all, who is to decide if our "tor-tell-ah" is right side up or upside down?

With deepest gratitude to my family who provided the love and support I needed to face the challenges of this life and the "angel brigade" who stood with me during those challenges.

Special thanks to my dear friends Ginny and Heidi. These two suffered through what Anne Lamott, my favorite author, describes perfectly—"shitty first drafts." Thank you, dear friends, for hours of proofing and encouragement. Your support was and still is priceless.

Finally to my partner Stephanie, whose courage to be who she was created to be serves as a living example of what this book is about.

CONTENTS

Chapter 1	DIXIE	2
Chapter 2	DEWARD	12
Chapter 3	THE ROCK	22
Chapter 4	SCREAMING TUCANS	32
Chapter 5	SAVING SISTER PEGGY	42
Chapter 6	ANGELS AND VISIONS	56
Chapter 7	OWNEE'S WORLD	68
Chapter 8	NO BOOTSTRAPS	78
Chapter 9	THE DANCE OF THE POLAR BEAR	98
Chapter 10	LEAVING	120
Chapter 11	HAPPY STREET	132
Chapter 12	THE HOT COAL CHA-CHA	150
Chapter 13	CRYSTALS, OBELISKS, AND ENERGY	166
Chapter 14	"LIVING JOYUS"	180
Chapter 15	VISITORS ON DEARBORN	198
Chapter 16	"JUST A LIVIN'"	214
Chapter 17	THE ALPHA, THE OMEGA	222

CHAPTER 1

What is it that causes us to seek refuge in being the same? Walking reflections of what we see outside ourselves, we mirror back a parroted existence like spoons stacked neatly in a kitchen drawer. Longing so desperately to align with another, we make the ultimate sacrifice. We extinguish the expression of our true self, losing our way and stumbling into arrangements unintended.

Our possibilities are limitless and infinite, our diversity so beautiful it cannot be described but must be lived in a rhythm that is uniquely our own. Each of us brings to the dance our one clear note that we alone express for creation. With enlightenment or without, when in alignment with our divinity, the tone rings clear.

DIXIE

WE REALLY DON'T HAVE TO look far or have to walk on the planet for too many years before we begin to notice our differences. Then, because we live in a world of duality, we become acutely aware of "right-wrong," "good-bad," "acceptable," and "have you lost your mind?"

On the other hand, when our parallel journeys intersect and we are touched by another, we observe our similarity. Although unique in our being, we are still much the same. We want to love and be loved. We want to be heard. Somewhere within our deepest longing is the need to feel like we are following the "right" path—which, of course, is duality at its finest!

Growing up in the South was slow and easy, like pouring molasses. Oh, I guess if you're not from the South, you don't know about our Southern delicacy, do you? Molasses is a thick, dark syrup. You pour it on your plate and mix it with rich creamy butter. Then you take a hot, steaming biscuit, break it open slowly and drag it through your creation with a little twisting motion at the end to break the clinging string of sticky moisture from its source. Bringing it to your mouth quickly, you taste the sweetness mixed with just a hint of bitter. A description lived into, bite by bite. Growing up in the South is sweet, slow, a little twisted, with just a hint of bitter, but then all life has just a hint of bitter. That is why we so enjoy the sweet.

Telling stories is a way of life in Dixie. We take the time to tell a good story, giving attention to all the details. Oral tradition is still alive and well. We love to laugh at ourselves while we bring to life the characters that have entertained us, enchanting our listeners with images larger than life. Accuracy is not so important, but it must be colorful, otherwise, what's the use of telling it?

These stories are told around the kitchen table, in the churchyard, or across the neighbor's fence. I have sat for what felt like an eternity on a two-lane winding road, the only road on this particular patch of earth that can get you from here to there. With work to do and a job waiting, irritation begins to creep into your hurried mind. No matter, both lanes are blocked, while the drivers chat with each other through their car windows. No rush, just being in the moment. You wouldn't dare honk your horn, an action considered rude beyond words. After all, this interchange is sacred. You are witness to the love and concern of two neighbors. From your vantage point, you understand this is their daily bread, revealed before you on the altar of this asphalt artery. Never mind this particular artery is the only way for you to get to work.

So you learn to slow down, you learn there are more important things than arriving at your destination. It's a great practice for being in the moment. Might just as well look around, soak up the scenery, notice the birds singing, or close your eyes, and breathe in the fragrance of the fresh-mown fields of hay alongside the road. At the same time, you're hoping there is not a pig farm within the radius of your olfactory senses startling you back to the reality of country living. Guess you might look at it as the Southern practice of mindfulness, meditation in a way. Although it is important for you to understand, meditation or any of the other practices of the East—may be frowned upon in "God's country."

Buddha was never a part of the kitchen table conversation. I don't think I knew there was a Buddha until I was in my late twenties. However, I find it interesting that you learn a few of his tenets when growing up south of the Mason-Dixon Line or nearby. While living in the rural regions of Kentucky, I was forced into a quiet mindfulness, which becomes a rhythm for living. Not Buddhist, mind you, but the Southern Christian version of quiet mind. "Jesus is the reason for the season" in the South, and the season is 365 days long and yearly thereafter. There is no room for other tenants or queries; don't even go there.

The Southern Bible Belt is pretty tight. Not much room for moving left or right; you stay on the straight and narrow path, or else. The Bible holds the key to accommodate any dilemma or ethical decision you might be called on to make, and most folks there can quote it to you, scripture and verse. There are multiple flavors of the Christian traditions, and each one understands theirs is the key to eternity and truth—theirs and only theirs, thank you very much, amen. You cut your teeth on the fires of hell—not a place for the faint of heart. Dante has nothing on a good Southern Bible-thumping preacher.

My teething began in a very small Methodist church that sat quietly on a little hill in the country. When I say I grew up there, I mean it. When those doors were open, Momma had my little butt in the pew—which, for a Methodist, was usually three times a week for the regularly scheduled gatherings. On occasion a good old-fashioned revival would roll around, that would be every night of the week. Those wooden pews were hard, straight, and long—kind of like the sermons, no cushion between you and the oak.

The little frame church was always freshly painted stark white, cradled by a few massive oak trees standing as sentinels surrounding my bastion of truth, Trinity Methodist. We had many preachers over the years, but Brother Breedlove was my favorite. He was a big man, especially handsome with raven, black hair. One lock typically ended up curled over his brow as the sermons heated up. His dark eyes held a gentle intensity, reflecting his love. You could also see the fires of hell, depending on the message he was delivering. He was young, a bit chubby, and his deeply dimpled smile was contagious. It made you feel the joy of the Lord just by looking at him. He usually wore a dark blue suit with a matching narrow tie along with a crisply starched white shirt.

That man was passionate about his preaching. What started out as a slow, soft, serious conversation would build into such a frenzied crescendo, it could make the Baptists envious. They could probably hear him three miles down the road where their little bastion of truth stood, Hickory Baptist. He would raise his hand up to the heavens and then slam his fist down on the pulpit, startling awake the old men in the amen corner that had quietly drifted off to sleep. None of them ever had a heart attack, and I find that a miracle in itself. You have to believe in God after witnessing their survival.

I totally expected the pulpit to split half in two or watch Brother Breedlove's head pop off from the incredible force of his conviction. His face would turn blood red, sweat popping out on his forehead as he would pace back and forth, shaking his Bible in the air while explaining God's love and tender mercy followed by "You're going to hell!" Although we sang "Softly and Tenderly Jesus Is Calling," there wasn't anything soft or tender in the way Brother Breedlove told the story. By this time, his suit jacket was flung dramatically on the floor, his tie loose, cockeyed and catawampus around his neck. His white Sunday go-to-meeting shirtsleeves were rolled up and "ready for bear." I was convinced, present, and accounted for when it was time for the altar call, on several occasions. Although the Methodists believe once saved always saved, I didn't think it could hurt just in case the first time didn't take.

Now there is a part of the sweetness I told you about, the altar call. After all the shouting and testifying—as well as the violence inflicted on the pulpit, our psyche, and my pew-worn butt—the altar call would come. You could always count on it as you sang the final hymn. Silence would descend over the church while we sang, now alert, watching and waiting to see if someone would walk down the aisle. It was not unusual to find yourself holding your breath. There was such an expectant sense of wonder. So much was at stake in that moment—heaven or hell, in fact. Finally, after much begging and pleading, silent and aloud, someone would stand. Man, woman, or child would make their way down to the altar.

Joy and happiness would spread across the little church like a wave as the energy shifted from anticipation to relief. The hymn being sung would come alive as Brother Breedlove would open both his arms to greet them. It seemed to me the whole world could be embraced by those strong arms. Maybe it was on some multi-dimensional level. It was not unusual to see tears streaming down the big man's face that suddenly turned gentle and tender like the song. As a child in that moment, I felt like this must be what God's face looked like.

Kneeling at the altar meant stepping into a deeper, although human, awareness and understanding of an all-knowing, omnipotent God. Forgiveness for all shortcomings was granted, lifting the heavy weight that was once their mantle. Then, one by one, as the Spirit moved them, others would come and stand behind the chosen. They would stand there, a bit like the oak trees that graced the church lawn—quiet, unimposing, and strong. It was almost palpable, this deep faith and all-embracing love. If this lost sheep had ever felt alone, it was only a memory now. Today, they became one with the flock, brought back to the fold. They were home.

Much of the mystery surrounding religion in my childhood was about trying to figure out who was right. Never mind the Jewish, Hindu, Buddhist, Muslim, or Krishna; I didn't even know they existed. My worldview was a bit limited as a little white middle-class kid transplanted from the Midwest to the border of the Deep South. I just wanted to know who was right among the Baptists, Methodists, Pentecostals, Catholics, and Church of Christ members. The Catholics hardly counted either because they were segregated over in the other side of the county, and I never met one until I was sixteen.

My Aunt Margaret was a hardcore Southern Baptist, my father's sister, and one of my favorite aunts. She was my first introduction to something outside the boundaries of my Methodist experience. She taught the adult Sunday school class at Hickory Baptist and was well respected in the community. On any Saturday night, you would find her on the couch sitting next to the lamp, cheaters perched low on her nose and in her lap a well-worn Bible from which she studied regularly. Born somewhere in the middle of thirteen children just prior to the Great Depression, she was well acquainted with hard work and poverty. When Jesus said "feed my sheep," she took him quite literally. Not only did she feed his sheep with the Word of God she made it her business to be sure the children within her reach were not overlooked. If she knew there was a child in need, she had a hand in seeing they had clothes for school and food on the table. She probably never went hungry as a child but suffered what, for her, was humiliation in having, what she considered, less than the other children. Her clothes hand sewn and bread homemade, she longed for what she thought was better, like the beautiful perfectly shaped white bread bought in town. As kids can be cruel, someone must have lord it over her, as the remnants could be seen in the tears welling up in her eyes anytime she spoke of the poor, especially the children.

A perfect Christian lady in word and deed, but of course, the congregation and her Sunday school class didn't know she was sneaking over to the Bottom on occasion to buy Mogen David wine. That would have blown the whole saintly thing right out of the water. Aunt Margaret didn't drink, mind you, but she did soak her fruitcakes in the "sauce" every Christmas. The wine was not included in the cooking process, so those cakes were about one hundred proof.

Soaking the cakes was quite the process, and I'm not sure how she kept from getting a little tipsy off the fumes. Maybe she did. No sparing the hooch for these culinary creations of merriment. I'm surprised they didn't get up and walk to their intended destinations on their own. My aunt was a great Southern cook, and she put an equal amount of love into her baking, probably the only ingredient larger in amount than the wine. Although purchased strictly as a part of the recipe, she did seem to feel a little naughty about her trips to McCracken County to buy alcohol. With an impish twinkle in her eye, she would giggle as she told us about sneaking in and out of the Bottom, a place no respectable Sunday schoolteacher would ever set foot.

The Bottom was just a low place in the road that separated Graves from McCracken County. Graves County was dry during my childhood. Not to say we didn't get any rain, because Kentucky can be a bit like a rainforest during some months. Dry as in no alcohol was sold there—well, not legally. You could find a bootlegger. They were out there, but that was just a bit too far over the edge for my aunt. So she would have to drive to the county line where a liquor store or two stood at the edge of the woods. The way to perdition wound through rich farmland, the road lined with corn and soybean fields, a tobacco barn or two, and an occasional small farmhouse. Everyone drove that way to go to Paducah to shop; it was our version of the big city. The ladies kept the road hot, especially on Saturdays. So you didn't dare go on a Saturday as they might, and probably would, see your car parked in front of the den of sin. You can believe every sister from the neighboring churches took a gander at the parking lot on their way to JC Penny, just to be sure no one they knew had wandered from the fold. Depending on the sister, that could earn the offender the embarrassment of being pulled out by their ear. All in a day's work for the Christian soldier; one had to remain ready and vigilant.

Before moving to Kentucky from Iowa, we made regular visits to Aunt

Margaret's. I was five when we eventually moved to the South but much younger during these annual trips to my father's homeland. I was always so filled with excitement when the announcement came that we were going to Kentucky. As far as I was concerned, Santa Claus had nothing on my Aunt Margaret. Going to her house was always like Christmas. I was the spoiled, and she was the spoiler. I so loved these visits. I would follow Aunt Margaret around the kitchen telling her long-winded tales as she would go about cooking. I always knew she was listening and very interested because she would look down and explain, "The thunder you say!" I felt like I had really driven the point home if I got a "The thunder you say." It wasn't until years later that I was told she couldn't understand a single word coming out of my three year old mouth. Such a disappointment to learn I was not the grand orator I thought myself to be. However, there was still something special, a sort of communion that took place between us while she used this old tried-and-true expression of wonderment, thunder and all.

The other phrase I loved to hear was "What you want, baby?" I can still hear the sweet Southern drawl in my ears. You can believe if my desires were anywhere within reach of her power, baby got what she wanted. This was obviously my first lesson in manifesting abundance. The fruitcakes were not the only thing my Aunt Margaret made well. Love in the South meant feed them, feed them well, feed them often, and let no one leave this house hungry. In fact, if they are miserably full, then that's even better. Homemade pies and cakes lined the kitchen counters. Although I was too short to see over the counter, I still knew they were up there and mine for the asking. Happy days!

When Christmas rolled around, there were copious amounts of homemade candies filling plates and platters. These candy plates seemed bottomless; no matter how much you ate, they were always full. I felt sure it was magic until I grew taller. Then I discovered they were replenished by the other stash kept in Tupperware containers sitting on the washer in the utility room. It was cooler in there, so the confectionaries stored better through the holidays. I don't think I ever went into a sugar coma while I slept, but it was nothing short of a miracle that I didn't. Coca Colas were also up for grabs, and there was no limit placed on quantity—you had all you wanted until Momma got wind of it and then the party was over. Although irritated and disappointed in having limits set by my mother, Momma was probably the only thing that stood between me and profound, possibly terminal, hyperglycemia.

Momma was a Yankee and a Methodist. Lord, that was almost too much to take! Iowa was hardly east, but it wasn't south and that meant *Yank*. The combination was suspicious in itself, but she was a part of the family now, and so it would be tolerated. I think my singing "Do Lord" and "Jesus Wants Me for a Sunbeam" convinced Aunt Margaret Momma wasn't bringing me up to be a heathen—although she was dead serious about the dunking thing and the Methodist sprinkled. To make matters worse, I had the words wrong on some of the Sunday school songs. I would proudly march through the house with my head thrown back singing "I got the peaches patches understanding down in my heart" instead of "peace that passes understanding down in my heart." I know; it didn't make any sense at all. But that's what I thought they were singing, and so I sang it like I heard it. This was more blatant evidence that my training in the Methodist church was falling a bit short.

There was much debate around the kitchen table about theology and baptism as they understood it. Again, this was a heaven-and-hell issue, so the debates were taken very seriously. As much as I loved my Aunt Margaret, the feeling was mutual. So she had something to say about it, it being my salvation and upbringing. Finally, Momma gave in to the argument, conceding that maybe Poppa would go to church if they'd go to Hickory Baptist instead of Trinity Methodist.

So I became a Baptist at the ripe old age of five. That only lasted about six months or so, and I was a Methodist again because Poppa never took the bait. Momma wasn't convinced about the dunking thing, and besides, she missed her friends at Trinity. Aunt Margaret was a bit heartbroken, I think, but lived peaceably with Momma's wishes.

In my innocence, I really thought the debate was over, and we would tolerate each other's differences. The Baptist and Methodist could get along; we just wouldn't discuss the baptism issue. In fact, it's best to stay away from any topic that had to do with water, just in case it reignited the debate. Of course, it wasn't going any better over in Fancy Farm, which was the small Catholic community in our county.

The faithful had gathered at the church for the wedding of a young Catholic couple. As the priest walked down the aisle blessing his congregation with holy water a small but vocal budding little Baptist looked up at his mother and sang out, "That son of a bitch just slung water all over me." Probably not exactly what the bride and groom had hoped for as far as setting the tone for their special day. It seemed everyone was having issues around the water. Regardless, I felt we might still work it out or ignore it altogether and live peaceably. It seemed to be working—the silent "don't talk about the elephant in the living room" approach. So all was right in God's world and mine at age six. Things flowed smoothly for several years until I butted heads with a Church of Christ zealot in the tenth grade.

Cynthia Stairs was a beautiful girl. She was very quiet, with incredibly clear, blue eyes and wavy locks of blond hair that fell well below her waist. She didn't have much to say until you got her started on religion, and then "Katie! Bar the door!" If the subject of religion came up, you could count on a fight. Suddenly she became a different person. Her eyes would change from blue to black, or so it seemed to me. If I closed my eyes, I could easily imagine her wearing the garments and cross of the Crusades. I'm telling you, the Knights Templar had nothing on this girl. Blows were never thrown, but when I walked away from these discussions, she had me wondering about the "peace that passes understanding."

They didn't believe in the Old Testament, just the New. How could that be? Who was right? And, to boot, they didn't use musical instruments in their services, which really worried me because I was now the church organist. I would hate to think all my sinful playing of Methodist hymns was going to cancel out my perfect attendance and assured passage into the kingdom, but I wondered about it.

After much deliberation, I decided, as president of the MYF (Methodist Youth Fellowship), it was my duty to set her straight. I mean, there were a lot of good stories in the Old Testament. You just couldn't throw out the baby with the bathwater, could you? What about Adam and Eve? What about the creation story? What about the Psalms? The debate lasted through high school, and we never came to an agreement. As with the baptism issue, we agreed to agree we didn't agree, politely avoiding discussions on the Old Testament or musical instruments. Unfortunately, now I was really hard-pressed to find the answers—dead serious about it, in fact. Obviously, I was not so unlike my friend and classmate.

After all, I was quite sure I was placed on this planet to find the way and then to show everyone else how to get there. The problem being, I wasn't the only person on this quest. In fact, a more accurate account might be, it was me and countless others walking the planet. Be that as it may, surely I could figure it out, and then I could save the world. And so, the journey continued.

CHAPTER 2

More than we can realize or comprehend, if left unchecked, our past commands our present moment. It is in releasing the past and stepping away from the stage that we begin to see with clarity. Our awakening is dependent on our willingness to embrace an ever-expanding universe, which is new with each eternal breath.

DEWARD

NOT FAR FROM MY LITTLE piece of paradise and enlightenment in the tiny corner of Western Kentucky, my friend Griff was experiencing her own lessons in duality in Western Tennessee. The thing about duality is, we have all lived under its influence and come to see the world through the lens of right and wrong. Either we are striving to fit in "the right" (as interpreted by the generations past and present), or we are railing against "the right" because we think it's "wrong." And so the story goes. My friend Griff would be a *railer*, defined as "one who raises hell with the status quo." At a very young age, she questioned authority, knew her own truth, and was not afraid to live it.

I was, on the other hand, trying to find a way to be in alignment with what was "right" because I knew, also at a very young age, that coloring outside the lines brings with it stern condemnation—at worst, separation from the pack. I was strongly influenced by group mind. Group mind is the uninvited, ever-imposing presence we swim in daily. The thoughts and beliefs of the group begin to control our thoughts and actions. I was all about being a "good girl," but whose "good girl"? I was dancing all over the stage trying to find the spotlight of "the light" or "the right," totally losing track of myself. I was hard at work trying to "choose the right" long before people were walking around with engraved CTR rings on their fingers.

You would be hard put to find much difference between Western Kentucky and Western Tennessee. It is rural farmland for the most part. Hard work is tempered by community gatherings—school, church, and sporting events. Neighbors truly care about one another, and for the most part, this was a welcome support—that is, until caring crosses the line into a Gladys Kravitz kind of voyeurism. You know the character, even if you didn't watch *Bewitched* in the sixties. Gladys was a plump little bitter woman with a voice that resembled nails on a chalkboard. Bored with her own life, she spent most of her day nose pressed against the glass, peeping through the window at the neighbors while watching their every move. Then she would report to her disinterested husband, Abner. There was something going on over there that just wasn't quite right or perhaps even sinister. So caring is one thing, until it becomes that Gladys Kravitz kind of concern. Then it works your nerves a bit—one of the pitfalls of living in a place where everybody knows your name, and your daddy's name, and his daddy's name.

Churches are scattered across the countryside, steeples and crosses reminding those called, and the few chosen, that God is ever present. Ultimately, from these spaces we found our path to absolution and rebirth. Sure and certain was our less-than-complex understanding of life and the promise of our ultimate death. Somber granite markers stand in silhouette right outside the church doors, as if to say, "Death knocks." Death knocks, and you had better "get right with God." This phrase is used liberally from the pulpit to the radio and plastered across highway billboards, most handmade. Moral codes were pretty rigid and outlined in a sort of cookbook recipe for everlasting life. The Ten Commandments were taken seriously, and although Jesus turned the water into wine, we weren't supposed to have any of it. This self-imposed commandment was jacked up a notch or two as many places would not even allow the sale of alcohol. As discussed before, those regions were dry—chosen prohibition. It was voted on, county by county, and some counties were holier than others. Griff grew up in a county that was "wet," as opposed to my neck of the woods, which was "dry." I wonder if there is a deeper symbolism in this metaphor. It conjures up images of dry, pruney, uptight, rule followers (that'd be me) as opposed to wet, fluid beings who drink up life with an unquenchable thirst (that'd be my friend Griff).

When Griff and I were in college together at Murray State, a small liberal arts university in Western Kentucky, we frequently drove to the border of Griff's county to stock up on beer for the weekends. If you wanted hard liquor, you had to drive a few more miles into Paris, Tennessee. "Gay Paree" took on a completely new meaning for the college crowd. It was not a far drive, just fifteen minutes south on a two-lane highway infrequently traveled. This was probably a good thing as some of the kids would hang out at the Cotton Club, which encouraged beer-drinking games and pool-hall antics. Just saying, not everyone left Tennessee in the same state of sobriety as they arrived.

The rallying cry of the school was "LET'S GO SOUTH!" It was particularly fun during football games when we had the ball and the goal was on the south end of the stadium. We would stand and chant "LET'S GO SOUTH!" It was the student body's favorite cheer. Although meant to urge the Murray State Racers on to the touchdown, it was also our college code for "let's go drink." There was something freeing about abandoning the moral codes presented to us by our various denominations and families for the folly of our own experiment with stupidity. No judgment about drinking as much as the amount we typically drank, which really was stupid. In "the day," it was as close as I ever got to challenging authority and sticking my toe outside the very well-worn path of conformity I typically followed.

On occasion, we would travel south on an entirely different mission—to load up on Southern home cooking, prepared with love by Griff's mom Merlyn. Sunday dinner was an experience of communion, Eucharist reflected in Southern fried chicken and all the "fixins." Our feasting came with its own ritual. No sweeter incense ever burned by comparison to the fragrance of chicken frying in a black iron skillet. The priest in his stole had nothing on Merlyn in her apron. She too was in command of the table she set before us. Feeding homesick college kids must not be so different from feeding the poor. Everyone coming to her table felt loved and welcomed. What would our world be like if it had just a few more Southern cooks with open tables and equally open hearts?

Merlyn cooked for all the strays Griff could bring with her—their home the epitome of Southern hospitality. Usually they were kids that lived a little farther away and could not go home for the weekend. The rest of us attended because we liked good food and being spoiled by her momma. Griff would throw open the door, and we would all trail in behind her. Merlyn stood with arms outstretched in a living image of the cross we had come to know so well. However, there was no suffering in this offering of herself for her children; she was laughing and full of joy as we shuffled past to find our place at the table.

Murray was a suitcase college, a lonely place for an eighteen-year-old kid after the locals went home for the weekends. The school was located in the very tip of Western Kentucky, and most of the students who attended there came from small towns across the bordering states of Tennessee, Missouri, Ohio, and Indiana. We were really a narrow mix of mostly white, middle-class carbon copies of each other. This smattering of mix didn't provide us with much of an opportunity to experience expanded beliefs or new world views. Murray State was not exactly a cornucopia of diversity. The college students brought home to the kitchen table were all similar in background and upbringing. There is a comfort in being the same, but then growth becomes a challenge.

Merlyn was one of those rare individuals whose open heart drew in those who were not only alike but different. She was willing to experience something outside herself and her well-worn beliefs. It was an unusual gift for a woman who viewed the world through the lenses of Southern Baptist homemaker born and raised in rural Tennessee. Even more bizarre was the fact that these colorful characters would somehow find their way to her door. Metaphysical practitioners were hardly common during those years. Hell, they are not common now, but especially in Paris, Tennessee, in the seventies. Regardless, one managed to find his way to Merlyn.

Merlyn's house sat on one of the many back roads of the small town—not in the city proper but the country well lived. If you were traveling down that road, it was because you lived there or you were going to see someone you knew. The house was pretty isolated, sitting under the shade trees as most small Southern homes do. On this particular day, Merlyn was having a yard sale. So you can imagine, she didn't have a large number of customers for her sale, but she still wanted everything out and perfect for those who did make their way over. It was certain the ladies of the church would be dropping by for inspection.

She was placing all her old knives out on one table when she looked up to see a stranger making his way toward her. She didn't know this man, unusual in itself because she knew everyone in the county. She lived there all her life. She didn't notice anything odd about him at first; he seemed friendly, smiling as he walked up to the table display. He was interested in her knives—fitting, given his perspective of living on the edge or, better stated, far from center. This was her first customer, and she was still rushing to get everything out and organized. Distracted by this newcomer, she grabbed the wrong end of one of the knives (kept razor sharp by her loving husband) and cut her finger. A good-sized cut—missed the arteries but still bleeding pretty freely. She was embarrassed more than anything else and grabbed a dish towel to wrap the wound and stop the bleeding.

The stranger saw this as a perfect opportunity for a teaching moment and immediately began to instruct her on how to heal herself energetically. Now let's stop here for just a moment and remember we are in rural backwoods Tennessee where the only healer is Jesus, the end, praise the Lord. A person might be shot or, at the very least, run out of town for even suggesting such a thing. Although he didn't know it, this guy should have been thankful it was Merlyn he was dealing with and not one of the shotgun-toting vigilantes living in those parts. He was a lucky fellow is all I'm saying.

Merlyn listened intently as he explained she could easily control the bleeding by manipulating her energy field. Merlyn didn't even know she had an energy field. By now, I'm quite sure she thought he was a kook but played along. What could it hurt? I can hear her now, "You don't say?" stated with curious attention. He asked her to close her eyes and direct her energy to the wound, commanding the capillaries to seal. Merlyn was still giggling about the situation, but she closed her eyes and participated, intently following his direction. As the tea towel was becoming more soaked in blood, the stranger became more concerned his exercise might not do the trick. Perhaps because she was a novice and needed more time to learn the skill. So he decided to add a more traditional first-aid skill, instructing her to raise her hands above her head. So there they stood, Merlyn with her hands above her head, holding the blood-soaked dishrag with the metaphysician standing in front of her holding a rather large butcher knife. About that time, the Bunny Bread man rounded the corner in his delivery truck, saw the unfolding scene, and drove right into the ditch. I guess that was more excitement than they had had in a long while. Bottom line is, Merlyn's first experience with alternative healing really didn't turn out so well, but at least she was willing and open to try it.

For all Griff's railing, mostly at the Southern Baptist Church and organized religions, she couldn't kick much about her parents. Well, maybe they could have supported her more by stepping outside the culture and times of the day. In short, they could have stopped treating her "like a girl." Obviously, this was not hers to have at the time, nor was it for any of us in this incarnation. Most of our mothers followed the status quo, but many held space for our taking the next step. Taking would be an accurate description because the good ole boys were not quite ready to give up their piece of the pie. It was a good pie. Why would they want to give it up?

We were born in the fifties, finding our way into college by the mid-seventies. Unfortunately for most, being a girl child in the South, or any of the four directions for that matter, meant you were going to be groomed to become a wife and mother. That went over like a lead balloon for my friend who was fast becoming a radical lesbian of epic proportions. Her idea of living life fully was living on the edge, challenging authority, and seeing how many illicit substances she could experiment with before the age of twenty-one. Griff was not about wearing ruffles and lace or learning to curtsy while being molded for future matrimony. This was about the last thing on her mind. In fact, it was the farthest thing from her mind unless it showed up just long enough for her to either explode or implode, depending on the company she was keeping at the time. She chose her battles well and knew when to be silent and when to pitch a hissy fit. I have been there to witness a few of the fits. Great fun, really. She is true to her ancestors and heritage. There was, and still is, a fierce Scot residing in her DNA who is neither timid nor Southern, but rugged and outspoken and certainly not given to conformity.

Always longing for the support she saw her brother Ben receive, her formative years grew more disappointing in their lack of validation. Ben was sustained with ample confirmation on his way to realizing his dreams and place in the world. There were no limitations. If anything, he may have been challenged a bit to stretch beyond what he envisioned—a sure sign of parental confidence. Of course, he was the boy child. On the other hand, Griff was encouraged to go to a technical school. Their underestimation of their daughter was profound, and she felt it. Griff wasn't a scholar; she didn't care much for school as this was not her way of learning—chained to a desk and obediently accepting another's understanding of her world. In college, she kept a calendar by her bed that contained her Skip List. If she skipped biology last week, that meant she needed to be sure and be there this week. Pretty creative, I'd say. Her parents didn't realize her brilliance or creativity because it could not be defined by the rules and measures of the day. Trade school should be good enough, they thought, just in case something happened to their dream and the imaginary husband was a no-show. Well, obviously, "he" was not coming in the first place.

Had they understood her vision and spirit, things could have been easier, but then, easy wasn't in keeping with Griff's path. She was always ready for adventure, fighting the "good" fight for creatively expressing herself. Herself was not acceptable at that time and place, which called for steadfast courage and unbending determination. That was the challenge that helped to mold the person she became in the world. That was on the one side, but the other side of that plank was, for the most part, pretty easy. She grew up in a household reflective of Ward and June Cleaver's place. The Beav had nothing on her. Parents, siblings, aunts, uncles, cousins, and neighbors wrapped her in a loving safety net that would sustain her through a lifetime. Our families eventually leave us alone on the planet, left to walk without them. However, we are imprinted by our brief encounter in their presence and carry it with us always, for better or for worse. Supported and held safe during her formative years, there would be no excuse for giving back anything less than "full measure, pressed down and running over," as the Good Book says. And so she did.

Griff's mom and dad counted their blessings. They had a nice home with three beautiful children who were mostly obedient. There was money enough to live comfortably with a little leftover. Life was good. However, living in a small town is a wonderful thing—until it isn't. What can make it challenging is everyone knows everyone else's business. Feeling understood and well known can bring one a sense of comfort and belonging, but there is a flip side. Like Santa Claus, they know when you've been naughty or nice. And Griff could be a little naughty by rural Western Tennessee definition.

Being pulled over by the local deputy on her way "South" for a traffic violation would not normally be a problem, but her buddy left a roach in the ashtray—unfortunately, not the kind with legs. Even more unfortunate was the newly rolled joint in the glove box. These regrettable placements of Friday night's entertainment led to the unfolding of Griff's arrest. She and her friend were taken to the county jail and booked on possession. This was followed with in-the-buff calisthenics under the watchful eye of the jail matron to ensure there was nothing else tucked away in another compartment. This may seem to be a little extreme for two college kids caught with a joint, but not in the day. The "demon weed" had to be stamped out. This turn of events was not what she and her friend had in mind for their Friday night on the town.

With a little luck, the deputy might have mistaken the joint for a home-rolled cigarette, but this was not to be. Needless to say, Daddy wasn't pleased when he had to go to the town hall and bail his baby daughter out of jail. The whole town knew the story by morning. However, the plus side of knowing the entire town unfolded during her court appearance; Daddy knew the judge. All charges were dropped, something about unauthorized search. You have to admire the girl's spirit; living life in the seventies absolutely called one to color outside the lines. Griff was more than happy to challenge the system, calling us to expanding horizons, redefining old boundaries. The Age of Aquarius was a good time to be alive and well on the planet for my adventuresome friend.

Griff's antics were a subtle reflection of her extended family, also quite the characters. Merlyn's sister and brother-in-law, Griff's Aunt Beanie and Uncle Deward, lived right around the corner. Family gatherings were commonplace. They were regulars around the kitchen table, which I remind you, was the place where we shared our understanding and experience of life with each other. Aunt Beanie ran the show, was a fast talker and wide-eyed with wonder while Uncle Deward experienced life silently, like a dutiful monk, having little to say and always obedient. There was no argument in Deward from what I understand; he was slow and easy, maintaining a low profile around his wife. The waters remained calmer that way, and in a sense, he brought ballast to the wild boat ride Aunt Beanie commanded.

In case you are wondering, Uncle Deward came by his name at birth (pronounced in the South, "Doo'erd"). *Aunt Beanie* was a nickname. Many of us were blessed with nicknames, our Southern terms of endearment. Most of the time you certainly wouldn't think of them as regal, but you could count on them being colorful, usually with a good story attached.

Aunt Beanie and Uncle Deward, unlike Griff's parents, had never left Paris, Tennessee. As Griff's mom and dad grew older, the kids left home freeing them up to travel across America. Griff's father loved to travel, and even at the age of seventy-five, he was still driving across country, graduating to world traveler not long before his death. Because the Griffins traveled and were very generous people, they commonly shared their experiences with family and friends. On this particular occasion they invited Aunt Beanie and Uncle Deward over for Mexican fare. Now this was really a treat for the aunt and uncle having never been out of Tennessee. Food is good in the South. It may not be healthy, but it's good. However, being invited to experience international fare was really a treat. Not only was it a treat, but it was also a little nerve racking. One didn't want to appear simple and unaccustomed to the ways of the world—*one* meaning Aunt Beanie. Uncle Deward could care less about keeping up appearances. Experiencing another culture's food could be tricky, like trying to figure out which one of those forks to start with at the more formal affairs.

The table was filled with everything that was needed to construct their fajitas, which Aunt Beanie pronounced "fa-gee'tas." The food was served family-style as was our custom. Everything in bowls or plates spread before you on the table in ample abundance. The feast was about to begin when Deward was handed the plate of tortillas. He watched the others take theirs to ensure he was following the proper protocol for fajita making, well trained by Aunt Beanie's rules of etiquette. Gingerly taking the tortilla, he laid it on his plate under the watchful eye of his wife. Aghast, Aunt Beanie quickly leaned over and whispered in stage voice, "Deward, your tor-tell-ah's upside down!" Mortified, Uncle Deward quickly and dutifully—as was his nature—reached down and turned the tortilla over. All was then right again in Aunt Beanie's world; she was hoping no one noticed her inexperienced husband's obvious blunder.

No one said a word, but the story has circulated over half the country now, and the stifled giggles around the table that day have turned into riotous laugher—no doubt heard through time and space, beyond this dimension and into the next because the story is profound, not just comical. There is a reason Jesus taught with metaphor. It touches something far more profound in us than logical reasoning, moving beyond the heart into the soul. Most of us, unwilling to look deeply at our own choices, feel akin to Uncle Deward. How many of us, like him, have quickly and silently turned our "tor-tell-ah" over, turned our lives over, because we dared not trust our own wisdom? No matter how ridiculous the order, we change our direction out of lack of clarity, need for conformity, or just plain failed courage. For the sake of calm waters, we sacrificed our truth. At the very least, we just get caught up in the group mind and follow the others blindly. It's far easier. Who's to say our "tor-tell-ah's" upside down anyway? Only we can know our true path and bring to the table the gift that is ours to bring, right side up or upside down.

How unfortunate for us and for our world. There is no up or down, there is no right or wrong—duality is illusion at its best. When we are living consciously and in light of our deepest essence, there is no need to look outside ourselves for supportive understanding or in fear of judgment. We have only to rest in knowing wisdom is transcendent, found in the core of our soul. Instead we look to religion, philosophy, infinite fact-finding, and no doubt, some fiction to find our way. We need only to understand, like Dorothy in *The Wizard of Oz*, we were home all along. We had only to click our heels together to find our grounding and center in the Divine.

Duality has served its purpose during our evolution. It has kept us, in the best of cases, living in peace and harmony with each other and, in the worst of cases, at war with others and ourselves. It commands boundaries, along with rules and regulations that are meant to keep us safe and guide us mindlessly through the cookbook of living. The message has been "follow the recipe of duality for a good and happy life now and in the hereafter, amen." The problem with recipe living is, we are robbed of our soul's expression. Creativity is lost, and we look more now like clones, losing the piece that is uniquely ours to bring into the world. The symphony waiting to be heard by our planet, created by the singular notes of our diversity, has sadly never been written. The melody of our past, in some respects, is a strangely flat work devoid of dimension.

We are here to create, not conform. Conformity is safe, and creativity is delightfully messy in its process. Sadly, many of us have forgotten why we signed up to come to the planet in the first place. Fortunately, this is changing, and we are on the cusp of all consciousness shifting an octave higher, maybe more. The energy on our planet is speeding up, sometimes uncomfortably so. It's a "shake, rattle, and roll" kind of transition, which can be disconcerting. Beanie and Deward could not have imagined it, it was too soon, but you can believe they laid the groundwork for the awakening we are now experiencing. Our ancestors have blazed the path before us, as generation after generation leapfrogged into the new creation from the shoulders of those who passed. The past is blessing and curse. It provided us with a solid foundation, but that very foundation can, at times, feel like an anchor around our necks. The new energy is not so solid. It is fluid and moving, alive with possibilities. It is only in letting go of our well-worn customs and expectations that we are catapulted into expressions of the yet unimagined.

CHAPTER 3

Through the looking glass, past the illusion created by our ego, there is a profound wisdom waiting to be born. Our vision, altered by the ego's creation, will soon be shattered by our soul's evolution. The earth is awakening. There was a brief quickening, a felt presence of new life; then we were thrown into the sudden and powerful phase of transition leaving no mystery. New birth is certain.

THE ROCK

THE EGO IS A FUNNY thing, isn't it? Our playmate for life. We come into the world clear—so clear, in fact, we are easily lovable. At first, there really is no ego because we don't realize until a much later date that we are separate from anything or anyone else. Our interaction with the adults who pick us up, also clear. They are not concerned about what we think or how we will affect their lives because they believe we are powerless and incapable of thinking, which is why we have to endure their goofy baby talk and silly noises. It's fun to watch, really. I'm sure babies are very amused and soon learn to laugh at our "baby jokes"—which are usually one-liners, with little or no punch line. Sometimes there are no words at all, giving us our first experience of the mime. It probably is the facial expressions that save the show. It's always the physical comedy that really makes us laugh, don't you think? Recent generations really don't know what they've missed for not seeing an episode of *The Three Stooges*.

Now there was the play on "the play." *The Three Stooges* gave us a glimpse into the comic expression of the human drama through Larry, Moe, and Curly Joe. Moe was the boss of the triad. He wasn't very bright, but he was very forceful. Larry and Curly met with sure and certain wrath with each error in judgment or failure to follow Moe's instructions. Slapped, poked, and belittled by their fearless leader who was, quite obviously, full of fear and ego. Always in trouble these three, making their way through the best they could with their limited understanding. Larry and Curly gave up their power, their understanding, and their wills to simply follow the leader. Sadly, this is an all-too-familiar story for most of us.

Then there was the *I Love Lucy* show, the whacked-out redhead who never learned to conform but, instead, asserted herself in a freestyle fall of comical escapades. Unfortunately for our heroine Lucy, it always seemed to run amok. She wasn't the best at following her husband and fearless leader Ricky Ricardo, the Cuban bombshell. Ricky was a strong, manly man—handsome and sexy. I'm sure many housewives could relate to Lucy and her need to break free of the rules of the day. Ricky was to be served and adored like all men in that era. As the show implied, this was to be performed with stylish grace and ease. He comes home and dinner's on the table; the children are dressed in their evening attire, waiting adoringly around the table. The house is clean, the beds are made, and she has on the cutest little housedress with hair and makeup just perfect. Her energy is endless. He doesn't see all the preparation it takes to get everything to this point and, over the years, thinks it just happens magically somehow. She sacrifices all to keep him happy, following his rules regardless of their adverse effect on her dreams. Of course, I'm sure there had to be some benefit in pleasing this Cuban hottie. It's easy to understand losing one's resolve to be heard when you could just melt into those arms. I wonder how many housewives enjoyed that fantasy. Move over, Lucy! Nevertheless, he brought home the money, which paid for the house, and it was her job to provide the home. This exchange worked well for a time.

Comedies filled the airways when television was young, and so was I. Life was a bit simpler then—not without challenges, but there was a clear understanding of right and wrong (at least in our minds). No one really had to think; no one had to be conscious. They just had to follow the rules laid out by society and whatever brand of church one embraced. People lived through terrible, unspeakable atrocities during the Second World War. When the war ended, we needed a simpler time, a time to regenerate and look away from the harsh realities lived. So Americans created their dream world and made very clear boundaries. They cherished what they fought and died for on "foreign soil" without understanding this soil was also their own. Our separation from one another is ego driven. These "foreigners" were, in fact, a part of us. On some level, those involved shared in the profound loss seen in the faces of these strangers. They saw clearly what could happen to their own homes and families. They knew that we came very close to losing all we loved. So our boundaries grew stronger and our egos out of control. Born of a new fear, our country became lost in its own illusion of separation. As with all conflicts past, present, and future, war always leaves an indelible mark.

Those of us who were not on the planet at the time will never truly understand what our families experienced. The threat was very real for those fighting abroad and at home. They knew, in a very real way, they could lose their home and country. Many of us born to those veterans knew little of these harsh realities. As infants, we had no understanding of our separation from the people in the room, let alone people across the world. For the infant, we are all one. We are all one: the mantra of the way seers. Those who point to this new creation, they urge us to leave behind the wounds that bind us to a past, a past that no longer serves. So it is easy to understand why newborns are looked upon with gentle love and caring, held without reservation or judgment. In that moment, the adult is invited to experience the love of another without the shadow of ego's separation, at least in part. We are still looking through the filter of our own ego.

One does not have to fight a war to experience the wounding of a warrior.

Once we step through the looking glass, we become aware of the other, apart from ourselves. We are now asked to perform according to the rules of the day, the group-established norms. No matter where our tribe or continent, we all participate in this contest while being judged. Like the three stooges, we are poked, slapped, and undermined by those in power—or at least those in perceived power. We, like Larry and Curley Joe, hand over our rights in exchange for civil rest. Unfortunately, many times, we place people like Moe in power. Although not too bright and not too enlightened, they are allowed to bully their way through our shared existence while projecting their fear onto the screen in their effort to control the masses.

So now you're wondering who I'm talking about. Or maybe you are not wondering and have already filled the playbill with your own villain; there are many of this caliber-filling roles of power throughout our world. We can point to national leaders, but in fact, the people we have put in power are but a reflection of our own maladies. They lead the way and take the heat. They provide the forum for the great debate of right and wrong, good and bad, while pointing their finger at "the evildoers." They are "the deciders," but who put them in this place, and why? It was not our votes (quite literally I am told), but it was us. Well, how could that be you ask? You think me confused; not at all. It is our habit to project onto another all our fears and unconscious limited understandings so we can see more clearly our own maladies. We create outside ourselves what lives within, and we do it quite well. We are master creators regardless of our awareness. In fact, until we look inside ourselves and identify this madness that separates us from each other, we are doomed to continue this same stale existence. Unfortunately, there is no limit to the number of times we can blow each other up. We are living in fear, interfacing with our world not from our core essence, our divinity; but instead, we live out of a collective wounding. Until we can enter within and hold gently and without judgment that part of ourselves that we fear most, exposing the darkness, we will continue to point to others out there and create tighter, more protective boundaries. The witch trials of Salem have never stopped. We did not learn from this time, and even now, we are "burning at the stake" those who embody understandings that challenge our left-brained expression of life.

We live from a tribal perspective, molded from a very young age. This happens in part from observations, but maybe more importantly, from the permeating group mind that is in constant interplay with the unconscious. This influence spreads like a virus from person to person, generating old fears in new ways. We are preoccupied, keeping rhythm with a beat not our own, and in so doing, we forget our own song.

For the first five years of my life, I lived in a very small town—a village, really. Oakville sat on the rich black soil of bottom farmland not far from the Mississippi River in Iowa. My brothers and I totally understood the adage "It takes a village to raise a child." We knew we were accountable to the village, and if we were in trouble, the village would be there for support or correction depending on who was causing the trouble. It didn't matter that Santa Claus was watching; he didn't have to because all the neighbors were doing the job for him.

There was a small boulder that sat at the end of our driveway. It was from the vantage point of this stone each of us, in his or her turn, witnessed the unfolding of our world. There were times when Momma would let us go play in another yard or ride our bikes down the sidewalks of our metropolis, but most of the time, the stone marked the boundary, and so there we would sit and study life in the fifties. I never knew until I was an adult that my brothers—seven and twelve years older—also shared what I thought was my rock and my experience, but they sat there as well at the same young and tender age of five. Interesting, as the number five in numerology signifies change. Five years into life, our worldview began to change, although ever so slightly. From our front-row seat, we watched the comings and goings of our little town. We began to entertain the notion that the world outside our immediate family was not just like us.

From this vantage point, we viewed the homes of our neighbors, the occasional car that passed down Main Street, and our thriving business district, which included a school, a gas station/restaurant, a small grocery, and a bank. We could observe almost everything in town from our small granite throne. Oh, and there was also a tavern that sat catty-cornered from the little Methodist church where I got my start in organized religion. So the light and the dark side sat in juxtaposition not far from the corner of our driveway. I knew the tavern must be a very evil place as my uncle was severely punished for going there.

Uncle Al visited the tavern on occasion in his younger years, but his trips were short-lived. Frequenting the tavern was not OK with my aunt who was quick to act on her displeasure. The domestic violence unfolded as he was met with a swift whack on the head when returning home one evening. The offending weapon was a baseball bat, wielded by Aunt Audrey. She knew he had been in the tavern. She mounted her surprise attack from behind the front door where she stood hiding on top of a kitchen chair. She was a short little woman and needed the advantage of added height to strike a well-placed blow. Didn't break the skin or cause a concussion, maybe a small hematoma. Regardless, it was quite the attention getter. Personally, I think she watched too many episodes of the *Three Stooges*, as this could have caused serious injury. She must have had several practice swings before he arrived to be certain she didn't really damage her handsome husband and father of her children. I've always wondered if the writers of *I Love Lucy* secretly came to Oakville to study Aunt Audrey for the character of Lucy—as character she was and one of my favorites.

So there you have it, good and evil playing out before us packaged quite neatly in small village style, easily observed from the rock. The tavern, the church; the fallen, the resurrected; the strong of heart, the sore of head—all became a part of our entertainment and training. Far smaller than the surrounding blocks of third-dimensional learning was our understanding of the world. Although limited, this began our training. This is where it started, our experience of life's play.

We knew there were people who entered the bar and people who entered the church. We were a part of the churchgoing people—well, all of us except my dad. He didn't attend either place; poor guy worked seven days a week most of his career. My Aunt Audrey didn't go to either place at that time in her life, unless it was to pull Uncle Al out of the bar by his ear. I don't think she ever had to do that again after the baseball-bat incident, or so I'm told. It wasn't until much later that she joined the churchgoers and embraced becoming the born-again Christian, which held her safe and secure in knowing she was a follower of "the way." My uncle soon joined her. Well, wouldn't you? Either that or he would have to start wearing a helmet around the house. She was and still is quite the presence. In reality, I don't believe it was the baseball bat that brought the sheep back into the fold. There was another driving force behind our churchgoing family: Grandpa (Levi) Whitaker.

My family was a little different from the *Father Knows Best* and *Leave It to Beaver* models played out for us on the living room television set. My mother and her bat-swinging sister Audrey married brothers Johnnie and Alfred, sons of Levi Whitaker. I don't know exactly how this happened, brothers falling in love with sisters, but it made for a closer-knit family in all respects. As I understand it, Johnnie, as the eldest son, was the more responsible and mature of the two. When and if a problem arose, Johnnie was the one they came to for help. Although they were poor, in the grand scheme of things, life was good. Then the unthinkable happened. Johnnie was killed.

My brothers were two and nine years old, and my mother was twenty-nine. Momma was working in the munitions plant where Johnnie was killed the day of the explosion. The plant was a composite of multiple buildings, each used for a different process in bomb production. Some were more dangerous than others. They referred to the buildings as lines. After the explosion, the alarms sounded, and all the workers left their lines and went to the cafeteria (as instructed) where they were safe (in theory). They were to remain there until it was determined safe to return to their jobs. When they reached the cafeteria, Mom learned the explosion was on line 9, Johnnie's building. She began to shake uncontrollably. Then she looked at her watch and knew it was time for him to be in the cafeteria for lunch. Guarded relief flooded through her, allowing her to catch her breath. She quickly began to look across the crowed room for Johnnie's face only to see his supervisors walking slowly toward her. As soon as she saw them, she knew, crumpling to the floor as if all life had passed from her as well. Later she would find out Johnnie's coworker had a headache, and so Johnnie sent him to lunch first—a decision that sealed his fate. Mom could not return there after the accident; it was too terrible, and she was too traumatized. Oakville rallied around her and the boys. A job was created in the post office for my mom. Uncle Al and Grandpa Whitaker became the guardians for Johnnie's family, watching over Mom and the boys just as Johnnie had watched over them.

I cannot say what those years were like for Mom and the boys, the years without husband or father. Randy has no memory of his dad—he was two and, by nature, is a guy that rolls with the punches. Each picture of his childhood reflects light. His smile is always there, looking into the lens of the camera as if to say "isn't life grand!" Burr haircut, freckles scattered across his cheeks, you knew he was sending you an invitation to come and play. Not the story for my oldest brother Dick, a sensitive who came into the world with heavy burden, his pictures quite the opposite. Even when smiling, there is a sadness that is palpable. His pain easily recognized now as I look back through the black-and-white photographs that chronicled our life.

Something was frozen in my brother following this tragedy. It is as if a part of his soul was ripped away when my mother came home that night and screamed through tears, "Dickie, your daddy died!" Not exactly how one might want to break the news to a nine-year-old (as if there could be a good way). In my reflection on the event, I imagine it was not the words that haunted my brother over the years; it was the energy that came toward him in those horrible moments. This is not the time for a boy to lose his father, at the age of nine.

In fact, there probably could not be a worse time with regard to childhood development.

Dick would relive this moment over and over in his mind, and even now at sixty-five, he's still living through the shadow of the event. He never recovered. Over the years, I found my stomach tightening up into knots when he would talk about his grief. He told the story over and over—each detail, each thought, each feeling forcing the experience deeper and deeper into his psyche and into mine. It was as if he would grab us by the collar, pulling us down with him into his torment, his self-imposed corner of hell.

A sensitive feels with far greater emotion; it's a double-edged sword. His torment in that moment filled every cell of his being, overshadowed his life, robbed him of joy. It is sad to watch and harder to live out. I moved through many stages observing and living out his process with him. The first stage as a child was unrequited grief. There were times I felt guilty for having been born, wondering if Johnnie had to die to set the stage for my dad and I to enter the family. The second stage as a teenager was anger; enough was enough! I didn't want to hear the story one more time. I didn't want to hear it the first time. Why focus on something so terrible? The third stage as an adult was a determined resolve. I was a healer. I would help him quell this madness. This stage lasted for many years. Finally, at my father's funeral came the final stage, acceptance.

Dick was asked to give the eulogy. In his remembering, I could feel the knots returning as I realized, he is going to tell the story again. I fell silent. He had me by the collar once more, pulling me into the loss of his father at my father's funeral. I wish I could say I was numb at this moment, but I was not. I was reliving his childhood pain while living the pain of my own loss simultaneously, pain squared to the ninth power. Not the tenth, but the ninth—as nine signifies completion, and the cycle was now complete for me. It was final. There was resolve in knowing some things cannot be changed. Some wounding will never be healed. I cannot help my brother find his way out of the nightmare. So I will stand with him where he stands and let it go.

My father worked on the river. He traveled the Ohio and Mississippi, wherever the rivers took him—sometimes to very small towns like Oakville "Ioway" as they called it in Kentucky. Poppa was twenty-eight years old and a dredge operator when he arrived in Oakville about two years after Johnnie's death. Let me tell you, Ricky Ricardo had nothing on my father. He was gorgeous, bronzed from the sun, and ripped with muscle from working construction. He had a deep baritone voice that resonated in his chest in a way that commanded attention when he spoke, which wasn't very often. He was a quiet man. I'm sure he must have made the girls swoon when they saw him walk down the street. His work clothes were always pressed and clean; you could cut your finger on the crease of his pants. He had the most beautiful smile, and an impish nature reflected in the cock of his work cap. Add to that equation a generous dose of Southern charm, and I suppose one might say he was irresistible.

Poppa moved in across the street from Mom and the boys in Mrs. Duncan's boardinghouse. His stroll by the house was a nightly affair. The summer nights were warm and humid in our little village. Air conditioners consisted of whatever you could fan yourself with, so I would imagine there were lots of folks sitting out on their porches. Randy was four years old, sitting on the rock, our rock, when Poppa came home from work each day. The two of them made their acquaintance during these evening strolls. Soon, Poppa was carrying candy bars in his lunch box to give to Randy. So who's to know who was wooing who? My dad had his sights set on Randy's momma after a brief meeting in the post office. I suspect my brother's contagious invitation ("Come be my buddy") was helpful in bridging the gap between a shy single man in a strange town and what was to be my family. It seemed their unfolding relationship helped load Cupid's bow with an arrow as the romance between the two—AG and Jeannie—was soon to follow. As for me, I was not even a twinkle in my daddy's eye. Not yet.

Well, that was a long-winded introduction to my brother's grandfather. He was a defining force in our religious heritage. Grandpa Whitaker was a beautiful and extraordinary man. I've never seen another express their love for their Creator with any greater conviction than our grandpa. He, of course, was not my grandfather, but I didn't know that until years later when I started to understand the biological lines of connection. Grandpa settled with his family just across the levy from the river that bordered our tiny town. They lived off the land with abject simplicity in what some would consider abject poverty. He raised his children and supported his wife on his farm, taking only what he needed from the river, the woods, and the land. A big man ever so gentle, walking the planet softly, Native Americans would have considered him an unusual white man as he lived in harmony with the earth. His way of being exemplified sustainable living long before this turn of phrase was in vogue or became a part of our understanding. I think he understood living in the present and honoring all of creation. He walked in wonder of all the miracles he saw in his day. Most would miss these tiny but extraordinary wonders, but not him. With obvious delight, he would simply exclaim, "My, my." He was a simple man of profound faith. His worldview was quite small by most standards. He wasn't at all convinced there should be a space program and felt certain his chickens didn't lay their eggs each time we launched another test flight through the stratosphere. He was never convinced Neil Armstrong walked on the moon and openly reported to us all that it was probably staged on some Hollywood set.

Grandpa Whitaker's relationship with his God was personal and unyielding. I believe his intercessory prayer probably had a profound effect on all our lives and our beliefs. He was living in his essence, and even in that day, with a somewhat limited access to this place of connection, he created his world. And in his world, his family went to church and loved the Lord. Poor by our standards but quite rich in reality. In his eyes one could see a love and kindness that spread out over his family like a river, which they all eventually floated upon. To this day, his children, his grandchildren, and his great-grandchildren are following in his footsteps. When my brothers lift their voices in prayer, you can feel their connection and the love for their God. It's like hearing Levi pray through them, and maybe he is. With clarity and a profound, unusual mix of power and humility, you know their words are not hanging in the air somewhere near the ceiling but have ascended to the realms of the angels.

And so our foundation was created by a family who loved us, a village that supported us, and a worldview that existed in a microcosm all our own. *Micro* being the operative word here; we were limited in our understanding of the whole. Our love and our joy, our struggles and our tragedies, molded our understandings and views in understandable but limited ways.

Life was certain, simple, and our perception of our Creator was never challenged. Our vision was limited by the illusion that the whole of life, the world at large, was really just like our world. And if not, well then, it should be after all. Our comprehension of right and wrong was concrete, literally—unyieldingly firm and as hard as my Aunt Audrey's baseball bat. The road to heaven, to our bliss, was a straight line. A very straight line. One dare not vary to the left or the right. The path was carved in stone, which we each in turn observed from our special stone that sat at the end of the driveway. All over the planet, there must be similar stones with like beings sitting on their rocks observing their universe and, ultimately, their creation.

CHAPTER 4

Deep within, you will find the strength and wisdom needed to align with your divinity. From this place, all culture and counterculture becomes a mute point. Life, through the expression of the sacred, reveals the true self—once hidden, now revealed. With this unfolding is born new life. Duality falls away, for it is no longer needed. The rigidity of rules and commandments become obsolete with this long-awaited atonement. Instead, there is created a flowing river of pure energy springing up from your core, the water of life.

SCREAMING TUCANS

THERE ARE COUNTLESS SMALL TOWNS scattered across rural America. Trying to find a big difference in these places, and the people living there might be challenging because, for the most part, they are very similar. Typically, hardworking born-again Christians raising families in the same little towns their parents and grandparents lived life. However, for all those folks who maintain the status quo, there are a few rare and colorful characters. Their job is to challenge the mainliners to see beyond their well-defined boundaries.

For the most part, each generation passes on the rules to the next. Rules are handy; they keep us focused and typically support living in community. The challenge comes along when someone decides the rules just don't apply, or they question how they could maintain their own integrity if they followed these tenets and decrees. When you are asked to compromise your integrity and inner wisdom for the "greater good," one might want to stop and ask, "What?"

Most of us, whether aware or unaware, have touched our core essence, the place deep within our being where we experience alignment with life force. We are able to touch and be touched by creativity, regeneration, and new life. Living from any other space can become an unconscious melting into something you can't even name. It reminds me of those old horror flicks when the "blob" was slowly bubbling across the countryside. This black, tar-like radioactive mass would devour everything in its path. Soon there was nothing but "the blob." That's the best way I know how to describe unconscious group mind. We've all been there. We are all guilty of having lost ourselves from time to time; many unfortunately live from this space. The blob is a perfect description of an unconscious modeling of behaviors and energy. You become one with whatever you are surrounded by on a daily basis. On occasion, someone has the courage or determination or calling to step outside the blob. Let me tell you, stepping outside the blob creates chaos for the blob-ettes, those mindless followers of the blob. So it does not come without a price.

If you think you can live differently in one of these small towns and remain invisible, well, you better think again. Any broad stroke of color applied to the canvas of this black-and-white existence creates quite the stir. So you have two choices. The first choice, the one I embraced, was leaving home to look for community that might honor my expression of life, or at least ignore it and leave me relatively unharmed. The second choice is to stay put and live like a screaming toucan in a wood filled with sweet, precious little brown sparrows. The first choice is really the easier of the two. The second choice requires wisdom, courage, and just a little bit of "kiss my ass if you don't like it" attitude.

I suppose a couple of my favorite toucans lived in a small town called Madisonville in Western Kentucky. They are known by their friends as ChiChi and Ms. Murphy. I heard about ChiChi before I ever visited this small town. When I was in college, it was not unusual to hear about one of ChiChi's parties after the weekend when the kids came back to school from Madisonville. Rumor was ChiChi was a lesbian. Well, we would have said *queer* in 1975 because we didn't care about being PC (politically correct). Really, there was no need for rumor. ChiChi would be glad to tell folks she was gay if anyone had the courage to ask outright.

I had friends at Murray State University who were also of this persuasion. I was trying very hard not to look at my own sexuality, as were they. So we did not talk about the parties much. I just knew that this woman existed and that she did not seem to worry or care about people knowing she was gay. That rocked my little world because, well, just call me blob-ette. We just never talked out loud about "those kind of people." Rarely, someone might whisper about it, but even that seemed to make people uncomfortable. It wasn't until the next generation that the out-loud name-calling began. Homosexuality was not the hotbed of discussion in those small towns. Of course, there was always an underground of sisters, but they were not seen or heard for the most part. This was the reality of the day. As women, we were still trying to have a voice, to be acknowledged. We didn't dream of living an out-loud expression of our sexuality. I mean, really. It was unheard of in those small towns. Well, not really.

While at Murray, I changed majors—for a very brief period—to physical education. Now there was your hotbed of dykes and the other reason I heard about ChiChi. I was a freshman and very naive. A couple of my upperclassman friends who were also physical education majors knew the scoop and watched me like a hawk. It was as if they thought I could be persuaded to turn to the dark side. Of course, they did not know "the force" was already with me. Neither did I at the time because I was running hard and fast from any association with homosexuality. Maybe that was just a part of being a teenager. I mean, could there be anything worse for a small-town fundamentalist Christian than realizing you were gay? So I very unconsciously chose not to realize it, which worked until I fell in love. Then things got a bit sticky. Surely you can understand, trying to get all the tar off after being encased by the blob, for what was now years, wasn't an easy job.

ChiChi was like a legend. I often wondered what she was like, then I was invited by a friend to go to one of the parties. I didn't go. I was afraid to go, and I didn't even know why I was afraid. I think I imagined this frenzied orgy happening under black lights on leopard skin rugs. Of course, that was crazy and probably me picking up on the group mind of Western Kentucky. It wasn't an orgy; people weren't in the back room having sex. It was just a party like any other party, although ChiChi didn't become a legend for throwing just mediocre parties. Thankfully, the universe continued to nudge me in her direction until, one day, I was privileged to experience her hospitality.

I met ChiChi years later through a mutual friend. College was well behind me and, thankfully, so was my denial. Living in Louisville at the time, I was finally out to myself and was in relationship with the second love of my life. The first love left me high and dry when I graduated from college. I was heartbroken and convinced God was punishing me for being gay. This was obviously why I was suffering. Then came the "I'm not gay I just fell in love with this one particular woman" game. For those of you who don't know, that line is about as old as they come and has long been used by countless gays and lesbians who have yet to come to terms with their orientation.

My first love was an incredible breaking open of my heart and the hard cast shell I built around my sexuality. Unfortunately, the next step was to move beyond "breaking open" to "heartbroken" when she left me for another. So for the next seven years I was celibate and miserably lonely, but I wasn't GAY! I prayed a lot—not so different from the character Annelle in *Steel Magnolias* who "prayed about everything," even the run in her panty hose. I would never do that again. I would never be gay, and for me, that had—quite literally—a dual interpretation. I was one sad pup for a long, long time. In the next seven years, I moved eleven times across Kentucky and Tennessee, finding refuge in different towns and cities. I kept my head down and my heart closed. I was literally imploding. I survived by focusing only on career and taking care of others. I closed, barred, and locked my "closet"—the problem being, I was standing on the inside of this living tomb. I felt I would be doomed to live there always, but I did not think about it. This seven years of transition lasted until I fell in love again. Then I had to take a long hard look at everything, including the tenets and cultural mores of our time. I felt like Jacob wrestling with the angel. It wasn't until my hip was pulled out of socket that I had the courage to face me. The real me. After all, please remember, I wasn't the free radical. I was the antioxidant, trying to stamp out the bad guys, and the bad guys were obviously the homosexuals.

ChiChi on the other hand—well, I don't know. I never asked her if she had to wrestle with the angel. Many of us did. There was a bloody battleground created in our conscious and subconscious minds by our families, communities, and the well-meaning preachers of our day. Homosexuality was a sin and, depending on your brand of religion, that might mean "Oh, poor thing, God will forgive you" or "YOU'RE GOING TO HELL!" I didn't like either one of those options, and frankly, they were really starting to piss me off. I especially hated the "Oh, we love you but not the sin." Doesn't leave much wiggle room for discovery of self and understanding of one's nature now, does it? Of course, you know all the heterosexuals figured out it was just our choice. Some came to this understanding because most of them had had a carnal thought or two in their lifetime, and they were able to resist the temptation of the devil. Those were the most vocal of the crew, and yes, you all know one—probably in your state legislature and most certainly in your churches. They are the ones turning red in the face while damning all the rest of us to hell. Somehow, they missed Masters and Johnson's studies that put us all on a continuum either really straight or really gay or somewhere in between. Those in between, who live unconsciously, are the really scary ones because they live in fear they might fall over the edge. As a result, people like Matthew Shepard get to experience the second crucifixion of Christ. Being beaten to death and left tied to what used to be a tree. His cross was a fence post—different day, same incredibly sad story. The story is people disconnect from Source and become evil incarnate. No different from Hitler and the SS in Nazi Germany or Pol Pot or Stalin or Bush for that matter. So my point is, standing up for homosexuality by simply being in a small community and living life out loud and out of the closet meant more than just being shunned by the ladies auxiliary. It meant you were putting your life on the line for your integrity and for others who didn't have the courage to do it themselves. Guess that is why I think ChiChi is a legend and one of my heroes.

When I finally met ChiChi through a mutual friend, I was surprised. She wasn't what I had imagined at all. She was a very small woman, red hair and beautiful blue twinkling eyes that crinkled around the edges. She was almost impish. There was such a joy about her. She laughed a lot, and she liked to tease you into laughing with her. She talked straight about everything and didn't have much patience for trivial nonsense. She told it just like it was, as she defined it, and if you didn't like what she had to say, she said it anyway and just a little louder. I was carrying on one time, whining about something very trite, when she handed me a dime and said, "Here, Bo, go call somebody that gives a shit." It wasn't as though we were long-term friends and she could take such liberties with my tender little ego. However, very quickly, I was brought back to reality and thought, "Well, she's right. Who would want to hear this shit?" I think that encounter happened at our first meeting. From the start, I knew she was brutally honest about everything and there was no room for compromise, even when the human ego was involved. I soon learned that, as small as she was in physical stature, she was inversely a magnificently huge spiritual being with a heart to match.

ChiChi lived out loud in a small community and with quite the flair. She was a photographer and a very good one, taking wedding pictures and senior school portraits. Her partner, Ms. Murphy, deserves a whole chapter of her own. What ChiChi missed in physical stature, Ms. Murphy made up for with her physical presence. She was a big woman and also a very big being, matching ChiChi in the heart and soul arena. Murphy was Ms. Murphy because she taught school, and so ChiChi called her "Miss," like the kids. It was sweet really, like the very old and courtly gentleman that called his wife Mrs. Smith. They mirrored each other's hearts and loved one another openly in a small Western Kentucky town. Not unlike any other couple, gay or straight, there was no public display of affection on the court square, but everyone knew they were a couple. Although I did know a couple that drove to a small-town court square and had sex on the lawn in the middle of the night just to thumb their nose at the straight community. Of course, it was dark and no one saw them, so it didn't make a damn bit of difference in terms of furthering their cause. But they felt better.

That wasn't their way, ChiChi and Ms. Murphy. They just loved each other quietly but openly, without apology, and certainly not under the cloak of darkness. They gave to their community and to each other and to anyone who wanted to come play with them. Their hospitality was true to Southern tradition. They lived in small unassuming homes—very simply but in a grand style that was remarkably their own, true to the characters they were.

One of my first encounters with Ms. Murphy was on a hot day in July. Hot in July in Kentucky means "Don't come out of the house, it's miserable." The heat is bad enough, but it is accompanied by a humidity that takes your breath away. So you can't breathe; all your clothes stick to you while at the same time your hair goes limp and looks like someone broke the curling iron. Ms. Murphy had a way to deal with the "dog days of summer." Her house was a small white frame home in the middle of Madisonville proper. Understand, it's a very small town, and *proper*, in this case, means heart of the town (defined as small neighborhood with trees and other little wooden frame houses). In contrast, there was nothing terribly proper about Ms. Murphy. I came around the back of the house to find her in her underwear, sitting in a child's blow-up swimming pool with a martini in her hand. "Come get in the pool, Bo. I got on my sex panties." Sex panties for Ms. Murphy meant the ones with little flowers on them. They all looked like big momma panties—you know the ones, the ones our mothers wore. There is nothing terribly sexy about them. However, for Murphy, the little flowers made them sexy; her everyday panties were devoid of flowers. "Hell, it's hot out there. Come get in." Now understand this was not an invitation to have sex in the kiddy pool. It was just Murphy's way of making light of life and enjoying the moment. I didn't get in the pool, but looking back on the day, it's too bad I didn't. Come to think of it, I've missed many rare moments or opportunities like this. Another example of living unconsciously.

Not too long after I met the girls, my partner and I were invited to one of the famous parties I had heard about since undergraduate school. It was their Halloween party and was held in Hansen, an even smaller town down the road from Madisonville. The party was to take place in one of ChiChi's properties; she was also a realtor and had bought up most of the little town to hear her tell the story. Main Street was lined with a few wooden structures, most empty and all built about the time of the Civil War or "thereabouts," as we say in the South. We drove up to the house, built literally when Abe Lincoln was in office. It was an old Confederate-style dwelling, paint peeling off the wooden clapboards, with a wonderful porch that ran the length of the house on both levels. I swear the house was leaning to one side, and I wasn't at all that sure it wouldn't collapse with us in it. I mentioned my concern to a friend who blithely replied, "Oh, we have the party here every year, and it hasn't fallen down yet." The party was rocking when we came through the door, and my fear grew stronger as I noticed the dance floor moving up and down to the rhythm of the dancers who were totally consumed by the music blaring loudly from the stereo.

I imagined a fun party filled with people just like me: gay, white, and middle-class. I had moved past my previous vision of imagined orgies, black lights, and leopard skin rugs. However, I never dreamed of what I would see when I walked into the old frame house that in its day was probably one of the finer homes of the aristocracy. I don't think I can describe how wonderful it was to find something totally unexpected behind the doors of the old homeplace. Remember, we are in Western Kentucky, the rural Bible Belt in the mid-eighties. The eighties in Hansen could be equivalent to the forties anywhere else on the planet. Well, not that bad, but almost. To help you understand, Rosa Parks was still not deemed a hero by most of these folks. Prejudice was still rampant in the South, and sadly, on many levels, it still runs the show.

Black and white people did not mix, let alone party together in the South. And "oh my Lord," as they would say, it would be unthinkable to see heterosexuals enjoying an evening with the homos. But as I looked across the room, I had one of those defining crystal-clear moments when time stands still and you touch something much larger than yourself. The image held in your mind is shattered like a cloudy pane of glass, and now you see clearly a new vision. The room filled with laughter and conversation, I looked across the dance floor to see black and white, gay and straight, poor and wealthy, powerful and powerless—all in the same place. It was as if I had walked into a mystical portal, and for a night, bigotry was released into the ethers, and in its place, the kingdom of heaven was among us. It seemed an appropriate party for All Hallows Eve. As far as I could tell, I was experiencing alchemy at its best. The lead of prejudice had given way to golden enlightenment. At least for the night, all joined in communion without attention to anything but what made them all family: their divinity.

No one was aware of his or her differences; they came to join in a celebration. Everyone from the white mayor of the City of Madisonville along with his lovely wife to the rather large black schizophrenic gentleman that came from the equivalent of Madisonville's homeless shelter, which by the way was managed by ChiChi. She gathered them all under one sagging roof and invited them to enjoy one another. No thought given to class, color, or creed. There was diversity at its finest, even in Hanson. I realized I was being given a rare and precious gift. The gift was the opening of my eyes. In that opening, I was privileged to see Christ incarnate in a little redheaded fired-up lesbian who defied the laws and regulations handed to her from the Pharisees. Although we seem to be unable to hold this energy for any length of time, there are glimmers of light and transcendence shining through to the surface. The more enlightened we become, the easier it is for us to see this light in every person. For a moment, God is palpable, calming our stormy sea. In this stillness, this peace, we find ourselves!

I was busy looking for the hostess when someone said, "She's upstairs." I found the staircase and climbed to the top, feeling a little more secure above what looked like a living dance floor. It was still moving up and down like a trampoline when I looked back over my shoulder. I shook my head, thinking, what keeps them from falling through? I had to live with that mystery for the moment because I wanted to find ChiChi. Directed out to the old second-floor porch, I found her. There she was alone, leaning over the banister looking out over Hanson—which was now asleep (anyone awake was at her party). The town had a main street, and that is about all I remember it having, with maybe one stop sign or two. The storefronts boarded up long ago. It wasn't big enough to have a court square. Most of the old buildings looked a bit like the one we stood in, leaning but still standing. If the town had had a heyday it was now long past.

ChiChi was smoking a joint when I walked up to her. She had just taken a big toke when she turned to me. Half-holding her breath to keep from losing her big drag, she gestured out over the little street. Her thumb and forefinger formed a tight circle pinching the joint in between—symbolic, as I saw it, for the life she was creating around her. Still holding the burning roach as she gestured out across the banister, smoke ascending like incense over the community, she said, "Bo, you see that town?"

She was obviously looped, her eyes now matching her red hair. I said, "Yes, ChiChi, I see it."

"Well, I own it," she said as she released the burning smoke from her lungs. She turned back to look over her little kingdom, swaying just a little and probably thankful for the banister.

I was very thankful for the banister. It was hard for me to keep from laughing. There was something surreal about the whole evening, the place, and the people. ChiChi probably did own the little town, but that wasn't what impressed me about her. It was her ability to live life without apology. She fully embraced her total self, never pretending to be someone she wasn't. She knew who she was and what she wanted in life. She allowed the people who crossed her path to have their own choice as well. I was in awe of her courage and honesty. I didn't care that she was stoned at the moment; I could still see her quite clearly. I could see the light, a light that shown through her as a beacon for the rest of us. ChiChi changed a community; in fact, ChiChi and people like her change the world. If you are wondering where she got the nickname ChiChi, I have no idea. *Chi* however, in some traditions, means pure energy. I have to say, she lives up to her name. Chi squared.

ChiChi calls us out and invites us to become aware of our inner power and wisdom. As divine beings, we are living in a time of great change in our world. Changes so profound they leave us shaken, disoriented, and confused. The vibration and energy we now live in is related to the changes taking place in our universe and especially here on this planet. Many of you have experienced this vibration on a physical plane. Others of you have experienced the vibrations through the form of sound or light. In all its forms, you are having this experience in a way that will help you with the shift into this next level of our evolution. A higher dimension is now unfolding.

Much will be different as we travel through this portal of atonement. There will be confusion and chaos, and we will be asked to rise above these forms of energy as they do not serve us. Walking through the crowds and in fearful places, we are being asked to hold a space of peace and safety that will help those around us. We are asked to center in our core self where we are in alignment with Source, the God of our knowing.

CHAPTER 5

There is an ever-changing interface with our Creator, over and beyond anything we can imagine—a living, breathing expression of the Divine. It cannot be held or defined; it can only be lived. And in that living, the sacred is born through us not once but through all eternity.

SAVING SISTER PEGGY

IT WAS A WELCOME BREAK after two semesters of core curriculum to leave the University of Kentucky for the Appalachian Mountains. The family nurse-practitioner program was intense, to say the least. Our internship would take place at the Frontier Nursing Service founded by Mary Breckenridge. In my mind, there could be no greater work for a nurse-practitioner, and Mary Breckenridge was the mother of all role models. She literally rode into the mountains on horseback during the Great Depression and established a health care system that would save the lives of countless people, reducing the infant mortality rate exponentially. She was forty-three years old when she returned from her midwifery study in England to begin her practice. Born of the aristocracy of Memphis, Tennessee, her father was the ambassador to Russia. She must have been tempered with an odd mix of rural America and old-world cultures. Following World War I, she traveled to France to help in their recovery. She used what she learned there, in a country of lost resources following the ravages of war, as a model for an area of our country whose resources were lost to the greed of land, timber, and coal barons. There was no area of America more impoverished. The people suffered without health care, many starving and living in substandard housing. Mary rode into town and made short work of pulling together the resources she needed to make their lives better. A survivor of one of the greatest tragedies that can befall a woman, the death of her children and the loss of her soul mate, she turned her grief into a greater love for all people.

Mary Breckenridge would raise the funds to build a hospital in Hyden, Kentucky and, from this central hub, directed the outposts that would be staffed by other nurses. These small clinics, where my classmates and I would be stationed, were scattered across the hills. There was Beechfork, Red Bird, Flat Creek, Mud Creek, and Buckhorn to name a few. I know the names are a trip, but all these tiny clinics resulted in improving health care for hundreds of people. The people, in turn, held a profound admiration for the nurses who came from all over the country to do this work. With their admiration came a trust and respect that carried with it the burden of living up to those expectations and beliefs. I found it quite daunting. I had no idea if I would be able to live up to the level of those nurses who came before me.

What started as a placement in graduate school ended up beginning my career as a nurse-practitioner. In my starry-eyed romanticism, working in Appalachia with the poor seemed like the ideal place to "do God's work." I prayed about it and prayed about it some more, long and hard. It was hard because I was absolutely up in the night. I didn't want to live alone on the side of a mountain as the sole health care provider for a large group of people straight out of graduate school. "What? Are you nuts?" Well, yes, yes I was nuts. "Crazier than the pony you rode in on" comes to mind, but unlike Mary B., I did not arrive on horseback. Still, I left school and made camp in a little cabin on the side of a mountain in the middle of nowhere. As a social being, I'd have to say, "What was I thinking?" "God," God was all I was thinking. I was on the quest, the "Hound of Heaven." I was doing "God's work." Somewhere between college and graduate school, something shifted in me, taking me ever deeper into my fundamentalist understanding of God. In those days, I still had a father-daughter relationship with God. Being moved around like a pawn, I felt totally comfortable in knowing God would take care of me and, as long as I was doing "His will"… no problems. Well, *not*; there were problems. And the biggest problem, I was suffering the torture of the damned by my loneliness.

When I arrived in Buckhorn, Kentucky, I was a Methodist Fundamentalist charismatic who was on a quest. Everything was a quest. I was determined to live my life according to God's will and be sure that everyone else did too. We were given choices and descriptions of each outpost. I wanted to be sure I was in the place God wanted me to be, so I prayed about it. Those were my "pray 'til your knees bleed" days. I prayed about, well, just everything. I was certain the God of the universe had an extra-special plan for me. I was not about making or taking responsibility for my own plan. In my mind, if I prayed hard enough, I would be led—albeit blindly—into just the right place at just the right time to do God's will and "save" someone. That's what good evangelical Christians do; it's our life's work. So when asked to choose a placement for my graduate internship as a nurse-practitioner, I felt sure I was led to Buckhorn. I wasn't certain why God wanted me in Buckhorn, but later I found out my internship preceptor was a Catholic nun. Oh, that made perfect sense because obviously I was supposed to "save" her! In my experience, Catholics needed to be saved as they were a bit misguided and could be lost, as I saw it.

Buckhorn was literally a one-stop town nestled at the base of the mountains. Really, to be more descriptive, you would have to say "hamlet squeezed between the hills." This is a biased reflection. The people who live in Appalachia feel held by the mountains, cradled by the hills surrounding their hollers. I felt like a sardine in a sandwich. Some days, I felt like the hills were going to swallow me up. By the weekends, I had had it and would drive frantically across the mountains to emerge somewhere near Lexington where I could breathe again.

It was a beautiful place really, incredibly green and rugged. The mist lay over us like a gray, moist cape on most mornings—especially during the summer, burning off later in the day. Until then, you never knew if it was a sunny or cloudy day; it remained a mystery until about ten or eleven o'clock. The humidity so high, books on the shelf would mold. Literally you could open a book to find black mold sprayed across the pages like a gunshot blast. So you can see how sardine is a perfect description, packed in and wet.

I drove into Buckhorn on the first day looking for the clinic. As described by my nursing instructor, the clinic consisted of two trailers arranged side by side near the baseball field. Those were my directions. The town consisted of the general store, the church, the public school, the Presbyterian Children's Center, the clinic—oh, and Rosie's ice cream parlor and hamburger stand, which sat on the edge of town. In the middle of all these establishments was the one stop sign I told you about. You drive up a winding two-lane mountain highway, sometimes so close to the ridge you hope your angels are outside the car keeping the tires inside the painted lines. Not so many guardrails on those highways, and personally, I would trust the angels far more than the little guardrails. After driving up the mountain, you drive down the other side of the mountain. This up-and-down process of winding road and calling on the angels repeats itself about a hundred times before you finally arrive, white knuckled, at your destination. Only to find you can drive through and out of Buckhorn in about two minutes, literally, unless someone has stopped in the middle of the road to visit with a neighbor. Then it could take considerably longer.

I found myself anxious and excited. I didn't know what to expect, but I felt sure I was on the right path because I prayed about it. Our instructors described the settings and preceptors to us. They were right on about the town, but they had no idea about Sister Peggy Duggan, OP. They got that all wrong—well, mostly wrong. I was told Peggy was a bit gruff but a good preceptor and nurse-practitioner. This statement was true. She was a good nurse-practitioner, but she was far more than their narrow description. I wasn't too excited to think I was going to be working all summer with someone described as "a bit gruff." It conjured up images of cranky and mean. Peggy was far from cranky or mean. However, my first impression had me a little concerned.

I found the clinic, walked up on the porch, and took a deep breath as I reached out to turn the doorknob. Little did I know, my life would never be the same after walking through that door. What I expected was an internship in family practice. What I got was far more. When I stepped inside the small white trailer, I was standing in a little waiting room. To my right, where the bedroom used to be, was an office where the secretary receptionist sat—Julie Gay. Julie smiled quietly at me, but I could see a questioning look on her face. I was a stranger in those parts—Julie lived in Buckhorn all her life and she knew everyone, man, woman, and child. I told her I was the nurse-practitioner student from the University of Kentucky, and I was supposed to meet with Sister "Doogan," mispronouncing Peggy's name. Now she looked even more confused, but after a moment's hesitation, her smile returned, and she said with a very Eastern Kentucky Southern drawl, "Oh, you mean Sister Peggy. I'll let her know you are here." She walked past me and through a narrow, short hallway that connected the business office/ receptionist/ waiting area trailer to the clinic/ lab/ clinician office trailer. In case you haven't gathered, this was not the Mayo Clinic. My wait was brief, and Julie came back out to escort me in to meet the woman who would forever change my life.

Peggy was sitting at her desk, which was in a small bedroom now converted into an exam room. I could see the woods out her window that bordered the baseball field and school. Peggy's hair was short cropped and starting to gray. She wore khaki pants and a button-down plaid cotton shirt under her white lab coat. Her small desk was crowded with charts, yet they were very neatly arranged, and on the corner, her stethoscope lay next to her prayer book. She didn't smile at first and looking out at me through steel-gray eyes said, "I didn't expect you until tomorrow." I had two immediate thoughts. They were "Oh, here comes the gruff part," and "Oh shit! Did I screw up?"

Fortunately, there were no patients waiting, so Peggy was able to redirect her day to include me. I was given the tour of the clinic, which took about the same time as driving through the town had taken—two minutes. There was one more exam room at the other end of the trailer equally as small and austere. The center of the trailer contained a scale for heights and weights, the medical library (which consisted of a couple bookshelves), and a laboratory that used to be the kitchen. A microscope and centrifuge, in addition to a small autoclave for sterilizing medical equipment and supplies, were arranged purposefully on either side of the sink. Specimen jars and glass blood-collecting vials lined the counters; multicolored stoppers topped the tubes in shades of purple, blue, red, and green. This was about the only color in the place, which seemed extremely small and dark to me. However, I soon learned that the color was not in the décor but in the people who walked through the door and, most especially, in Sister Peggy.

After the tour, I walked with Peg back out into the administration and waiting room trailer to be introduced to the administrator, Mary Ann Sparks.

Mary Ann greeted me with a warm smile. She was a small woman in her mid to late forties, and she cradled one hand in the other in an odd sort of way. I later learned she had suffered a stroke during pregnancy, which left her with a paralyzed hand. She seemed a little anxious but very friendly. We exchanged a few pleasantries and then I was shuffled out the door. Peggy seemed to need a little time and space, and she wanted to get me settled. While I was talking to Mary Ann, Peg was trying to decide where I would stay for the night.

She made a few phone calls, and arrangements were made for me to stay in the administrative building of the children's center. Peggy introduced me to the pillars of the community as we walked through town. HC, who helped run the general store, Mary Ann's husband; Maude, the owner of the general store, Mary Ann's mother; and Charlie, the director of the children's center, no relation. They all greeted me with courtesy and warm welcome.

We met a few other friends along the way, and I was shown to my room, I think, so Peggy could regroup. I immediately felt lonely in the small room, wondering if my prayers really had been answered or if I had failed in my discernment. At the same time, I was wondering how I was going to bring up the subject of the big G with the sister. I would have to be subtle, not too forward, yet charming. Charming was important as I wanted to win her over and gain her trust and admiration so I could "save her." I knew God would guide me in my efforts, so I wasn't worried. Well, not much.

The center of town held three main structures that surrounded the one stop sign I told you about. The general store, the children's center, and the Presbyterian church formed the tiny trinity of their metropolis. This was where community was formed, where neighbors greeted neighbors, and old folks watched the children play while talking about the weather and their ailments. This was about all there was to talk about. The Presbyterian church was a log cathedral. Literally built with logs, a beautifully designed, relatively large two-story structure—people were very proud of their place of worship, which was understandable. There were other churches scattered over the hills. Some of which were led by self-proclaimed preachers who got "the call" and started their own brand of Pentecostal religion. These were places where people lifted their voices in foreign tongues. Indeed, they lifted more than their voices. On occasion, what was lifted included poisonous snakes. Poison—quite literally, poison—was doled out like Sunday morning cocktails for the faithful's consumption. All these actions proclaimed their undying faith—undying as long as they didn't piss off Mr. Snake, who, by the way, probably didn't abide by "churchgoin'."

The little community was well cared for and home for the Appalachian peoples who had lived here all their lives. These folks were very connected to the land and to each other. Their families migrated here from England. Many of their colloquialisms and seemingly odd expressions hailed from the queen herself, I suppose. Very few ever chose to leave. The web of their ancestry covers the hills and the hollers, permeating the life force that binds them together like the aspen trees of the Rockies. Aspens form a community bound together by one enormous root system, all the trees interconnected. On my way up to Peg's, I stood at the stop sign, looking up to see the hills surrounding me and the town in all directions. I felt like I could reach out and touch the face of every hill, as if standing in a small closet of hillside. *Tightly knit community* took on a literal meaning in the topography of this place.

A small lane wound up the side of the mountain where Peggy lived in a cabin provided by the children's center. There were several small white clapboard houses on the side of this hill serving as housing for the "dorm parents" who worked at the center and a few strays like Sr. Peggy and me. Peg invited me to come up later for dinner. As preceptor, she not only had to serve as teacher but she had to house and feed me as well. There was really no other choice. Well, except Rosie's burger stand at the edge of town or the Fred Burgers at the general store. Fred Burgers—what an Eastern Kentucky delicacy. The "burger," which wasn't a burger at all, was named after Fred who worked at the general store. Fred's namesake was a full-bodied bologna sandwich. He sliced the bologna one inch thick off a huge hunk of processed meat from the cooler. Loaded down with tomato, lettuce, onion, and copious amounts of mayonnaise, it was a real artery stopper! The cholesterol contained in just one of his sandwiches had to hold a world record. He was famous for this culinary art of bologna sandwich making, which was topped off with potato chips and Pepsi. Either choice of dining establishments would get old after a while, and we won't talk about what they would do to your lipid levels. So Peggy's dinner invitations were welcomed.

I walked slowly up the lane with excited anticipation and began thinking of St. Paul and his mission work. Still mulling over how I was going to bring up the God conversation, the speed of my cadence up the hill picked up, and what a hill it would be. More like Thomas Merton's *Seven Story Mountain*.

I arrived at Peggy's front door where she invited me in. She seemed more at ease now and a bit friendlier. She was having a beer and offered me one. Now it had been about four or five years since alcohol had passed over my born-again lips, but I thought, well, as St. Paul would say, all things for all people for the sake of the Lord's work. That's not a direct quote, but you get the gist. So I said, "Sure." Pretty soon I was also a little more at ease and a little friendlier. It doesn't take much hooch after that length of time to get you a bit tipsy. I drank with the college kids a little after college, but when I recommitted myself to the Lord while in Nashville, I decided I should not drink, no matter how much wine Jesus made. I could not afford to get off track.

We were to be feasting on tuna fish sandwiches and beer. Now you can't beat that when you're in graduate school and poor as a church mouse; if it's free, it's great! Peg's house was small and simple. She lived her vow of poverty literally. I saw her recycle tinfoil and paper towels regularly. Her meals usually came from the scraps they threw out of the backdoor of the children's center. They threw the scraps her way, mind you; she wasn't collecting them out of the trash cans. Entry through the front door left you standing in the living room, which doubled as a dining room. There was a very small galley kitchen on the right. Her table hugged the wall between the entrance to kitchen on one side and bathroom on the other. Straight back was a closet with two little bedrooms on either side of the house. All of that held in about five hundred square feet. The house felt warm, and I felt welcomed—maybe this wasn't going to be as hard as I thought? A crucifix hung on one wall, and on the other, a picture of Jesus with his lost sheep draped over his shoulders.

Peggy and I talked freely about the internship, and she shared a little about herself. I smiled as a bit of her Irish brogue came through, mixed with a strong Boston accent. It was really fun for me, having never spent time with someone from the East or that Irish. Peggy's mother, Bridget, was born in Ireland. She came across the sea as an adult, where she met Peg's father, a longshoreman. They raised five children together in South Boston.

Bridget was a no-nonsense Catholic, passionate about her family and the Irish Republic. She raised her family with love and a stern hand. Peg learned early how to bob and weave as it was not so unusual for a glass milk jug to sail by her head as it made its way to the intended target, one of her teenage brothers. Her brothers met their match with Bridget but, on occasion, forgot who was boss. The flying milk jugs were gentle reminders. Peg was one of two girls with three brothers. There was nothing dainty about her. She was fierce about her work, swore like a sailor when it was appropriate, and would hang upside down on a cross for those she served if need be. It did not take long to realize the gravity of this woman's work. She wasn't just tending the wounds of the flesh; she was caring for their souls as well. Watching Peg with her patients was like watching Jesus heal the sick. It was, for me, the first time I could plainly see Jesus in another—as if he were incarnate through this loving, strong, salty saint. I was in awe and in love almost immediately. Before long, I knew I would have hung upside down on a cross for Peggy if need be. And as it turns out, I did. Well, metaphorically.

We weren't too far into the conversation, and I was still obsessing about how to mention God and start proselytizing when, suddenly, Peggy looked across the table and said, "Well, how are things with you and God?"

I thought, "Wow, this is going to be so easy. The Holy Spirit must be right here sitting at this table."

And she was, sitting directly across from me. So who was going to save who? I'll spare you the suspense. One year later, I was Catholic.

I often think back about that night and our friendship. Sitting on the side of a mountain, in a cabin, in the presence of JC (as Peggy liked to call him), talking about God over our communion of tuna and beer. I laugh out loud sometimes as I think about what a sense of humor there must be in the Almighty. I came to save Peggy, and Peggy converted me to Catholicism. It has to make you laugh. I am still laughing. It's all perfect, the unfolding of our lives. It just may not turn out exactly as we plan.

She always seemed to have the candles burning when I walked into the front room; their reflected soft glow of illumination flickered across the sanctuary that was her home. Cream sherry stored in the kitchen cabinet was always available to warm the body, while our conversations warmed the soul. In this place we sat, night after night, through the summer of my internship, sharing the Spirit—a little of both kinds. Peggy opened a whole new world for me, that of the mystic. I never imagined how rich my spiritually would become because of her presence in my life and the seeds she planted. Prior to Sister Peggy, my line to God was one-way. I did all the talking and never really listened. Although I believed in a living, personal God, I treated God like a foreign deity, trusting in divine intervention but not given to being a part of the plan.

During one conversation, Peg asked, "Well, how do you envision God? Is he like an old white guy with a beard sitting on a throne?"

I laughed. "No, of course not." But I found myself blushing as I thought, "Well, yes. I guess that is kind of how I envision God."

Peggy began talking to me about her directed retreats. Experiencing God through visions, prayers, and symbols was all new to me. My perspective was narrow, one-dimensional. What she described was far more than I ever dreamed of or hoped for in this lifetime. So if she could experience this depth of relationship, then why not me? My experience of communion with God had been through a stale cracker, tiny one at that. She was talking about standing face-to-face and having a two-way conversation with the Almighty, the great I AM. I felt like someone had just shown me the Arc of the Covenant.

Peg entered religious life older than most women in that day. She completed nursing school before she found her way to the Order of Preachers. Being a novice was no easy feat, and many returned home, including Peg's best friend who entered with her. As Peggy blossomed, her friend withered—which created, for Peg, a great sadness. Typically, those who didn't make it left silently in the night, and it was not talked about. Peg endured; religious life suited her. If I was the Hound of Heaven, Peg was the Bull Dog. She gave up everything in her quest and thirst for God, throwing herself into her profession, heart and soul. Life was good, prayer was good, things were plugging right along, and then it happened, Vatican II. Life for all vowed religious would forever change; Pope John Paul threw a wrench in the works.

When Peg entered and eventually took her vows, she became Sister Mark Daniel, leaving her past identity behind to become the bride of Christ. Her vows included poverty, chastity, and obedience. She was in the full habit. The Dominican habits were quite beautiful: solid white from their veil to the tip of their hems, which reached the floor. Prayer beads hung at their sides, looping long and deep, symbolic of their devotion. This was all to change now as Pope John Paul unleashed a tidal wave of reform. He called his followers to throw off their trappings. Sisters came out of the habit as he challenged the faithful to understand all are called to this depth of personal relationship and service to God, not just the religious orders. These changes shook the church at its very core. It shook Sr. Peggy too, now thirteen years into the habit, on all levels.

How would that feel if you left everything to follow Christ and serve the church you loved only to find out you could have your cake and eat it too? "Celebrate, not celibate," as the old joke goes. I would think it would be a bit like someone pulling the rug out from under you. It seems this is not new for the followers of the way. Jeremiah wailed, "I have been duped, oh Lord, and I let myself be duped!" Poor Jeremiah, poor Peggy—poor religious orders, for that matter. Before this moment in time, it was all about devotion, hard work, rote prayers, and obedience. Difficult but doable. Now everything changed. Simplicity gave way to organicity. Relationship with the Creator of all became far more complex on all levels as they were called to step out from behind "the habit" and step into a constantly evolving, living expression of their deepest longings and divinity. In many ways, at that moment in time, the Catholic

Church modeled for all peoples a new paradigm. There are many habits of faith that need to be disrobed in order to bring about a living expression of spirituality. Religion has very little to do with it.

This shifting of consciousness resulted in a crisis of vocation for many in religious life. And so it was for Peggy as she realized she still didn't really know God. This is why she entered religious life. She wanted this more than anything. More than family, more than home, more than relationship with another—she wanted to know God. After years of listening, praying, and waiting, it became clear to her she had not reached her goal. She did not really know God at all. She knew God through her head, but after all, she was one of the brides of Christ. She wanted to know God through her heart.

Peg met with her superior to tell her she was leaving. This was it. A very wise and gentle woman, the superior listened to Peggy's rationale and suggested she do one more thing before she left. After all, this was very serious; there would be no going back after such a decision. She asked Peggy to make a directed retreat. They had to wait for the Pope's dispensation anyway, and that would take a little while, so why not make good use of the time? Many were experiencing this crisis of religious vocation following the Pope's revelation; poor guy had to wonder if he made the right decision. After he "threw open the windows of the church," lots of folks started jumping out.

So Peggy, in keeping with her vow of obedience, agreed. The retreat was scheduled for eight days and would be made with a director trained in the tradition of the Jesuits, a religious order of great theologians who were also quite heady. Their retreats are directed from the head with the help of the scriptures. This was a familiar place from which to start. Peg's most dominant expression was mental. The Jesuits' style provided a place in which she could be comfortable. The "directee" would spend anywhere from seven to thirty days in silence during these retreats, meeting with their director once a day for one hour. Usually one would be lodged in a place of hospitality, like a convent or motherhouse. As their guest, you would receive hospitality for the week or weeks of your process. Everyone knew you were in retreat, and so they would not bother you, typically smiling and nodding without engaging you in a conversation.

This was a huge decision for Peg; discerning whether to stay or go was only a small part of her discernment. Her heartfelt question was not about the expression of her life as a religious or layperson; it was "Who are you, God?" Peggy put her heart and soul into the retreat, and on the seventh day, she felt no closer to her answer than she had in the last thirteen years. Peg met with her director to tell her how disappointed she was, to which the director replied, "I think you are angry with God because he has ignored you."

At first, Peg could not believe the director would suggest such a thing, "Angry with God?" Now she felt even more disappointed and disillusioned, but as she walked back to the cabin where she was staying, the anger began to surface. She could feel it welling up inside her with the force of a repressed fury she had never allowed to surface. Well, not when in her "right mind," but "right" was about to get the boot in keeping with the Pope's example.

As she stood in the cabin, the tirade started, and it did not stop until Peggy had her say with her oft-too-silent lover. Looking at the wooden door, the exit from it all, she did not leave. She stayed and exclaimed, "Yes, she's right! I am angry—very angry with you, you woodenhead!" She told God, "You are mean! Here I have spent thirteen years in this order following you around in this monkey suit! Working, praying, following all the rules, and you have ignored me. Here I am right under your nose in the sheepfold, and you run off and save the one dumb sheep that falls off the cliff?" The anger continued to spill out until, at last, all had been said except the last word, which was, "If you don't come across tonight, I am out of here in the morning!" She picked up the Bible that had been her constant companion and slammed it facedown on the table, making her point. Having said it all, the anger was gone and Peggy felt "surprisingly free," soon falling into a deep sleep.

It was four in the morning when Peg was awakened by the sound of voices singing. As Peg tells it, they were singing, "My Word is flowing like a river, flowing out of you and me, flowing out into the desert, setting all the captives free." When the singing subsided, the room was filled with light as if dawn had come early. Looking at the clock, Peg knew it wasn't sunrise. It was four in the morning. She knew something was happening and felt certain she should do something—return to the prayer, read the scriptures, something. She sat up and looked where her Bible lay. It was still facedown, but now words appeared on the back cover, which was blank the night before. It read "The Word." She found it odd because the words were arranged so that you had to read the text from right to left, "Word The."

As she sat there filled with awe, she heard, "Let my word, rich as it is, dwell in you." Peg responded with her whole being, "Yes!" She sat in the silence for what felt like a long time, as time stood still. The sound and light show was not over, however, because soon there was a knock at the door. She opened the door, but no one was there. She could now see the dawn beginning to appear over the horizon. Closing the door, she turned to see the clock again. It was six thirty. Quickly dressing, she went to the seven o'clock mass. The gospel was so alive for her; every word penetrated her whole being. Her lover had finally showed up, or maybe she was finally able to feel his presence. "I felt like every cell in my body was being soaked by the incoming tide"—a very familiar sensation for a woman who grew up in the high tides of the East Coast.

The Tide finally came in for my friend. She was able to be clear about and focus on what she wanted more than anything, and so it became hers. The bridegroom stood at the door knocking, and she opened the door into a new life. "Woodenhead" came through as promised! Thanks be to God.

Years later, Peggy's retreat was to be affirmed again—typical or, I should say, typical for my experiences and Peg's. It's as though the universe is saying, "OK, just in case you forgot or just in case you don't really believe this happened, I'm going to give you another little reminder." While at a Bible study, the instructor brought in several bibles. Among them there was a Hebrew Bible written in this ancient tongue. Peg became curious because the text had to be read from right to left, and the title was written on the back cover, just as it was written during the retreat of her rapture. In that moment of quickening, Peg asked, "What does this say in English?" The teacher responded, "The Word."

I listened in awe to the story of Peg's first directed retreat. I trusted Peggy. There was no concern that she made up this story; I knew she was telling me the truth. A whole new world of possibility opened before me as I never dreamed one could actually have a living, interactive relationship with the Almighty this side of hereafter. Before this time in my history, it was truly all about love and adoration from afar, and I do mean far. God was in "his" heaven, and all was right with the world as long as you followed the rules as written and interpreted from the Word (Bible) and were saved, amen. Learning that I could have a one on one with the Creator of the universe was more than I could get my head around but became my sole desire.

The next step was obvious. I had no romantic love interest; I was avoiding that like the plague. Suddenly, I understood the reason for my coming to Buckhorn. I was not here to save Sr. Peggy. I was here to begin my process of entering religious life, and obviously, Peggy was to be my mentor. It was all so clear now. Don't you just love how we jump from step A to Z without all the LMNOP steps? Somehow, I missed that whole thing with the Pope telling his flock one is called to this depth of relationship with God regardless of their vocation, religious or laity. Since I missed out on that part, in my mind, the only way to have this kind of prophetic, mystic relationship was to become a nun. Of course, there were a few preliminary steps, like becoming Catholic.

This took entirely too long for my schedule and lack of patience, a year of study and classes. That was a little disappointing; my previous experience of joining a religion took about thirty minutes.

I became Peggy's shadow, listening intently to every word that fell from her lips. I was sure she had a direct line to the Almighty, and so this was a little like being on the extension. I began working toward entering religious life and taking my own directed retreats. The outer layers of my God-in-a-box started to fall away, and something new began to take its place. A bigger box. Yes, unfortunately, I was still in the boxed model of spirituality. Like processed food, it's a far cry from the real thing but there are some similarities.

CHAPTER 6

There is no magic without faith, no understanding without heart, no just cause without total abandonment of pre-constructed ideals. The journey of the wayfarer is always uncharted but divinely guided and never alone, no matter how it may seem.

Angels and Visions

IN ADDITION TO PLANNING MY entrance into religious life, Peg was also helping me plan my entrance into my professional life. In keeping with following in her footsteps (because, again, she obviously had a direct line to God), I made it my intent to take over her practice so she could follow her dream of practicing midwifery. Peg would be leaving to join other nurse midwives in Harlingen, Texas. Now as I've said, how crazy can this be? Stepping out of the classroom with a brief internship into solo practice in an isolated region of Appalachia, does that make any sense at all? Absolutely freaking crazy, I tell you. No backup, just out there by yourself—not even a green doctor but a green nurse-practitioner. Practitioners are good at what they do, but they have a limited scope of practice. This community of people had more than limited needs. I knew my scope of practice—problem was, the people I served did not.

The people I cared for thought "the nurse" can do anything, and over the years, "the nurse" has done everything. The difference is, those nurses were seasoned; I was not. To make matters worse, some of these folks would not leave their hollers even when told their problem was more than I could handle. If I would not help them, they simply just let nature take its course using whatever remedy their granny had passed down to them over the years. I learned quickly enough: either help them or they are on their own. So much for scope of practice.

There was no way this decision to take over Peg's practice made sense, but Peggy put a little sign above my desk that read, "Nothing's going to happen today that you and God can't handle." Well, that's just special until the phone rings at 3:00 a.m. and "MaryAnn's in the shock" is what you hear on the other end of the line. Insulin shock, and me without even a glucometer to test her blood sugar, no emergency room close enough to save her. It was me driving down the holler to push glucose and pray to God this was the reason for her coma. There is no 911 in Appalachia. Did I say I prayed a lot? Prayer is the only 911 available there, and the bottom line is, you are at the mercy of your neighbor and the nurse. You hope you have a good one on both counts.

Through the summer of my internship, Peg and I continued to plan my transition into career and vocation all wrapped up in one neat package. I would go back to UK to complete my last semester and then return to work at Frontier Nursing Service while waiting to receive my board results, officially becoming a nurse-practitioner. The summer passed too quickly, and I went back to Lexington for another wicked hard semester of coursework before graduation in December of 1983. I took my boards and traveled back to Appalachia. I was required to pass the boards and work for at least another six months in joint practice before I could legally take over for Peggy in a solo practice.

So, as with many before me, I started at Mary Breckenridge Hospital in Hyden, Kentucky. This was big city compared to Buckhorn. I think they had two stop signs. I would live on the side of Thousandsticks Mountain in housing provided for students and residents. The large cabin provided rooms for the "outlanders" like me who came to work in the hospital or outposts. The people living there shared a common room, bathroom, and kitchen. I didn't know a soul and spent most of my time in my room praying. I think I was praying for confirmation about my decision to move there and praying that I wouldn't accidentally kill anyone by making a poor management decision about their health care.

I don't remember who shared housing with me during those brief months in the large dorm like cabin of Thousandsticks. However, I did meet an angel while living in Hyden. Her name was Elizabeth. Incredibly lonely and scared, I felt like I had bit off more than I could chew on all levels, with special emphases on clinical practice and social isolation. I continued to see Peg every weekend, which was incredibly helpful, but during the week, I was alone in a foreign land. Then one evening, Elizabeth knocked on my door.

The unannounced visit was unusual in itself. No one was particularly friendly in this place, including me. I opened the door to see a very young and beautiful woman standing in my entrance, gently smiling at me. She had dark eyes and long dark-brown hair pulled back in a braid that trailed down her back. She was slender and her features balanced into a delicate beauty. Her smile alone was healing as she asked if she could come in and visit. I don't know how she knew about me or why she showed up. She did not live in the cabin. Story has it, she was an RN working in the hospital. Rumor also had it, not a very good RN. Her poor incarnation as a nurse put in mind the story of Clarence, the angel in *It's a Wonderful Life*. He was naive, kind, and a bit clumsy and awkward in his attempt to save George.

I found out more about her, including the part about being a poor nurse, much later after she was gone. It seems we met, she left her message, and then she was gone. I guess that's what most good angels do. There was an energy of purity about her that is hard to describe, but it was palpable. When she walked into the room, it was like someone unplugged the circuits, and all my anxiety promptly drained through the floor into the earth, leaving only silence and serenity in their place. Suddenly, everything seemed more transparent, and I was transfixed in the moment. She stayed only briefly, and I don't remember all the details of our conversation. It seems like there was only small talk for a few moments, and then she looked up to see a poster I had on my wall depicting the universe. She turned back, looking into my eyes for what seemed like a very long time. What would normally have felt awkward was not uncomfortable at all, but mesmerizing. She was smiling all the while and, after the pregnant pause came to a climax, she simply said; "You are our sky gazer." She said this with such love and adoration; I just stared back at her in stunned silence as she continued to smile. She was right; I was a sky gazer. I had always been drawn to the heavens, but even more now as it was the only thing in my world that was familiar—like having a piece of home, no matter where my wayfaring journeys took me. It didn't seem to be what she said as much as the transformation that happened for me during her visit. It was as if something had been downloaded into my psyche. I was left feeling loved and no longer alone.

It was not until years later when I reflected on the experience that I began to think. Elizabeth was not a good nurse because she was not a nurse at all. She was an angel, a messenger sent from the heavens I was so fond of gazing into. In the shamanic world, when an animal looks deeply into your eyes in this manner, it is said they are giving you their medicine. Their medicine is their power, their energy, their particular gift—which is uniquely their own. In retrospect, I will always believe this is why Elizabeth knocked on my door. I needed her magic, this energy, to meet the challenges that were to come.

The clinic I was working in while in Hyden was physically connected to Mary Breckenridge Hospital. This is where I was to go through my orientation before being dispatched to the outpost at Mud Creek in Clay County. I walked down the hill to the clinic just yards away from our backdoor. I really didn't like my living situation on the Hill as they called it. Many people from all over the United States came to this place to do "good work" and had lived on this hill. I was in good company, but still felt quite isolated. On occasion, all the practitioners and physicians would meet, coming in from the outposts scattered all over the mountains. This is how I met Rose.

Rose was the nurse-practitioner now in charge at Mud Creek. Like most of the nurse-practitioners, she had a little bit of a hippie-chick feel to her. Soft flowing skirts, tunic tops and feet dawned with matching socks and Birkenstock sandals. Rose hailed from the East, like my sister Peggy. East but not Boston, there was no real accent. The nurse-practitioner she worked with at the clinic was leaving for a six-month vacation. She was planning to tour the world in her well-worn Birkenstocks. This is what provided me with the six-month practicum I needed to ready myself for the Buckhorn practice. It all fell together quite neatly. So I would work with these two women briefly after my orientation, and then Susan would leave Rose and me to take care of the practice while she was gone.

Rose lived in one of the original outposts, a relatively large cabin not far from the Mud Creek clinic. As the years went by, they moved the clinic out of the nurses' home and built a separate clinic down the road a piece. The cabin was filled with dogs, cats, and a goat or two. Seems like there were also chickens, but they didn't come in the house. Well, at least they were not invited into the house. The place required work, and Rose really didn't like the idea of living there alone while Susan was gone, so she invited me to live with her. Now I had no problem living with Rose, but the goats were a tad much for me. I'm a bit of a neat freak, and you can imagine we could hardly eat off the floors with all the animals running around. We had electricity but no television and, at that time, no Internet. The phones worked, if it wasn't raining, which in Kentucky was about a fifty-fifty proposition, especially in the spring. I imagined Rose and I would become good friends, and even the goats couldn't keep me from seizing the opportunity to leave my cloistered existence on Thousandsticks Mountain.

I made my home in the attic of the old cabin. It was used for storage and didn't really take much to dust things off and set up my bed in the corner. There was a wonderful sleeping porch off my makeshift bedroom where you could slumber in the summer months while listening to the night sounds of tree peepers and crickets creating the symphony of spring. I chose the attic because I could close it off and keep the animals, goats included, out of my space.

Unfortunately for Rose and for me, I continued my cloistered existence even there. As it turns out, it wasn't others that caused my isolation, it was me. It seems only God could fill this hole I had created for myself. I was determined to experience God in the same way Peggy had; I wanted my mystical experience. When I came home at night, I quickly retired to my attic "apartment" to read my Bible and pray. *Apartment* is a good term because I had withdrawn to be apart from the world. Looking back, I feel sorry for Rose. She didn't know she was inviting a religious fanatic into her home. She probably thought she was going to have a little company and a little help. I am embarrassed to say I was neither, but in my mind, I had to be totally focused on my pursuit of God. I could not be bothered by the mundane.

Each night after work, I climbed the stairs to my room. I would read and pray until it was time to go to bed. Then I would close my eyes, drifting gently off to sleep. I can't say I was happy, but I was definitely determined, waiting expectantly for God's arrival. Spring was waking up the woods, and now it was warm enough for me to leave the windows and doors open to the sleeping porch. On some nights, I would lie out on the porch and listen to the song of the night creatures. One night, as I said my last amen, a gentle breeze stirred, touching my forehead and leaving me with the feeling of being kissed good night—a sensation I had reveled in over the years. Every day of my childhood ended with my mother's gentle forehead blessing, one soft kiss. I was sure this kiss was from God and a prequel of what was to come.

My hunger for God grew each day, and my determination to remain ever faithful expanded along with my hunger. My habitual study and prayer filled my evenings, while my days were consumed with healing the sick and reflecting on the beauty of the people I served. We were a few days away from Holy Week, my first Catholic celebration of Easter. I loved the feasts and special holy days, observations of the life of Christ and all the saints that followed in his path. The rituals were a feast in themselves. Later it became clear to me why these symbolic acts touched something deeper than could ever be expressed through language. The spoken word is impotent in comparison to the artistic expression of the godly. The art form always invites us to something that is far deeper than can be defined by words in any language. To experience this place, you have to step out of the mind. That sounds really strange, doesn't it?

"Are you crazy?"

"No, I just stepped out of my mind for a minute. I'll be right back."

Sometimes this stepping out sneaks up on you as it did for me on this night. It was not unlike any other evening in my cell of the soul complete with study, prayer, and reflection. But on this night, as I lay there, my mind sank into the silent gap between wakefulness and sleep. Suddenly, although my eyes were closed tightly, I was looking at a large rocky cliff. The details of the image so clear, it was as if I was standing there in front of it—so real I felt I could surely reach out and touch the face of the precipice. From the center of the rock was a triangular opening, and from that opening water was exploding out at me as if the source on the other side was attached to a fire hose. It was no trickle; it was a large forceful outpouring of water. I did not want to open my eyes because I did not want to miss this! So I lay there with my eyes closed, acutely aware and taking in every detail. My mind was back in all its glory, trying to explain how this was happening. I went through the checklists of reason. "Am I asleep? No, I can hear Rose and the animals downstairs. Am I dreaming? No, I can't be dreaming if I am awake. Am I having a vision? Wow, I am having a vision.

God must be talking to me in a vision!" Then the next thought was, "I have no idea what he is talking about. I'll ask Sr. Peggy, she'll know." Sound familiar, *Wizard of Oz* fans? "Let's ask the wizard, he'll know." The vision quietly faded, and now I was bouncing off the walls, alert and excited. But it was too late to call Peg. And besides, it was raining, and so the phones were probably out.

I burst into Peg's cabin that weekend, and the words exploded out of me not unlike the water I saw bursting through the rock. I recalled the whole experience in finite detail as Peggy sat listening. She wasn't nearly as excited as I was; I saw not even a spark of wonder. She took it all in as if listening to the morning weather report. Then when I finished with my tale, she said quietly, "You will see it."

"See what?" I said.

"See it."

"You mean see it, the cliff? See it, the water? See it, as in understanding?"

"Yes," she said, "you will see it."

And that is all she said. Well, I had to feel a little akin to Dorothy who got all the way to the Emerald City and the Wizard would not give her entrance or answer to her questions. So I stared back in silence and thought, "Well, maybe I have to figure this out by myself, but what does she mean 'I will see it'? Where are my ruby slippers when I need them?" I'm thinking, "I am definitely going to need more magic here."

Holy week arrived, and Peggy and I kept our plan, attending the celebrations and liturgies of the week with the sisters of her community. On most weekends and every holiday, I would accompany Sr. Peggy to the motherhouse, St. Catherine's. The Dominican sisters did not take a vow of stability; they were itinerate preachers, like their founder St. Dominic. As such, they were scattered across the Sates and beyond to countries abroad. St. Catherine's was home for these women who had left all to follow their vocation into the religious orders. During this time in their history, the motherhouse was home for the older, infirmed sisters and the governing board. There were a few others living there in between missions or serving the community in various odd jobs.

St. Catherine's was located in Central Kentucky. It took us about two hours to drive there across the mountains. Two-lane roads carved their way through rugged mountain passes, which gave way to rolling hills and farmland as we neared Neilson County. We came up over the rise to see the motherhouse standing there like a sacred icon. My breath was taken away the first time I saw this structure emerging out of the rolling fields, a place not unlike my childhood playground. The edifice was incredible and looked like something you might imagine seeing in Europe where the ancient Roman Catholic Church had its birth. It simply felt surreal here in Central Kentucky.

Everything about the place was formidable—its history, its energy, and what was held within its walls. Founded by nine women during the 1800s, these sisters lived in a one-room cabin on Cartwright Creek. From this place, they began their work of educating the children of the pioneers who settled in this valley. The early sisters were to be teachers, followers of Dominic Guzman's Order of Preachers. Their roots reaching back to Europe, the Kentucky Dominicans have the distinction of being the first Dominican community of religious women to be founded in America. Their call to hear and proclaim the Word of God took many forms throughout their history. What stood before me now was far from a one-room cabin. It was a huge four-story structure complete with the most beautiful chapel I had ever seen. I walked into their sacred house of prayer and lifted my eyes to see an enormous rose window casting its rosy glow over the sanctuary. The energy of the place called for an immediate reverence as I heard the words from scripture, "Take off your shoes, you are on holy ground."

In keeping with Southern tradition, the Kentucky Dominicans provided abundant hospitality. Peggy walked me through the motherhouse introducing me to the women of her community—all of whom seemed warm, loving, and cheerful. I was soon to find out that laughter was as much a part of their chrism as their zeal to hear and proclaim God's word. Peg and I walked up to the fourth floor, ascending the steps that would become, for me, symbol of my journey. I could close my eyes and imagine the sisters who came before me, walking two abreast on the beautiful wooden staircase. Rising before dawn, they would make their way to chapel at four in the morning, prayer beads sounding the rhythm of their march. Only the steady rustle of their habits and striking repetitive clack of the wooden beads would break the vowed silence of their descent. Hands folded neatly beneath their scapula, heads bowed in humility, the image of piety and holiness revealed only a shadow of who they were in truth. These were women of incredible strength and courage, who laid down their lives for their God.

Peg and I made our beds in the dorms for our week of holy retreat in preparation for Easter. In earlier years, the "dorms" located on the top floor were full of novices in training. Now empty, they were used to house visiting guests. There were three dorms, each holding somewhere around twenty or thirty beds. The small twin beds were surrounded by metal scaffolding serving as curtain rods. The material hanging there provided some semblance of privacy for the young novice. In the corner of the dorm was a small wooden petition, which enclosed the superior's living quarters. The area was large enough for a small bedside table in addition to a twin bed. These were deluxe accommodations in the convent.

It was the superior's charge to keep the young novices in line. Understandable, as some of these sisters were only seventeen years old when they came to become the brides of Christ. Never thought of Jesus as being a cradle robber, but seventeen? A different age, obviously—they were more mature although some of the dorm stories would leave you thinking, well not really. Young women are really young girls, and they had to have a little fun, no matter how holy their setting.

My favorite story was told to me years later. When one of the particularly gullible young novices arrived at St. Catherine's, she was told by the others during "recreation" when they were allowed to speak, if she left her shoes outside in the hall, one of the sisters would come by and polish them for her. So she thought that was a grand idea, and what service! So she promptly and neatly arranged her shoes just outside the dorm door before going to bed as instructed. The other novices promptly hid them. The bell rang for morning prayers. It was especially important that you be on time to chapel, but Norah could not find her shoes. They were simply gone, and she could not ask about them because they were all keeping silence. What was a girl to do? So she went to chapel without her shoes, going unnoticed until they were all lined up on the kneelers. The superior looked up to see all her novices aligned in perfect formation except for the fact that one was barefooted. Even in a Kentucky order, this was not smiled upon. Not to worry, I'm sure Norah got even before it was all over.

At the ripe old age of twenty-two, I felt like I was arriving late, but better late than never. Although I could not formally begin the process of entering religious life until I had been a seasoned Catholic of three years, my heart would not be held by the tenets of the church. As far as I was concerned, I was starting today. After all, I had not taken the vow of obedience yet. I watched with amazement and awe, gleaning any scraps that fell from the table. These women were my rock stars—their gifts, their call, and their commitment was beyond anything I had ever experienced. I fell totally and helplessly in love with them all and remain so even until this day.

The week unfolded in the mystery of each new ritual. Like Alice in Wonderland, everything was beyond amazing. Yet I was still focused on my own mission. Between prayer and liturgy, there was time for silent reflection, and I was hard-pressed to decipher my vision. Each moment alone was spent looking for any clue I could find or imagine. In scripture, the only link I found with water coming from the rock was not exactly what I had hoped for. It seems, pissed off by his fate of leading an ungrateful stubborn people, Moses took his staff and struck the rock. He was instructed beforehand—by God, I might add—to tap the rock gently, not beat the hell out of it like a drunken Irishman wailing away at a snake with his shillelagh. Although understandable given his situation, this is just not what the Creator had in mind. There was an expected decorum to be followed when you were the messenger of God and leader of the people. The people, on the other hand, were pretty upset too about this whole "no water" thing. Dehydrated, tired, and disillusioned, they were probably quite sure this lunatic who talked to burning bushes was leading them to their death, all the while promising pie in the sky. At his wits end, he lost faith. As a result, the next forty years were spent wandering in the wilderness. Damn! I closed the Bible. That was not what I had in mind. Surely, there was another hidden meaning.

The week of fasting and prayer ended with a fabulous celebration of the Resurrection. Holy week flew by, it seemed, and now it was time to return to our jobs and the real world. I was disappointed because I felt sure I would be given a better understanding of my vision. The week was over, and I still didn't know what any of it meant. The scripture I found didn't make the connection. After all, I wasn't angry with God. Quite the contrary. I wasn't called to lead his people to the Promised Land, as far as I knew. So why would I see water coming from the rock? When was I going to "see it"? I still had not seen it, on any level.

"The vision has its time, wait for it," says my friend from Habakkuk.

Peg and I packed the car and started on our journey back up the mountain. The countryside seemed transformed. It rained most of the week, and Easter Sunday came complete with sunshine and daffodils lining the roads and scattered across the fields we traveled. Everything looked new and green. The energy was bright, and I was transfixed by every cliff we passed. I began to feel the anticipation growing. The creeks were full, and water was everywhere. I started to see streams running off the tops of the cliffs, channeled over the ledges in huge silver bands of reflected light. It seemed there were streams of water everywhere, but they were not what I saw in the vision. I was beginning to feel a bit like Richard Dreyfuss' character in *Close Encounters of the Third Kind*. It was that kind of relentless haunted searching; my head snapped back and forth from side to side trying hard not to miss anything, especially falling water, as Peg drove down the small two-lane highway. These seemingly endless tributaries were not obvious when we made our way down the mountain, but they existed in great proliferation on the way back up, too numerous to count.

Peggy sensed my anticipation, and she too began looking with me, obligingly stopping the car when I suddenly asked to be let out. I saw a stream off to my right. Although I could not see its origin, I felt sure this was the place. The unnamed foreboding came to a head. I jumped from the car and headed up the side of the hill, following the stream to its origin, thinking, "Surely this is the one." This is *the one* that would lead me to the source of my vision. Very shortly, it was clear this was not the one, so I turned and walked back to the car where Peggy was waiting.

"Wasn't it," I said in disappointment as I looked up at her. It was at that moment I saw it just as she said I would. There behind her left shoulder, it was just as I had seen it in the vision. The same cliff, the same triangular opening, and the same forceful rush of water blasting out of the side of the mountain was being now visualized in the physical realm. I stood staring in disbelief before I eventually walked silently over, knelt down, and looked up at the vision manifested in front of me. After a moment, I reached out to allow the water to run over my hands and then brought my wet fingers back to my brow to bless myself with the sign of the cross. The cool touch of water on my forehead felt strangely similar to the mountain breeze that left its gentle kiss there. I still had absolutely no idea about what any of this meant. I also knew I could never turn back.

CHAPTER 7

Through screens, like sifted sand, one finds entry. The portal of a reality profoundly our own provides entrance. Yet unimagined fortitude serves as guide to our greatest gifts.

OWNEE'S WORLD

I LEFT MY PRACTICE AT Buckhorn burnt out and disillusioned. I was disappointed in myself. I knew living in Appalachia would not be long term, but I planned on a four-year commitment. My pledge of allegiance to the people I served would crumble after a year and a half. The solitude of the mountains and the pressure of taking care of a community was a daunting task for a twenty-four-year-old. I lived in constant fear that I would make the wrong clinical judgment and something I did or did not do would end in hurting someone—or worse, bring an end to their already short life. There was no getting away from the responsibility. It was 24-7 unless I drove out of the hills and took refuge in Louisville, Lexington, or the motherhouse for the weekend.

There were three cabins on the side of the hill where I took up residence. Peggy was gone now, so two were empty, and then there was mine. One of the cabins sat lower on the hillside so I could actually step from the road onto the roof. I sat on that roof regularly, staring out over the little village that was mine to care for on a daily basis, always wondering if I would be up to the job. At night, I would sit on the same roof and look out at the stars with the same thought in my mind. It was like a constant drone, forever humming in the background. These thoughts would be interspersed with prayer and contemplation. Meditation would have been a nice addition, but I had no idea how to stop the constant chatter of my mind, so prayer would have to suffice.

One evening, as I was sitting on the roof, Mastie Blanck drove up the lane. As always, there was a little churn of my stomach as I saw the headlights winding up the lane toward me while I waited to see if someone was coming to get me for some emergency. When I saw it was Mastie and observed his casual slow movement as he stepped out of the car, I knew all was well.

Mastie was one of the elders of the community, a middle-aged man wise beyond his years with gentle demeanor. A beard covered what folks would call a strong jaw. He was short and stocky with steel-blue eyes. He wore typical farmer attire; bib overhauls covered his well-worn work shirt. He smiled at me as I climbed off the roof, never pausing to ask why I was sitting up there; I think he knew, a kindred spirit of sorts. He was only stopping by for a visit. Mastie and his family were Mennonites. Like my Grandpa Whitaker, they lived simply and walked gently on the earth.

I'm not certain why Mastie stopped by. It was not his practice to come up for a visit. My little lane was a dead end, so it wasn't like he was driving by and stopped when he saw me sitting there. It was as if he had a message to deliver, and so he did. As we stood in the small lane together in the darkness, he began to point out the constellations. His favorite, he explained, was Orion.

There was no light pollution in Buckhorn. The stars looked close enough to touch from our vantage point. It was a sky watcher's delight. The heavens provided a black canvas, holding space for the living dance of the spheres. In a slow, deeply resonant voice, Mastie looked intensely into my eyes as he went on to explain, "The stars are always there. No matter where your journey leads—if you look up to the heavens, this remains constant. A gentle reminder that you are always home."

The words echoed within me, awakening a soul memory. It was as if a long-forgotten imprint was reactivated, although not clearly understood. This was not new information. It was like an ancient key returning to unlock a secret door. His visit was short, the lesson profound. With that, he bid me good night and drove back down the lane. I returned to my perch in the silence of the rooftop and looked out at Orion, as if rediscovering an old friend. He pointed out many of these primeval astrological clusters, but it was Orion and the Pleiades that called to something unnamable, leaving me comforted and disturbed at the same time. Forever from that night, I would remember his words. The stars, the lights of creation, are always there, never changing. This universe is our home. We are not limited by counties, states, or nations. We are not bound by our mythical borders, creations of our own doing which imply separation one from another. Our small blue planet is the micro expression of community in the far greater design of the infinite.

I knew I was unhappy. What I didn't know at that young age was being unhappy is a clue. It means the energy is stuck, and you need to take action. Sidestep left or sidestep right; move forward, backward, or run like hell! Do something, even if it's wrong. Whatever the choice, you know it's time to shift when you find no joy in your day. No one who loves us, mortal or divine, is going to ask us to be miserable. In fact, being miserable is a pretty good indication that you are not in alignment with your purpose for being. It suggests you have wandered off your path.

I had one clearly defined intention. I wanted to follow God's will for my life. What I didn't understand was happiness and contentment are the barometers for this quest, not suffering. The other mystery hidden in plain sight is I am one with my Creator, and so when I am in touch with my deepest longing, our wills are also one. Sources outside us would have us believe we are separated one from another. As this is born of fear and control, it is easily exposed as a lie. Well, maybe not easily, as we have followed this paradigm of separation for what feels like millennia.

When I embody and I am in tune with the matchless note of my eternal resonance, I become the expression of Divinity. I am a single spark, dancing within the fire of the divine matrix. This energy is my fingerprint in creation. There is no other like it, yet it is a part of the whole. This knowing brings with it a great joy and an unlimited power. We are created to step into this power and express the gift that is ours to bring.

Your infinite Creator would not give you a beautiful violin and then turn around and ask you to play the bongos. Each of us has a gift that is uniquely ours—sometimes many gifts. When we pull the bow across the string of our particular Stradivarius, the tone created sends us soaring into soulful bliss. Our vibration begins to match this well-played note, and in so doing, all those around us are caught up in the music of our life's force. If we connect to this gift, it brings us joy. This is when we are in touch with our soul's deepest longing, when we are in tune with the all in all, our Creator, the ultimate maestro. Call it what you will, but know that it is connection with life force. There is a reason they call it life force. Obviously, I was playing the bongos—not the Stradivarius—in Buckhorn.

I never knew who was going to show up at the clinic or on my doorstep for that matter. It wasn't always life or death, but you can be sure it was always interesting. While Sr. Peggy was on watch before my arrival, a woman burst into the clinic, screaming, "My kid's a-dyin'! My kid's a dyin'! I gave it some worm medicine. Its eyes rolled back in its head, and it fell over!" May I just say, this is the kind of thing that causes you to go into arrest when you are the provider? Peg grabbed the emergency kit, which we kept ready at all times. She ran for the door with kit in hand to follow the distraught woman out to her car.

With the information Peggy had, the most obvious probable cause of loss of consciousness, given the woman's description of the event, was an allergic reaction followed by anaphylactic shock. While on the run, Peggy shouted, "Where is your child?"

"Child?" the woman replied in puzzled confusion. After a brief pause, her confusion lifted, and she shouted, "Oh no, honey Ownee's a goat!"

Sure enough, Ownee was a goat and was in anaphylactic shock in the back of the woman's truck. Peggy never argued about the lack of a veterinarian license; she just gave Ownee the appropriate dose of adrenalin for her approximated size. The goat batted its eyes, jumped out of the truck, and chased Peg back into the clinic. Ownee lived. The woman, now certain of Peg's capabilities, soon brought all her real "kids" in for immunizations and, well, child checks.

Working in Buckhorn placed you on the front line—alone on the front line. When I worked in the ER at Vanderbilt Hospital prior to graduate school, I saw just about everything. This was also a place where you never knew what was going to come through the door. The difference being, you made your assessment, walked over or called out to the secretary on duty, and she in turn called the pediatrician, neurosurgeon, cardiologist, psychiatrist, internist, neurologist, or any combination of several of those specialists according to your need. Within five minutes, these doctors were at your side. Just that quickly, the burden of life and death was now shared by a team of experts. In Buckhorn, there was no one at your beck and call. When it rained, the phones went out, and your one fragile lifeline to the greater medical community, which in truth wasn't all that great, was severed. Even if you drove with the patient in your car over the mountain roads, which gave passage to a hospital, it took forty-five minutes to an hour to get there in good weather conditions. You had to put them in your car or somebody's car because there were no ambulances, no emergency medical technicians to rush in and scoop the patient up and out to greater sources of medical miracles. So there you have it; the proverbial buck stopped with me.

I had two heartbreaking outcomes while in Buckhorn. Neither of the events was within my power to change; another provider may have had the exact same outcome. There was no malpractice, and yet I always felt an acute responsibility for both lives lost. Grace was an eighteen-year-old woman who came to the clinic for her prenatal care. She lived in dismal poverty with her parents and numerous brothers and sisters. Sr. Peggy decided I should experience the place they called home to understand their needs and challenges. So we took a day trip and made a home visit to see their living conditions.

We traveled quite a way down one of the hollers to reach their place. The lane was small and sparsely graveled. The trees and late summer's growth of weeds crowded our passageway. Queen Ann's lace graced the sides of the road like delicate, frail white discs of patterned light. These native perennials served as a reflection of the intricate well-planned design of the universe scattered across the underlying maze of random chaos expressed in the unlimited species of plant life there. An occasional wild tiger lily visually jumped out at you, with its glaring bright orange contrasted by the manifold shades of greens serving as a backdrop. The road morphed into a tunnel intermittently as the heavy overgrowth hung above us to form a living canopy, closing us in from every side. The entrance to their property was welcomed by me as I was feeling, as usual, like I could not get my breath in the presence of the mountains and their unruly children, no matter how beautiful.

Grace's family carved out and extracted a piece of this wilderness to build their home alongside a creek that ran though their property. The clearing held their house, their garden, and a few old broken-down vehicles scattered around the grounds of the old homeplace. Driving into the clearing gave way to blue sky above us. It was like a small living room carved out of the Eastern Kentucky jungle, which held them tenuously on the edge of the wilds.

The house stood two stories high, the wood speckled by the remnants of what was once paint. A few shingles were scattered across the roof, sagging above the structure, which was, for the most part, a half bubble off plumb. There were no straight lines, not anymore. The first floor of their home housed the animals and served as a barn. Grace's family included not only a large number of brothers and sisters but also a menagerie of goats, chickens, and pigs. The family lived above and with their animals.

Grace was one of the older children, which brought with it the responsibility of caring for those who came after her—all of them, both two-legged and four-legged. The poverty and responsibilities accompanying her place in the family was not an easy lot, and yet had not dampened her spirits. She was young and a bit rebellious, as would be the norm for all teenagers. In short, she was an incredibly cute kid, but *kid* is the operative word here. In addition, her living situation, her age, and poverty placed her at high risk from the beginning of her pregnancy.

Neonatal mortality rates dropped dramatically due to the outposts we manned for the patients we served, but I was not a midwife. I knew what to monitor during the prenatal months, following a strict set of protocols. However, knowledge never really outweighs experience. I was inexperienced, and the subtle cues of this culture and their medical management were often missed. I saw the change in Grace's blood pressure in her third trimester. I put her on bed rest, a low-sodium diet, and followed the protocol strictly. What I didn't know was, she wasn't following my strict protocol. In fact, she was ignoring my stern warnings and recommendations. I had her come back in for follow-up in one week; the blood pressure problem was worse. So I sent her into Hyden where she would see the midwives at the hospital in the prenatal clinic. She went in, finally, but not when I made the recommendation. When she finally left to make her journey over the hills that stood between her and the hospital, she was in labor. She had her baby prematurely; he was stillborn.

One of the doctors in Hyden called me, extremely upset. I am sure it was his intent to tell me I screwed up. However, when he traced back through the steps with me, he realized I had taken all the necessary precautions and directed the patient with the appropriate recommendations. The problem was, she was eighteen years old and wasn't doing anything I said. Sr. Peggy would have followed her like a pit bull, and she would have made sure Grace was following orders. That is where life experience changes outcomes. This was my first tragedy.

Not long after the baby's death, another family came to the clinic with a problem I could not solve. The parents brought in their thirty-year-old son who had obviously had a psychotic break. Delusional and hallucinating, the problem was very clear. Because he was not drinking moonshine and had no known exposure to drugs, the most probable differential diagnosis was schizophrenia, probably paranoid schizophrenia. If paranoia was a part of the equation, this placed not only the patient at risk but his family and others at risk as well. However, I was not a psychiatrist. I could not diagnose this patient or treat him. I could evaluate, assess, and recommend the appropriate referral. I might even be able to help the family with monitoring him after he was better controlled with medication, but there were several steps that had to be taken first. The very first step included driving the patient to Hazard where he could be hospitalized, diagnosed, and treated.

I explained to the family their son was having a psychotic episode. I was clear that he needed to be in the hospital where he could be cared for by psychiatric specialists. There was nothing else I could do. They responded with classic Appalachian etiquette and said simply, "Well." *Well* in Eastern Kentucky typically means the same thing as "I don't care to," which when interpreted clearly means "I will, I don't mind at all." Of course, I say this in jest because it is not clear; it is as confusing as hell for outlanders who come from beyond the mountain ranges these folks call home.

Well is a term liberally used and probably a throwback, as are most Appalachian phrases, to their Elizabethan ancestors. Although it usually means OK, it can mean just about anything, leaving interpretation up to the listener. These are people of few words. Deriving clarity from their expressions requires an understanding for the people and the context of the conversation. *Well* is typically a term of agreement, but not always. I'll give you some examples.

"It's snowing down the road a ways." "Well." (*Well* in this reference means "I didn't know it was snowing.")

"I think old Jack's dog Shep is about one of the best coon hounds in these parts." "Well." (*Well* in this scenario means "I would have to agree he is one of the best dogs for coon hunting in this neck of the woods.")

"I want you to take this medicine four times a day. It's very important." "Well." (Here, *well* means "Yes, I understand, and I will take my medicine.")

When I went through my recommendations for this patient, the family turned to each other and then back to me and said, "Well." So I sent them out the clinic door totally expecting them to drive from our clinic to Hazard where the patient could be evaluated in the emergency room and then hospitalized. This was my plan; it was not theirs. They never took their son to Hazard. They drove back up the holler to their home. A few weeks later, the son walked into a pond on their property and drowned. The action was probably directed by the voices that haunted his reality with relentless banter. All the while, I thought he was admitted safely to the psychiatric ward.

Two lives were lost. Did I do anything wrong? There was nothing you could point your finger at in a court of law, but that did not make me feel any better. I was placed in a situation where I could never completely meet the needs of the people I served. At least for me, it was a no-win situation. Would a more skilled practitioner have handled the problems differently? Maybe. This was the demon I faced daily. Would I be able to manage the problems they brought to me? Would their needs fit into my limited scope of practice? Ninety-nine percent of the time, yes; but one percent became too high when the lack of skill or experience could be associated with loss of life. After one short year in Buckhorn, I was done.

The dam broke on Christmas vacation. I went to visit my parents. They were away from home at the time, living in a small apartment in Florida. There was no guest room, so I was sleeping on the living room couch. Because their place was located in a small quiet neighborhood, you noticed the street traffic, what there was of it. In the middle of the night, a car pulled up to the stop sign near their front door. Waking startled from deep sleep, I was off the couch and halfway to the car outside when I realized I wasn't on the mountain. This wasn't a patient in crisis. There was no emergency. I stopped in the middle of the yard, dropped to my knees, and started to cry. I could not do this anymore. I was starting to feel like a post-traumatic stress case.

I left my parents' place and traveled back to Buckhorn, knowing I could not continue on there. Sr. Miriam was my relief for vacations from the clinic. She was a family nurse-practitioner like myself and taught nursing at Spalding University in Louisville. She enjoyed working in the rural setting when I needed to take time away from work. It was helpful for her to step back into clinical practice to keep her hands in the mix. It is imperative for teachers; otherwise, they lose their clinical skills. When I came back to the cabin on the evening of my return, I sat across the table from Miriam and told her what had happened. I could not do it anymore. I had to leave. I asked her to keep an eye out for a job in Louisville; any job would do. She listened and agreed, promising to give me a call if she heard of anything.

I knew I would be leaving, but I never dreamed Miriam would call me back in less than a week. She had a job. They needed a clinical nursing instructor at Spalding to teach community health and physical assessment. I could start in the fall. This would give the community some time to find another health care provider. Teaching in a formal setting was not the plan I had in mind for my life, but at the moment, it felt like a godsend. In addition, I had experience teaching nursing as an instructor before I went back to graduate school, so I knew what to expect. I wouldn't mind stepping away from clinical practice, not one bit. In fact, this sounded wonderful. I was one burnt-out crispy critter.

Spalding is a small inner-city Catholic university, well respected and especially known for its outstanding nursing school. I would soon be introduced to a great faculty of professors and instructors while looking out at the eager eyes of the students awaiting my wisdom, all twenty-five years of it. God have mercy. The pay was terrible, and working there meant taking a vow of poverty. I had to get a second job to pay the bills. However, I didn't mind. Teaching was like a perpetual summer camp after Buckhorn. In addition, all faculty members were allowed two free courses per semester as part of the perks. I took theology; who would guess?

Spalding would serve me in many ways. There I would be introduced to two of my lifelong friends. Because the days unfolded without surprises or emergencies, I was provided with a badly needed respite following my trial by fire in the mountains. The students placed me on a pedestal, healing my bruised and battered ego through the curative salve of their adoration, no matter how limited and naive their vision. All priceless gifts, yet Spalding's greatest offering was the springboard it provided, launching me into my greatest life's work, health care for the homeless.

CHAPTER 8

They lift their eyes to see you standing in the distance. Slanted expressions of unseen truths are mirrored in their being. You may come to understand another part of yourself in their presence, if you choose to enter, if you choose to see beyond the looking glass.

No Bootstraps

I WISH I HAD A nickel for every time I heard someone say they should just pull themselves up by their bootstraps. Eighteen years of my life was spent working with the homeless, and I can say clearly and without hesitation, they have no bootstraps. We were in the mid-eighties, and the "homeless problem" was getting bigger. I joined the ranks of Mitch Snyder and other homeless advocates unintentionally and quite by accident. Are there accidents? Of course not; it's all about the grand plan driven by probability and heart. There are infinite possibilities, and in those days, I walked without much forethought into the future. Under the grand umbrella of general good intentions, there was no well-defined goal. I was not aware I was a co-creator with God. I was totally unconscious for the most part, motivated by primal need. I just kept marching, and the parade led me to the steps of St. John's Homeless Day Center.

Very shortly after I arrived at Spalding University, I was busily working on a lesson plan when Betty Bednarski walked into my office unannounced. I looked up from my desk to see her bound through the door, posture perfect despite her years. As quickly as she entered my office, she sat down on the corner of my desk to rest her tired feet housed in stilettos. Stilettos meant for real women, not wannabe debutantes. Down plopped her butt and her purse on my desk, all with quick, deliberate no-nonsense style, which was totally Betty. Swiftly she opened up her purse to retrieve the ruby-red lipstick, which was also a part of her trademark. Stilettos and lipstick gave hint of her heyday, mimicking the glamour of the forties and Hollywood. I often felt she missed her call and should have been up in lights with Betty Davis, Joan Crawford, and the like. She had a personality that took up the room and commanded attention, of which she had mine.

"Hello," she said while liberally applying her lipstick with expert perfection. "I'm Betty Bednarski. I want you to know you have taken up residence with some fabulous Southern belles here at this institution, but I am a Yankee bastard," she proclaimed with great pride. She threw back her head and laughed while pitching her lipstick into her open pocketbook. This was quickly followed by an extension of her hand reaching for mine in welcome.

Betty was from New York and was a shocking jolt to my Southern distilled nature. Quick-witted, well-read, and extremely bright, she came to Spalding with a lifetime of nursing under her belt, most of it in community health. It takes all these qualities to understand the intricacies of this often-overlooked niche of the nursing profession. Most of us want the drama found in the corridors of hospitals and emergency rooms where life hangs by a thread. The rush of excitement and the power felt in having knowingly saved a life is very alluring. We can become addicted to the rush of adrenalin these situations demand. Betty was well seasoned. She was beyond this limited scope of practice and knew where the real challenge lay, the community. Well-planned intervention in the community could save more lives and prevent more suffering than any dramatic scene played out in sterile hospital settings. A wise woman, she understood the complexity of health care. She knew where we failed and where we succeeded, and she knew what still needed to be done.

Community health is where nurses make some of their greatest contributions to society. With wisdom and understanding comes responsibility. Betty obviously felt great accountability for the community and for her students. She was serious about it, and she was about to make a believer out of me. Direct and to the point, Southern courtesy be damned. She was all about business. I felt totally dwarfed in her presence but ever grateful for the extended hand that foreshadowed her willingness to reach out to me as a mentor. She would challenge me, offer direction, and serve as a confidant. When the time was right, she gave me one quick, swift, well-targeted push out of the nest, landing me in the most underserved population in the state. I quickly came to understand the poverty of the inner city can be far more devastating than the poverty I witnessed in the mountains of Eastern Kentucky.

My mountain friends had each other. They had a home. They were entrenched in a tradition that served them well, just as it had served their ancestors before them. They stood on the shoulders of a deeply rooted community, providing them with identity and purpose. The homeless did not share this wealth of resource. Their only commonality, it seemed, was their dearth of material wealth, hardly an issue when you consider the greatest poverty that can befall us. These men, women, and children of the inner cities have lost their homes, their purpose, their self-respect, and their identity. Nothing or very little in their day brings comfort. Instead, they are greeted with aimless wandering, no place to lay their head, no place to form community. For a time they were an invisible population, drifting through the streets by day, finding shelter at night within overcrowded, substandard missions or under concrete freeway viaducts. It took community advocates like Betty, and many others, to hear their silent cries and call the rest of us to accountability.

During this visit to my office, Betty slapped not her butt but the *Courier Journal*, our local paper, down on my desk. "I've found a great place for you to take the students during their community health rotation," she said while looking down at me. Her steel-gray eyes were slightly faded by time, but profoundly alive and strong. "They have opened a day care center for the homeless at St. John's according to the paper. I think you should go down there and take a look. I hear one of the nurses from Seven Counties has started seeing patients at the center in what they are calling the health room. Here, read this article. It'll tell you all about it. Let me know what you think." And out she went as quickly as she arrived. Betty could spin in and out of a room like Looney Tunes's Tasmanian devil. The whirlwind of frenetic energy created by her passing through always left my head spinning, trying frantically to catch up.

I picked up the newspaper and read the article as instructed. Obviously, I was given an assignment of great import. Important or not, I had no intention of doing anything contrary to Betty's instructions, even if it meant stepping outside my comfort zone. Betty was in charge of community health. As an instructor, I was her charge to keep. I made arrangements to go scope out the place they called St. John's Homeless Day Center. What I met there would bring me face-to-face with what was mine to do over the next eighteen years.

The old church was well-placed in the heart of downtown Louisville. Small in comparison to some of the greater cathedrals of the city, the building stood on a corner adjacent to the housing projects across the street. Convenient location, one step off the curb from marginal living, St. John's provided a place for those who now found themselves living past the margins. I slowly pulled my car to the side of the street and looked up at the twin spires, each one towering above either side of the central entrance. They provided a powerful masculine energy for the church's facade. This was appropriate because most of the guests were men, in those early years. As far as that goes, the Catholic Church was and continues to be the epitome of a masculine institution, so the architect was right on in his design for the little Irish Catholic parish.

A decline in numbers resulted in the closing of many of the archdiocese parishes, sadly leaving the churches sitting empty. The diocese rented the building called St. John's to the city for one dollar a year. In return, the city opened the day center, which was terribly needed on many levels. Within the walls of what was once a church, the homeless found a place to rest from their wanderings. They were provided with coffee and kindness. Under the cathedral ceilings, they were treated with respect and dignity, followed by a generous helping of social services and, ultimately, health care, both mental and physical.

I walked up the stairs to the entrance and opened the door. There was no way I could have been prepared for what I saw within this sanctuary of suffering. Tables were scattered across the room where benches and kneelers once stood, like some odd form of holy café. The guys sat at the tables, smoking and drinking coffee. Some talking lowly to one another, some talking to themselves, and others sat blankly staring across the room. They were held there with only their memories of better days and the promise that no one was going to ask them to move along, at least not until three o'clock when the center closed its doors for the day. The destitution was palpable, seen in downcast eyes and drawn, unshaven faces. Their features were carved deeply with the wear and hollowed expressions of lost dreams. I stood looking out at them and beyond them, above their heads where a twelve-foot crucifix commanded my attention from the front of the church. There he hung, the savior of the world, and here was his world seated beneath his feet. He knew their pain, their misunderstood plight, their loss of home and family. He shared in their communion, unwelcome wayfarers, misfits of the status quo who, without warning, looked around to find themselves alone in the world. I think the guys knew this; they knew at least in this they were not alone. I imagine this gave them comfort, sitting under the image of his outstretched arms. Somehow, I believe, on some level, they understood they were being embraced by another homeless brother.

I suppose I must have looked a little like I had been shot out of a cannon when Sr. Kathleen Mary walked up to me. She was frowning. She was always frowning or she was laughing, but you never saw her with a mediocre look on her face because she was far from mediocrity and had, like Jesus, very little patience for it. When I saw her approaching, I quickly tried to gather myself back in, which included closing my mouth and drying up the tears now stinging my eyes.

Mary Kathleen could put Betty to shame. She was hell on wheels, minus the stilettos. Nothing scared her, and nothing got in the way of her taking care of these men. She was in charge, and there was no question about who ran the show. If you wanted to be a part of her show, then you better be there because you had something of value to give them. She was not about pity or sideshows. Her mission was clear, and the boss she served hung right over her shoulder just in case anyone forgot who she worked for or where she derived her strength.

Sr. Kathleen stood several inches shorter than my five-foot-eight frame but, like many people of her spiritual stature and presence, she seemed to tower above me. Of course, she did tower above me on many levels. It would be years before I knew I was taller than her, but that never changed the reality that I continued to look up to her and still do to this day. I was quick to hear Sr. Peggy's brogue when Sr. Kathleen began to talk with me.

"Oh my god, it's another Boston Irish Catholic." My second thought was "Lord have mercy." What is it about these fearless women? They are almost scary, but beneath the tough unyielding exterior lies a tender heart, freely given over to all those who cross their paths in need.

I was right to think "Lord have mercy." I was just about to step onto a trapdoor that would drop me square into a population whose need no one could ever hope to meet. The vacation was over. Fortunately, this time I would learn I was not there to save them. I was there to walk with them. To meet them where they stood, in whatever condition they presented themselves. The unfortunate part is it took many years for me to learn this lesson. In the meantime, I hit the ground running, soon finding myself overwhelmed and emotionally bleeding.

Lying awake at night, I would wonder how in the world I would ever fix them. I could never meet all their needs; they were so broken. If that wasn't bad enough, we had no resources other than manpower provided by volunteers. Sounds like the same song, second verse, from my experiences in Buckhorn. I would learn over time I wasn't suppose to meet all their needs; no one could. They were broken, some of them beyond repair. For some, their world would never be brighter than the cup of coffee that sat steaming in front of them, or the felt presence of an arm thrown around their shoulders by one of the staff working at the center. "The poor are with you always," so says the boss hanging around in the background. If we want to take that admonishment literally, it was certainly played out in these people—although the greater lesson may be found on a deeper level. There is a part of us that is poor, always calling out in need and sometimes never to be repaired.

Totally beleaguered, I scrambled to regain my composure while trying to explain to Sr. Kathleen why I came to visit. The Sisters of Charity of Nazareth were the founders of Spalding University where I taught. Sr. Kathleen was a Sister of Charity. So she connected the dots far more quickly than I did and felt that bringing the students into the center to volunteer in the health room was a fabulous idea. I did not have to sell her on Betty's plan. She quickly introduced me to Teresa who was in charge of the health room. Teresa actually gave birth to the idea of health care for the homeless as a part of the center's mission. Betty was correct; Teresa was employed by Seven Counties. This organization provides mental health services for Louisville and six surrounding counties. I assume Teresa found her way to the center trying to track down one of the many mentally ill clients in her charge. I can also imagine she had a similar experience to my own when she walked through the doors. She saw the need, she met Sr. Kathleen, and the rest of the story is history.

First I would need to get my feet wet, and this started by my volunteering in the health room. Rapid assessment made it clear that this was an ideal setting for a nurse-practitioner. I could provide the unmet needs of hundreds and, eventually, thousands of homeless individuals—one person at a time, one step at a time.

There was a glaring gap in the health care being provided for these individuals. We had a very small team of volunteers, but we made a huge difference in their lives. Our motley crew included multiple nurses, one doctor who came for a couple hours once a week, a pharmacist, and one nurse-practitioner, that was me. Bob, our pharmacist, provided medication at cost, paid for by the funds raised by the center. Our volunteers were not unlike Fagin's orphans in *Oliver Twist*; they could be sleight of hand around any unused supplies left for the taking at the hospitals and clinics where they worked. Yes, we would beg, borrow, or steal supplies for our needs, for the needs of our patients. Our clinic was as poor as the clients we served, and yet somehow we managed to provide decent care.

The initial health room was about eight by ten, that would be eighty square feet of compacted service area. The little clinic contained a beat-up donated exam table, a very small wooden desk, and an even smaller white porcelain sink suspended against the wall in the corner of the room. This was accompanied by a couple of wooden chairs, one for the health care worker and one for the patient. On the desk, we kept our filing system, which consisted of a stained and tattered gray receipt box someone brought from their kitchen. Here we kept four-by-six cards where we recorded our patients' visit with vital signs and documented needs.

Our cozy little space was poorly ventilated. The one window desperately needed for fresh air was sealed above our heads, only partially exposed by a drop-down ceiling used to frame in our makeshift room. Ironically, the portion of the stained glass window that remained visible revealed the image of bare feet. I thought this profound as I was soon to learn our patients' greatest immediate need was wound and foot care. I jokingly began calling the healing room "Our Center for the Ministry of the Feet." This place, and our ministry, was obviously not meant for the delicate of senses or the faint of heart.

I met with the dean of nursing at Spalding, Sr. Mary Kathleen, and no, I did not make up their names. Sr. Mary Kathleen and Sr. Kathleen Mary were my bosses, and that's just how it was in my world. Also a Sister of Charity, Sr. Mary Kathleen was more than happy to excuse me from campus on Fridays so I could work at the center. Volunteering at the center through the remainder of the fall semester, I was ready to bring the students in by spring term. I knew the facility, I knew the staff, I knew the mission, and I was beginning to know most of our guests.

Now, bringing twenty-one-year-old nursing students into the center, which was filled to capacity by less than balanced men, provided more than one challenge, as you may be able to imagine. I usually had three students with me, as they rotated through this site one day of the week. My students were somewhat innocent, naive young women, most of them wealthy, all wealthy given the counterculture in which we were immersed. So they did not have a clue; neither side understood the other. With the exclusion of a small number of exceptional students, most were totally oblivious to what their patients were up against. In addition, this was probably not the safest of rotations as our patients had particularly complex morbidities, which included mental illness and substance abuse—sometimes one or the other, sometimes both. You don't have to be a world-class mathematician to figure out that equation. Let's just say I had to stay on my toes.

We set up a small triage area outside the health-room door where the first nursing student took vital signs and chief complaints. The other two students manned the clinic were the patient was treated according to their needs. I ran back and forth trying to calm the students' fears, some of which were real as our guys were not all upstanding citizens. I envisioned my job to be a bit like a safety officer. I was to make sure the student was protected while ensuring our patients were out of harm's way, *harm* being defined as student care. This by itself can be a big job depending on the student and the setting.

On one particularly challenging day, I walked into the health room to see one of my protégés cupping the patient's hands in hers, tenderly admonishing him to go out and find a job. This she was saying to a bipolar patient who was self-treating his disorder with Ripple on a daily basis for a dozen or so years. Ripple is a particularly neuro-hepatic toxin passed off as wine under various brand names. It is sold by the cases to the homeless for under two bucks a half pint, giving "Two-Buck Chuck" a whole new meaning. This habit, along with his underlying mental illness, left him with several pretty certain deficiencies for employment. I rest my case. I'm hoping this particular student went on to work for a health spa somewhere over the rainbow because Dorothy was not in Kansas at this facility or the real world.

Time passed, and our center morphed according to need and resources. Within one year of my walking through the doors, I became the new expert on homeless heath care. A title not self-assigned. The Veterans Administration received a grant to provide care to homeless veterans. The grant was to include one nurse-practitioner and one social worker. This was perfect because it would afford me the opportunity to work at the center full time and be paid for it. However, there remained a problem. Working with the homeless was gruelingly hard work. I was far from a state of enlightenment and was still frantically trying to provide for all their needs. This, of course, could not be done. On some levels, I wasn't far behind my misguided student who thought her patient could just walk out the door and apply for a job. We both were sorely misguided in our expectations. Move over, Dorothy.

My first response to this job opportunity came to me in unspoken silent clarity, "No! Hell no!" With further contemplation and insight, I knew this was mine to do. I had found my Stradivarius. I truly loved these guys in all their brokenness. I could meet a need for them that no one else could meet. Probably more aptly put, no one else wanted to meet. Taking this step into their world could make it a little better. A week later, I accepted the position and made arrangements to leave Spalding after three years of teaching.

Victor Gazelle was the administrator for the Veterans' Homeless Grant. He was as flamboyant as his name—a tall, well-dressed young man with slender lanky features and a wild tuft of dark, curly hair on his Lebanese head. He was funny, quick-witted, intelligent, and as queer as a three-dollar bill. I was immediately attracted to Victor; it was as if we were soul mates of a different sort. In addition to his administration of the grant, he was also an administrative assistant for the chief of psychiatry at the VA hospital. His hands were pretty full, but he managed all the balls in the air quite well.

It was my first week working for the VA. I was to meet the other part of our team, Nora Planck, at the airport. Nora had just completed her degree in social work. We were on our way to a three-day training program in St. Louis. The Homeless Program was brand spanking new, and the three of us would champion the cause in Louisville while others were beginning their programs all over the United States. We were head and shoulders above the others because we had St. John's, which provided a place to meet with the homeless, and I had over a year of experience working on the streets. This was important because taking care of homeless veterans meant you had to find them first, and St. John's provided an excellent interface between our service and their needs.

Victor drove me to the airport, chatting nonstop as was his custom. I was to meet the other half of my team as we got on the plane. Nora was a beautiful woman, dressed to the nines, sporting some remarkable stiletto high heels. "What is it with stilettos and Irish Catholics?" I thought. Seemed like a recurring theme in my life. I extended my hand to grasp hers while I stood there in my khaki pants and loafers. All the while I'm thinking, this chick has no idea what she's in for. She'll probably last one month, maybe. I don't know what Nora thought, probably that I could have dressed more appropriately for this very important national meeting. She was probably right, and I was definitely wrong.

I soon learned from Victor that the woman responsible for Louisville being awarded the grant for the homeless was Barbara Davis. Barbara was an ER nurse at the VA hospital. I knew Barbara because she was politically active in the nursing profession and had served on a committee formed by Spalding. She was a jolly, round, slapstick happy woman, and that is all I knew about her. Later I would find that she had a heart that took in the world with courageous abandon. After working about six months with the program, I learned she not only wrote the grant but it was her dream to work in the homeless program. I was in the position she wanted. She never mentioned this. She was totally supportive of Nora and me. Barbara was our connection to get our vets in quickly for hospitalization and workup when needed. We became a team of three. Barbara was career VA. She knew the system, which was broken, and she knew how to get around the fractures. She was almost a one-woman show and played the system like a brass band. We needed her gifts, and she shared them freely.

When our patients were admitted to the VA hospital, I would follow them through their stay. This is when the chief of medicine decided it would be a great thing to just have me work part-time at the center, and the rest of the time, I would be his. He needed another pair of hands on the medical floor, and the homeless program couldn't be all that important, so why not have me do both jobs? This, I was not happy about.

As this drama began to unfold, I was beginning to realize our homeless program really didn't need a nurse-practitioner. It needed a good triage nurse, and Barbara would perfectly fit that bill. She, by the way, did not wear stilettos. In addition, Mitch Snyder had worked his magic in Washington, and now a local community health center was awarded a grant to provide homeless health care. The crowning cherry on this unfolding of divine intervention included St. John's toilets backing up, flooding the place. This forced the center to close, and the repair was far more costly than their shoestring budget could support. This was the chaos before the creation.

A local contractor heard about our tragedy and came in with a team of volunteers, which included carpenters, plumbers, and electricians. He also managed to get the supplies donated. They would not only repair the place but they would build a new clinic in the corner of the little cathedral in what was once just a storage room. The new space was complete with triage area, two exam rooms, two offices, and a nurse's station. No longer just a health room, we would soon have an actual clinic.

Again, because I was considered to be the expert on homeless health care, now with all of two years of experience, I was approached by Family Health Centers to take on the role of clinic manager and health care provider. I was asked to quit the VA and come on full time to run the new clinic, which was complete with supplies and medications for our boys. There was such an improvement; I thought I was at the Mayo Clinic. This was a no-brainer. I would step into the clinic, Barbara would step into my position, and now our team was even stronger. Nora, Barbara, and I became a well-matched team. With the help of the community and our passion for those we served, we put together one of the best programs in the nation. I should add, none of this would have been possible without the help of Sr. Kathleen and the staff at St. John's. All came to the table to make a difference, starting with volunteers traveling all the way up the chain of command to the mayor of our city and the governor of our state, and that was just the incarnate portion of our team. We were obviously well supported by another team, far more superior. The angels watched our keeping, and let me tell you, the angels were needed. We were an army, and it took an army to meet the needs of those we served.

I accepted the position with Family Health Centers and was assigned a medical assistant, Terry Roach. Terry was another godsend. He was a naval corpsman, just starting in the private sector after completing his tour of duty. He had great skills, a far better temperament than mine, and he could always anticipate what was needed far before I could articulate it. He was underpaid, which made it hard as he had a young wife and three little boys: Tim, Jamie, and Mike. I fell in love with them all, including their dad Terry.

Terry was a beautiful man on every level. He had a tender heart for the guys. He grew up poor and African American in the South. The poor part wasn't so bad because, like the Appalachian people, his family was tight. The problem had to do with the horrible prejudice he endured, which is a part of that twisted tradition I told you about. Shortly after his return from the navy he was jogging near his home. Terry loved to run, not only did it keep him in shape, it helped him manage the stress he endured. Suddenly he was met with a patrol car screeching to a halt before him, blocking his way.

"What you runnin' from, boy?" exclaimed the officer as he opened up his car door. Just like a scene out of *To Kill A Mockingbird*. I couldn't believe it; this was the 1990's. Terry told me story after story until I felt almost ashamed to be a German Irish mutt. His experiences helped him understand the suffering of our men. Terry kept me grounded and would keep me calm on the days when the love of Jesus was not foremost on my mind and I wanted to knock heads together.

On any given day, we averaged about twenty-five to thirty patients. They signed in to be seen and waited. Unless they were bleeding or unconscious, it was first come, first served. The volunteers were good to spot anyone that needed immediate help. Most of their needs were simple: wound care, foot care, and upper respiratory tract infections. Pneumonia and bronchitis was not uncommon as most of the guys smoked. During flu season, our numbers could rise to forty a day. Then we had our patients with chronic illnesses. However, their lifestyle—which included walking everywhere they went and no in-between-meal snacks—left most of them pretty lean, which resulted in a low incidence of the major diseases of aging including diabetes, obesity, hypertension, and vascular disease. Although hypertension was pretty common, in part due to stress and the other part due to substance abuse. Their short lifespan also played a role in reduced morbidity from chronic illnesses.

Mortality rates among our population were high. AIDS and hepatitis C became a big part of my practice. We monitored the guys until they came to the point in their illness where they needed an infectious disease specialist. They were then referred to University Hospital. They would see the specialist, and then they would come back to see what I thought about the specialist's recommendations. It felt good to think they trusted me this much, and it also felt daunting, keeping me on my toes.

The other infectious disease that we combated was sexually transmitted disease. We handed out condoms like the Easter Bunny handed out candy. In fact, we kept a basket full of condoms at the window where the guys signed in to be seen. I think maybe Sr. Kathleen frowned on it, but she turned a blind eye to our cloak-and-shield campaign.

I lost many patients. None in the clinic; they met their demise on the street. Beaten to death by teenage thugs, found frozen in the winter, pulled out of the river, and on the list goes. They knew I cared about them; sometimes they would wait through the night, avoiding the emergency room so they could be seen by Terry and me.

One morning, George showed up at the clinic door. I saw him frequently. He was one of my regulars and one of my favorites. On this day, the volunteers brought him in and through the entrance without sign-in, which was not allowed unless there was an emergency. I looked up from my charting to see him standing there, his face a bloody swollen mess. There was no recognition until he mumbled through swollen lips, "Cindy, it's me, George."

George was an alcoholic. He was one of many men who had worked hard labor all their lives, and when they hit fifty, found no one wanted to hire an old man for the job. This, in addition to his addiction, landed him on the street, too ashamed to ask family for help. He had fallen asleep on a park bench, and kids from the projects beat him with bricks until he was unrecognizable. "Why?" you might ask, because I certainly did. George didn't know, could not give me a reason. He probably chalked it up to being at the wrong place at the wrong time. I have my theories.

The homeless reflected back to the kids a hopelessness and poverty even worse than what they endured in the projects. I assume they were trying to kill it, the very notion that things could get worse. They almost succeeded; George could have easily been killed. We took care of the minor lacerations and trauma, cleaned him up, and sent him on to the ER for treatment of his fractured arm and fractured facial bones.

Wound care was very common in our practice. I viewed more than one wound alive with maggots. One would have been quite enough. I'll say one thing for those little guys, they can sure keep a wound clean. The greater problem was infection and trying to avoid sepsis. Keeping a wound clean on the streets was no easy feat. They had no way to clean the wound or keep it bandaged until we appeared on the scene. Terry was the best wound care specialist out there as far as I was concerned. He took care of some very nasty wounds and kept an untold number of guys out of the hospital because of his skill.

The mentally ill were the hardest to help, especially those with paranoid schizophrenia. If you could keep them engaged long enough for a caseworker to be assigned, you might be able to make a difference. One of our patients, Mary, was case in point. She had wandered the streets for years, hallucinating and alone. Because the center provided a safe place, she could be approached, and soon we had her off the street and into her own apartment. Once on medications and with the assistance of a caseworker, her fear and madness turned into joy. She had connection with the world again, and although her illness was chronic, it was manageable and life was better.

I walked past her one day as she was meeting with her caseworker. I called out, "How you doing, Mary?"

She called back, smiling, "Oh, I'm good, Cindy, just a 'schizoprhenin' all over the place."

Others were quite elusive, which included one of my very favorite patients, Synota. Synota visited quite frequently. She had a list of what she wanted at every visit. This typically included Sudafed, aspirin, and multivitamins. I don't know how anyone could need that much Sudafed unless they were running a crack lab. Since crack had not arrived on the scene, this wasn't a concern. I was pretty tight with our medications because we still weren't rolling in the dough. You had to be sick to get a script filled, even if it was an over-the-counter preparation. However, I was trying to keep Synota on the line until Seven Counties had a chance to gain her trust and work with her.

Synota wandered into town from Canada. She was a Native American Indian. I didn't believe her at first, even though she named her tribe and seemed to be very proud of her heritage. She was so delusional, any information she gave could easily be her fact but our world's fiction. I got the impression she was probably from Cajun country.

Synota looked Creole, with high cheekbones and light creamy mocha skin. She was tall and wiry, her features striking. She always wore a brightly colored scarf wrapped around her head like a turban. I could easily imagine her standing over a huge cast-iron pot, fire crackling up from its edges. It seemed to me she would be at home cooking on some forgotten Louisiana bayou, surrounded by swamp, peering through the steamy vapors of a secret jambalaya recipe.

All was secretive with Synota. Through frightened eyes, you knew she was studying you, looking straight past the veneer presented to the general public and into your soul. So much a part of the gift given to the paranoid schizophrenic—although delusional, they still have better perception than most of us.

Set on hyper alert, her movements were typically quick and deliberate. Every encounter calculated, it was very obvious she was always afraid. Synota viewed the world as an unwelcome place, as if prey for an unknown predator. I thought her name was probably an alias because she was so secretive and paranoid. I would learn later it was her name. She was from Canada, and she felt she was prey for her family, who eventually showed up looking for her. She wanted nothing to do with them, with her native tribe, or with any of the rest of us—at least not for any length of time. The world was too much, too "evil" for her.

I worked hard to win her confidence by giving her anything she wanted within reason. I allowed her to be in control of every encounter, directing me through the maze that was her comfort zone. Most of the time, she wasn't too much trouble. The exception was the bathroom incident.

I was in an exam room with another patient when I heard all the commotion. Commotion we had on a regular basis, but I rarely heard Terry raise his voice. I ran out of the exam room quickly to hear Terry screaming, "No, Synota! Give me that! Put that down! Don't do that!" His voice was stern and almost frantic, very unusual for Terry. I imagined him plastered against the bathroom wall with a knife pressed to his jugular vein.

I rushed over to find them in a standoff. Synota was armed with an assortment of bathroom cleaners, one in each hand and one tucked under her arm. Terry backed into the corner with his hands up, bobbing and weaving to avoid a direct hit from the Soft Scrub. His lab coat was covered in tiny scrubbing bubbles. Fortunately, he escaped to safety with his eyesight still intact. It took us both to talk her down and out of the bathroom.

Synota was germ phobic, obsessed with being clean. I always had to make sure she saw me washing my hands before I approached her on the exam table. If not, then I could wash them again for her inspection because she wasn't about to let me touch her.

On this day, she decided she needed this particular arsenal of chemical protectors for her purse. When it seemed she had taken up residence in our clinic bathroom, Terry knocked on the door to see if she was OK. The door opened, and the altercation began with Terry's request to hand over the goods. When reasoning didn't work, she proceeded to fend him off with a few well-directed sprays.

Conversation was always interesting. You never knew what she was going to say or who she would include in the conversation. Many times she would say, "Cindy, did you hear that?" Then she would proceed to redirect her conversation between myself and the other person in the room, unseen by the rest of us. She would look at me curiously when I did not engage the others, as if to say, "Well, you poor limited creature."

She always kept her distance physically and emotionally, approaching only when she needed something. Then one day, as she was leaving, she threw her arms around me, delivering a full-on hug, and said in one moment of lucidness,

"I love you, Cindy." Then, just as quickly, she jumped back, threw both hands in the air, and shouted, "In the Lord, I'm not one of those 'gaud' damn lesbians!" The words curled off her lips, and each syllable of *goddamn lesbians* was drawn out slowly, as if making a pronouncement of a death wish.

"I know, Synota," I said gently. "I know."

What Synota didn't know was she was hugging one of those goddamn lesbians, but I thought it best I didn't share that little piece of information.

For many years, there were very few women on the scene. Most of our clients were men. The women we did see in those early years were either very mentally ill, had limited intellect, or had horrible backgrounds of physical and emotional abuse. As always, sometimes it was a combination of any or all three problems.

Sr. Kathleen always seemed to deal much better with the boys than with the women, and the coed thing just wasn't working for her. She could come face-to-face with a raving drunk, two feet taller and outweighing her by 150 pounds without batting an eye. Bring it on. However, she did not seem to know what to do about the sparks flying between the men and the women who showed up at our doors. Of course, there were some sparks; despite their illnesses, they still had pretty healthy libidos. They were sick and homeless, not dead.

Sr. Kathleen, like Terry, rarely raised her voice. I could almost say, never raised her voice. It wasn't needed. She had this look and, as I said, her presence was formidable. However, on this day, she not only raised her voice, she was shouting for me through the sign-in window. The tone and urgency sent me running to the window, certain someone was going into cardiac arrest.

As I arrived, I could see by her expression she was frantic, and I thought, "Oh, something is really bad wrong."

"You have to do something," she said.

I waited for the what.

"You have to do something about her."

I looked over Sr. Kathleen's shoulder to see a new visitor, a young woman sitting quietly on the bench. She didn't look so unusual, and she didn't look like she was in any immediate distress. She wasn't bleeding, she wasn't pale, and her airway seemed clear. I'm thinking, "Hey, we're good here! I'm confused?"

"What's wrong? What do you want me to do?"

"Just watch," Sr. Kathleen said.

Just about that time, the young woman stood up, looking out across the sea of men in front of her. She turned her head slowly from right to left like one of those old oscillating fans. Then with arms slightly bent and fists clinched by her side, she began delivering the most powerful pelvic thrusts I have ever witnessed. I was hoping Jesus, who hung facing this display, had his eyes closed. It was as if she was having intercourse with the whole room. I didn't laugh because I didn't want Sr. Kathleen to box my ears, but it took great concentration and control to keep from doubling over.

I walked out to the woman and approached her slowly. As I smiled at her, she was distracted and stopped humping the air.

"Hello," I said.

She was only with me for a minute, and then her face became contorted as she shouted, "The FBI is broadcasting through my hair! I've been pussy whipped in the bathroom!"

This was not helping Sr. Kathleen's panic attack.

"What did you have for lunch today?" I said.

Immediately she was back. "Soup," she said, as casually as if she were in her right mind. I kept redirecting her to a more concrete reality until the real mental health worker could be reached and brought to the scene. Oh yes, sister girl, you just grab those bootstraps and pull yourself on up.

Through the years they came and went—some we saw very briefly, others became regulars. My job was never boring and rarely routine. My favorite couple arrived at the center from Nashville, Tennessee. At least, that was their last stop. Who's to say where they started? The duo came into the clinic together; obviously, they had been a part of each other's lives for some time. The other apparent observation, she was hallucinating, with very few lucid moments in between trips to the other side. I took a breath and entered the exam room.

The woman was sitting on the exam table; her partner stood by her side. He was engaging, smiling at me when I walked in the room. He looked like an ole Grateful Dead follower, long hair and tie-dyed shirt. Totally laid back, I expected him to say "Peace, man," when I walked through the door. I sat down to take her history. I could not get her to engage me; it was as if I was invisible. So I talked to her boyfriend.

She became more and more agitated while we talked, rocking back and forth on the exam table. "Well, she is having a little trouble right now," he said.

"Obviously," I'm thinking.

"You know, they put her in the state hospital in Tennessee. I don't know why."

"Good decision," was my next thought.

About that time, she jumped off the table and began dancing around the room. I looked over at him and said, "You know, this is not normal behavior."

To which he replied, smiling proudly, "Ain't she a hoot? You ought to see her when she's got a radio."

The mentally ill never stopped coming. It took an enormous amount of work and connection to get them the help they needed. The caseworkers from Seven Counties were wonderful. We typically had at least one worker at the center, sometimes two. We had success on occasion, getting them on medications that would bring some normalcy back to their lives, sometimes even getting them off the streets.

Next to St. John's, the old parochial school served as housing for a few of our past clients. There they could have a small apartment while they were assisted with daily living skills and followed closely by case managers. Freddie was one of the few fortunate, helped to get off the streets. Although he had a place now, he continued to come to St. John's almost daily for the community the day center provided.

Typically, this was not allowed. You had to be homeless or working as staff or volunteer to enter the center, but Sr. Kathleen took exception with Freddie. He was like the teacher's pet. A large gentle giant, Freddie towered above the rest of us. He stood at least six foot four and was made of solid muscle. He was in his late forties when he finally found a home through the support and assistance of our caseworkers. Freddie always smiled. He looked a bit like the Cheshire cat as his white teeth glowed against his rich ebony skin. He had little to say, usually used the same phrases over and over. "Ah gee" was his standard byline. He always seemed a bit like a little boy, shyly peeking out from behind an unseen door, which separated his reality from our own. Freddie loved us all; you could feel his devotion. We served as his surrogate family.

Our clients were always appreciative. They understood the rules. They respected the guidelines Sr. Kathleen had in place to make their day a little brighter. The regulars rarely gave us any grief, although, on occasion, a fight would break out between them, and the police would have to be called. They might argue with us on occasion, but they didn't fight with staff. Fighting with each other, on the other hand, was pretty common. However, our out-of-town drifters were quite another story. Occasionally they would show up tired, angry, and drunk. Not a good combination. They had no connection with us. They were used to fighting for everything they wanted. These encounters never made for a pleasant day.

I followed in Sr. Kathleen's footsteps; fear was not a part of my equation with the guys. I typically remained pretty calm and could work with whatever energy showed up. However, on this particular day, I was frazzled, tired, and cranky when one of our out-of-town guys presented at the window to make my day even more challenging. Again, this was not a good combination.

This gentleman didn't like anything I told him about our process for being seen as a patient. He became more and more angry, demanding, and belligerent. This prompted me to go outside the clinic into the center and ask him to leave and come back when he could follow the rules. He continued to swear, and I continued to point to the door and invite him to come back later.

The angrier he became, the more I held my ground but, unfortunately, not my temper. I had had it with this fellow. Finally, he turned and walked toward the door. He was not a small man. He was not old and frail. He was young, strong, and pissed off. He got about halfway to the door and then wheeled around and started toward me. Obviously, this time, further discussion was not on his mind. I was quite certain he had it in mind to knock me into next week. I stood squarely on the ground and looked him in the eyes. I would not back down. I was so angry and out of control that my senses had obviously left me.

It was quite the scene; it happened very quickly. By now we had the attention of those around us, and everyone was braced for what would come next. Most of the staff remained on alert at all times and would be right by your side in just these cases—power in numbers, you know. For whatever reason, no one was coming. I was standing there alone. My opponent was inches away from me, every muscle in his body tensed, face contorted with rage, fist clenched and ready. I stood senselessly incensed and beyond reason. Suddenly the guy stopped. I noticed he was looking above my head and beyond me. It looked like all the rage suddenly drained from his body as he slowly turned and walked out of the center without another word.

"Well," I'm thinking, "guess I showed him." I was feeling a little cocky at the moment, thinking my powerful stare-down won out. As I turned to walk back in the clinic, I stood face to chest with Freddie. He was standing not two inches behind me like a huge guardian angel.

I looked up to see him still glaring at the stranger walking out the door. As was his way, he was not saying a word, but the look on Freddie's face was startling. He was not smiling. The change in Freddie's expression was even scary to me. Obviously, it was neither my power nor the power of the image of Jesus hanging over my shoulder that saved the day. I thought maybe that was what the man was focusing on when he suddenly returned to his senses. No, it was Freddie.

I stood there looking up at my gentle friend, my body starting to shake from the adrenaline rush. My heart was pounding from the huge fight-or-flight response brought into play by our encounter. The neurotransmitters flooding my system had my sympathetic nervous system on overdrive, leaving me trying to find my way out of my reptilian brain and back to reason.

As Freddie dropped his head to look down at me, his face melted, and he was transformed back into the gentle giant we all loved and adored. "Hey," he said as I looked up at him. Then he turned and silently walked away while I regained consciousness, realizing Freddie just saved me from hospitalization, or worse.

They have no bootstraps. They come from broken homes, broken brains, broken bodies, and fractured souls. They endure horrific suffering that, for many, finally brings them into a trance-like existence of hopeless despair. I learned through the years we would only be able to help a small minority off the streets, the rest would remain with us always, just as Jesus promised. They were poor on every level. The best we were going to do for them was stand with them where they were.

I often wondered how people could hold them in such contempt. I came to believe the heartless judgment coming from so many who looked down at them with scorn was born out of fear.

The homeless play out for us our greatest wounding, the worst-case scenario. They reflect the illness of our society. They are the result of our own unbalanced state. In addition, they embody one of our greatest fears, that of isolation and failure. It is no wonder we throw bricks to drive them away. They hold up for us a mirror, and we don't like what we see. They invite us to look within ourselves to find our own bootstraps because, of course, we still have ours.

CHAPTER 9

In all of creation, there are no two of us alike, and yet we are all one. Each of us brings to light another facet of the face of our God. What we create each day can be a masterpiece of evolution or pale echo of mimicked expression. It is our choice and our dance that creates our world.

THE DANCE OF THE POLAR BEAR

COMING TO TERMS WITH YOUR sexuality is "a hard row to hoe." For those of you who have never held a hoe in your hand or heard this turn of phrase, let me explain. When you come to the field with your brothers and sisters you are hoping for an easy row. One that doesn't have as many weeds and, if you're lucky, it might be just a little shorter than some of the others scattered across the fifteen acres you plan on clearing with your hoe-worn hands in the hot humid sun of the South. So what I'm pointing out here to you is the row left to gays and lesbians is damn long and filled with weeds. None of which we planted, mind you, but just the same, we need not only a hoe but an additional machete to chop through what comes up for us.

You don't just wake up one day and look in the mirror and think, "Yep, my eyes are green, my hair is brown, and I am a homosexual." You aren't given the cultural or social cues and nudges your straight brothers and sisters are getting when they start dating. There is no one there winking at you saying, "Now that's a really cute girl. Why don't you ask her out?" When they ask you what you want to be when you grow up, they don't include, "And which do you like, boys or girls?" It's just always assumed that you will be "normal," attracted to the opposite sex. That is until you're not, and then all hell breaks loose.

For some of us, it's a very quiet unspoken hell, but hell just the same. For others, there is nothing quiet about it. Coming out has resulted in being kicked out of our families, our churches, our homes, and our jobs. Some of us have been physically beaten, and all of us have experienced emotional beatings. Others have paid the ultimate sacrifice for coming out, having been brutally raped or beaten to death. So don't get me started on the folks who smugly call this a choice or a "lifestyle." I just won't even entertain that argument and chalk it up to ignorance in its most bigoted form.

My cues were subtle as a late bloomer. I was twenty-two before I even had a hint, thirty-two before I knew for sure, and thirty-seven before I accepted who I was—literally by the grace of God, which I will explain in a minute. However, when looking back now at my childhood development, when I was supposed to be playing with girls during my school-age years, I preferred playing with the boys. They had better toys. I favored basketballs, softballs, guns, and trucks. Baby dolls bored me to tears, literally. I usually cried when someone sent a dolly as a gift. Then when I was supposed to be getting all excited about the boys when in junior high and high school, I just liked hanging out with the girls better. I didn't feel the twitter that my friends had obviously bloomed into and felt out of step but curious over all the fuss. I can look back now and see all the crushes I had on girls starting around twelve or thirteen. But I had no clue they were crushes. I just thought it was normal to want to spend all your time with one "particular friend."

I had several particular friends before I woke up and realized my bread wasn't buttered on the usual side, or as Aunt Beanie might say, my "tor-tell-ah" was definitely upside down. I suppose I was a bit obtuse. The strongest of my schoolgirl crushes developed when I was a senior in high school. The recipient of my affection was my senior English teacher. There were no sexual feelings, just a shift in perspective. I woke up thinking about her, could never get her off my mind, wanted to be with her every moment, and went to bed thinking about her. Well, I know, duh! Unfortunately, my high school friends figured out my feelings before me, and halfway through my senior year, we were branded *lesbians* by another senior girl. She was quite vicious in her accusations. So in just a New York second, we became the talk of the school and the community, which were just about as big as that same New York second. In other words, everyone was talking about us. We were the scandal folks waited for in a small town. Finally, they had something to discuss beyond the weather. The teacher almost lost her job, and I was devastated that anyone would think I was queer. I turned in on myself and stuffed my feelings as rapidly as I could until that gave way to rage. I put my head down, finished out the last year of high school, and ran away to college. I left and never wanted to return. I still have an aversion to going back there, even today.

Although dating never interested me really, suddenly it became very important. The reason is obvious: I wanted to prove to myself and the rest of the world I was not gay. So when Louis called for a date, I said, "Sign me up, baby, I'm yours." Louis was a wonderful guy and became my best friend. The problem was I didn't get out of bed thinking about him. I could get him off my mind, and I didn't want to be with him every minute of my waking day. Our relationship lasted into college when Louis gave me a ring and we announced our engagement. I wanted to be engaged, I wanted to have a boyfriend, I wanted to fit in, and I really liked Louis. As we have established, for me it was all about being good and doing the right thing. However, now I was twenty-two, and the right thing meant being honest with myself and with Louis. I still had no idea I was gay, but I knew something was missing. I didn't know what was missing until I fell in love. Then it all made sense, and yet it didn't because I fell in love with a sorority sister, not what I was expecting or hoping for in the context of being normal.

First love is grand. It's big, it's freely given, and there is no fear. You don't have a clue how horrible the loss of a love can feel. How could you? This is the first one. You just show up with your whole heart and then you look into their eyes and say, "Here! Here's my heart, I give it to you," blissfully entering into the magic.

My first love crashed and burned in three years right after my graduation. I never dreamed we would not be together forever but that was not to be. Soon after I left school she stopped calling, stopped coming to see me and would not accept my phone calls. Years later I found out she didn't want to see me because she was having an affair with another woman. Obviously absence did not make her heart grow fonder. I left school and she was on the prowl.

There was no closure. I never knew why she left. I was twenty-two years old, and my heart was broken. I never imagined how painful this would be. I just wanted someone to tell me why it happened. I wanted her to tell me why she left. I cried for months. I had no support because no one knew about our love affair. I was so far in the closet, it took two hands and a flashlight to find my way out the door. No one knew I was gay; I still didn't know I was gay. I just thought I was in love with this one person. Remember I told you about that little game most of us switch hitters play before we come out to ourselves? I was no different. I finally came to the conclusion I was in this terrible place of pain because God was punishing me. Now there's a very old story. I hurt, therefore God did it to me. I don't think so. In fact, this is one of the few things I feel with great certainty. God does not hurt us or inflict pain or damn us to eternal agony. We are very adept at doing that to ourselves without any help from our benevolent Creator. However, that was the best conclusion I could come up with at the age of twenty-two, and so I accepted it. I decided I would never let this happen again. I would never let myself have feelings for another woman, the end, so be it.

Over the next eight years, I moved eleven times. I was dancing as fast as I could to avoid any prolonged eye contact with anyone I felt a closeness to on any level. I dated a couple guys—again, nothing special, but at least it gave me some sense of normalcy. I am quite certain I was totally in love with my best friend in graduate school, but I guarded my heart like a pit bull, never allowing myself to even think about acting on my feelings. This resulted in some lovesick moments daydreaming. Following graduate school, I moved to Eastern Kentucky for my internship and ended up staying there for over a year. It was easier in some ways—no one there to fall in love with. I was alone on a mountainside so could hardly get myself in trouble. In addition to that factor, I was also looking very closely at celibacy and becoming a nun.

It was all going pretty well until I left the mountains and moved to Louisville. I was teaching nursing at Spalding University and was in discernment with the Kentucky Dominicans. I was certain I was to join their merry band of itinerate preachers. I moved into one of the convents as part of my discernment process. It was not the typical convent but a house the sisters owned that provided a place for four sisters, or in my case, three sisters and an associate. I affectionately called it the Condo. I was living here when I was rediscovered by my soon-to-be best friends.

Tammy saw my name in the faculty register. She was in a long-term relationship with one of my old nursing classmates, Judy. Judy was the only person on the planet that knew with any certainty that I had had a relationship with another woman. She knew because I told her. We both stayed with a mutual friend in Louisville right out of undergraduate school when we were sitting for our nursing boards. I don't know what possessed me to tell Judy about my loss, but I did and finally got some relief in just being able to tell someone else my heart was broken. Judy responded with kindness and concern. She was always better at psychiatric nursing than I was, and it came in handy on that day.

I was quite the character in college. I suppose Tammy had been privy to some of the Bo stories, because she was very excited to find me on the faculty register and immediately had Judy call to see if I could come over and have dinner with them. So I guess, at this point, Tammy was the second person to know I had had a relationship with another woman. Partners share everything, you know. I gladly accepted the invitation and drove over to their home.

At this point in the journey, I was beginning to accept the fact I would never be a nun. I was sorely disappointed at this turn in the road, but it was very obvious religious life was not to be my vocation. I was also becoming acutely aware that I was truly lonely. I was so focused on career and God to this point that it was easier to be alone, but now I was starting to understand the gravity of my past decision to be an emotional recluse. The steel doors in front of my heart started to crack open from the pressure, and I started to get a glimpse of what lay behind them. It wasn't pretty.

Tammy and Judy had a beautiful house in the suburbs of Louisville. I walked in and immediately felt at home. Tammy was also quite the character, so we hit it off immediately. I felt like a hand in glove in their energy set, which included the deep love of two women for each other. I spent the last eleven years running from this expression of love. Most of that time, I was preaching to anyone who would listen about the evils of homosexuality. I quoted biblical chapter and verse as all good little evangelical Christians do. However, the door broke open and I was faced with what I didn't want to see or experience or understand. I felt so at home here and fit in so well because I was obviously gay. I was livid!

Talk about a "come to Jesus" moment. I walked out of the house, looked up at the stars in the sky, and screamed at God, "Why? I don't want to be gay! Why did you do this to me? I obviously didn't do it to myself." This was my line of reasoning. So I screamed, "Why did you create me this way? What am I going to do now?" I drove home to the condo with far more information than I wanted and a twist to the evening that I certainly wasn't expecting. The realization was bittersweet. The steel door stood wide open now. I could become whole again, but being whole and being honest would mean setting myself up for a permanent position in the dunking booth. It would win for me the honor of being the bullseye, the target for every bigoted fundamentalist I came upon for the remainder of my life. This was to be my lot. It was not a position of choice for the do-good girl.

I had a couple weeks to sit with these thoughts. I was in a bit of a crisis. The decision was made; I would leave the condo and move out into an apartment. I was at a loss to understand why I stood in this place. Disappointment is a pale expression for what I felt now. I would not be living out my life as a Dominican—at least, not as a vowed Dominican. This transition was in the works, and at the same time, I had to come to terms with being queer. Oh joy! As was my custom, I needed to talk to someone, and it had to be someone with whom I felt safe. I needed a person who could hear my story and hold space for my fragile state without judgment. I called Ginny Brown.

I suppose I was more nervous than a whore in church when I arrived at Ginny's doorstep. Actually, I would have preferred the position of whore in church; It felt much safer than my current predicament, the homosexual in church. Ginny was a theologian, a philosopher, a poet, a gentle soul and more progressive in matters of spirituality than anyone I had ever experienced in my travels. Most importantly she was a good friend. I knew I could entrust my heart to her. But my fears, like demons, "were legion."

As I walked in the door, I felt myself groping for the courage to come up with the right words. Ginny knew I was hurting. I'm sure it was palatable as I walked into the room, and as a sensitive, it probably was almost as unpleasant for her as it was for me. She had worked as a campus minister where we first met, and she was a mother of five. As a result, she had infinite patience and great skills in listening. I talked all around and under and in between what I really wanted to say when I finally blurted it out, "Ginny, I think I'm gay!"

She looked at me with a "so what" expression on her face as she replied, "I know."

"Really, you know? How do you know? I don't even know!"

"Well, I have known for a long time," she said. "It's obvious."

Now she was giggling as she reached out and gently touched my hand. I was in shock. I was not giggling, but I was totally relieved. There was no condemnation, there was no upset, there was not even a hint of disgust, which is what I feared. At the same time, I was kind of hoping for a "Oh no, darlin', you're not gay!" instead of a "Well hell, girl, you are obviously as queer as they come, get over yourself" kind of sentiment. Regardless, in that split second there was a deep healing, not acceptance on my part, mind you, but healing. Enough so that I could at least start to look at myself and begin the process of acceptance that would, for me, take years of work and struggle.

Ginny sent me out the door with four or five articles that discussed homosexuality. Not articles of condemnation but articles of acceptance. That was a switch. This would begin my study of the subject. I would read everything I could get my hands on as I struggled with the expression of sexuality in the context of spirituality. It's a bit of a weighty issue. However, it was not nearly as heavy as the ten-ton boulder I had carried around on my shoulders since my first kiss. That is to say, the first kiss that came with all the bells and whistles. I could not hide any longer; at least, I could not hide from myself. I didn't come roaring out of the closet that day, but I opened the door and peeped around the corner.

In the meantime, my two well-meaning partners in Lesbos were busy behind the scenes making plans to fix me up with a friend of theirs. I didn't tell them I was having a meltdown about being gay. For that matter, I didn't tell them I was gay. Obviously, that did not enter into the equation. Like my high school class and other folks near and dear, they figured it out all by themselves. As I was learning, statement of fact is not a requirement for being. I left Tammy and Judy's house abruptly following my "aha moment" when we last met. This did little to deter them. A couple weeks later, they called me up to see if I wanted to go out to dinner. This was followed with "And, oh, by the way, there is another friend going with us." My hesitation on the other end of the line prompted, "Oh no, we are not trying to fix you up." They were definitely trying to fix me up. Some years later, they finally admitted it through long-repressed laughter.

I was still living in the convent with my community, the Dominican Sisters, but by then we all knew I would not adapt to religious life. My decision to leave was made with the help of my friend and spiritual director who was also a Dominican. I was looking for an apartment and would soon relocate to the other side of town. I thought the hardest part was over with the conclusion of this discernment process. However, now with one very quick breath, I was submerged in another kettle of fish. Oh now, that was really a poor choice of metaphor, considering.

I told Judy and Tammy I would be glad to meet them for dinner. The plan was to meet at a central location and carpool into downtown. As the date came closer, I became more excited. I had no previous experience of what I was feeling. The anticipation was incredible, and although I didn't know why, I felt certain something very big was getting ready to burst into my life. And so it did, and her name was Carolyn.

You have heard of love at first sight. Some of you, the most jaded of us, don't believe in love at first sight. Well, I will give you a bigger bite to chew: my love for Carolyn was there before first sight. I feel certain this was the anticipation and excitement I felt before we met. I know it doesn't make any sense, but I was there living through the experience. Our life together began that night in the parking lot of a bookstore, but knowing what I know now, I can only imagine it was just one of many lives together.

Carolyn was a joker, playful and kind. Her cheerful presence of being served as a cloak of light, used to hide the tenderness of her all-seeing heart. Beneath the cloak, she held the wounded. The image is much like the Ghost of Christmas Present from Dickens's play, *A Christmas Carol*. An old soul, here in this lifetime to serve others, the sick and dying became a huge part of her reason for walking the planet. This you could not see in her face, but instead, deep laugh lines extended out from the corners of the eyes. Eyes that knew too much, had seen too much, but searched for even more.

As our eyes met, the steel door was now blown off the hinges and I was hopelessly in love. I felt like a seventh grader remembering in an instant the painful awkwardness of adolescence all over again at the age of thirty-one. I was back at square one, but now I gave in, at least on one level. I was tired of holding the doors closed, and besides, now I had no doors. My heart lay exposed before her, unprotected and completely vulnerable once again after years of hiding. Introductions were exchanged, and we were off to have dinner, the four of us.

I understood what Cinderella must have experienced at the ball. I did not want the night to end. It was magic. I tried not to be so obviously smitten, but I'm afraid I didn't do a very good job. I wondered if she was feeling what I was feeling. Surely she did, but she wasn't showing it. I was in agony before the night was over. She teased me without mercy throughout evening. I was hoping this was her way of flirting, but I wasn't even sure if she liked me or if she was just being nice. The night came to a close, and I did everything short of handing her my glass slipper so she would know I was interested, but I still had no clue about her feelings.

I floated back home to the convent. Our evening had turned into a marathon of laughter, and it was early morning when I unlocked the door and quietly tiptoed up to my room. I still had several I's to dot and T's to cross before I could settle into my new home across town. There was much to do, and I was thankful for something to keep my mind occupied while trying to get my footing as I drifted in and out of thoughts of her, my head in the clouds. Yes, all those goofy expressions now made total sense.

Soon I left my local Dominican community and moved to the Highlands of Louisville, a charming place with towering trees and old Victorian homes. I busied myself with painting the apartment and unpacking to make the place my own. All the while, all I could think about was Carolyn, wondering if I was ever going to see her again. When I could not stand it anymore, I called Judy to see if I could get any positive feedback. After chatting about this and that, I reverted back to the seventh grader and shyly asked, "Do you think she likes me?"

"I don't know," was Judy's reply. "You can never tell what Carolyn is feeling."

That was prophetic in itself; no truer statement ever spoken. I would come to learn over the years that followed, Carolyn was a master at hiding her feelings.

I decided it was time to have the girls over; I wanted to host the evening. I called Judy, and they gladly accepted the invitation. Then I asked her for Carolyn's number. It took all the courage I could muster, but I decided I had to do something to get the ball rolling. Judy gave me the phone number. I sat for a long time staring at the digits before me as if there were the winning lottery combination. Finally I called; I got the answering machine. I was relieved to leave the message, afraid she might say no. And if so, at least I wouldn't have to suffer the rejection in person. I quickly rattled off the invitation, probably leaving her wondering who the auctioneer was on the other end of the line. I dropped Judy's and Tammy's names into the mix, hoping that would help to entice her over to the party. In addition, I spouted off the menu, which included shish kebabs. Who the hell knows why I thought it was necessary to tell her what she would be eating? Then I said good-bye, hung up the phone, and took a breath, very near to passing out. I forgot to breathe, extending my long-winded invitation without ever inhaling.

So I waited, I paced, I reviewed the menu, I looked around the room, I stared at the phone trying to will it to ring. I wondered if she would call back. I wondered if the answering machine really worked. I wondered if my message sounded stupid, which, of course, it did. But that didn't seem to matter to Carolyn because she called back. The phone rang. I picked it up, and on the other end of the line, I heard her say, "Hey, what 'cha got on them skewers?"

Carolyn's language and English skills were far better than mine. She was slaughtering the King's English to make me laugh. In addition, I found out later she thought I was a bit of a hick, so she was teasing me again. Obviously, she could tell I was nervous; it wasn't because she was psychic. It would not take a Nostradamus to figure that one out. She was laughing on the other end of the line, and now I was laughing.

"All right," I said. "I know, I know. But will you come?"

"Sure, what shall I bring?" she replied.

"Oh wow," I'm thinking to myself. And all was right with my world.

The night finally came. Judy and Tammy arrived first. My new place was very small but nice, home sweet home. I was still teaching nursing at Spalding; the tiny apartment was about all I could afford beyond a room at the Y. What is it with private institutions of higher education? You need a sugar daddy to be able to work at one. I didn't have a sugar daddy or momma, for that matter, but I was working fast and furious on the momma.

I had the grill going in the backyard. We left Tammy in the front room to listen for Carolyn's arrival; Judy followed me out to be sure nothing on "them skewers" burned. I looked at Judy and in all seriousness said, "I don't know what to do."

"With the shish kebabs?" Judy asked.

"No, no. With Carolyn. I don't know what to do next."

"Well, flirt," she said.

"Really." I looked back, wide-eyed. "I don't know how."

Judy was the queen of flirt, and I mean that in all seriousness. She flirted with everyone all the time, and she was good at it. I was, on the other hand, so developmentally delayed, I had absolutely not one single skill in the gift of allurement.

Judy immediately got this little grin on her face that looked like part angel and part she-devil. Obviously up for the challenge, she jumped in with both feet. After all, it was the least she could do; coupling Carolyn and I was her idea in the first place. Under Judy's tutelage, Carolyn would not know what hit her. Time was short; this was a crash course. My beloved would be arriving at any minute.

"Leave those," she ordered as she waved her hand over the meat-covered sticks. "Come inside. They are not going to burn, and I need your undivided attention."

I followed her into my kitchen where the tiny table was set with my best fare.

"Now sit down here at the table," she said. "Pretend you are Carolyn."

"OK," I laughed nervously.

"Now when you're talking to her or if she's talking, look into her eyes and don't look away. Not even for a second, get it? Look really deeply into her eyes."

Judy demonstrated, casting a long intense gaze that would make a hooker blush.

"Oh," I said as I felt her seductive spell.

Then she said, "Where is she sitting?" She switched gears. "Oh, it doesn't matter. Just make sure she sits right next to you."

She was starting to get pretty bossy; I think it was the pressure she was under. She had five minutes to teach me to be sexy. I had spent the last thirty-one years trying to be asexual lest someone, especially me, figured out I was gay. So it was hardly an easy feat.

Judy picked up the salt and pepper shakers and placed the salt near the area where Carolyn might rest her hand. "Now"—Judy looked at me as if to have me understand this was important, extremely important in Flirting 101—"when Carolyn rests her hand on the table, reach over for the salt. When you do, be sure you brush up against her hand with yours." She stated emphatically, "Timing is key here. As your hand touches hers and she looks over, capture her gaze and hold it. Do not let her go. Now you practice, I'll be Carolyn."

I looked back at her thinking, "You have got to be kidding," but I followed every instruction with great attention to detail as outlined in my crash course. Course over, the doorbell rang. Carolyn had arrived.

Three weeks ago, during our first encounter, Carolyn sat and listened intently to my story with great curiosity. In all honesty, I was trying to impress her, and my friend Judy was trying to help me along. I was quite the musician in college. Fixated on this talent, Judy kept asking me to sing and play Tammy's guitar when we arrived back at their house after dinner. So I did, but Carolyn didn't seem all that interested in my talent show. In fact, she actually seemed a little uncomfortable, and I could feel her pull away a bit. That had never happened before. Then there was our commonality, we were both nurses. I think I was the first nurse-practitioner she ever met, but the fact that I practiced in Appalachia was a bigger novelty. However, what won the prize for oddity was my desire to become a Dominican. She seemed more curious to meet someone who was seriously thinking of entering religious life than anything else.

Most people don't get it, even if, like Carolyn, they were raised in the Catholic Church. So I wasn't surprised. In addition, I'm sure she found it hard to put it all together. I was living in a convent, and here we all sat, pretending we were not on a date, when in fact we were. To top it off, Judy and Tammy chose a gay bar/restaurant for our dinner engagement. I am certain I looked a bit shell-shocked with all that was unfolding. She was probably sitting across from me thinking, "Could this be any more queer?" My history and our evening provided Carolyn with more material for her stand-up comedic routine. She arrived at my dinner party with hostess gift in hand, an original album of the Singing Nun. I loved it. She always had a way of making me laugh and keeping things light.

The moment of truth came. We sat down to eat, and I stumbled all over myself to make sure Carolyn was seated strategically as planned, salt shaker at her right hand. It played off perfectly as designed by Judy's expertise—the deep longing looks, the soft brush of hands in the candlelight, a little wine. All the makings for romance unfolded in perfect scripted form under the watchful eye of the master of flirt. Poor Carolyn never knew until years later, the trap was set and she fell into it.

Judy and Tammy got up to leave for the evening. I totally expected Carolyn to follow their lead, but she didn't. Instead, she sat quietly on the couch and seemed to hope no one noticed she was still there. At that moment, I knew. Not only did she like me, the air was thick with pheromones and I was the lucky recipient. I walked into the hall with my other guests, calmly closed the door, and immediately started doing the happy dance. I looked wildly, first at them and then at the apartment where she sat waiting inside. Tammy and

Judy joined me as we formed a circle, madly flailing our arms in the air while dancing a silent Irish jig right outside the door. They snuck away in muted soft giggling, giving me the eye and high-five motions on their way out to the car. I walked back up the stairs, opening the door to see her still seated there. Now Carolyn was the one returning the deep longing gaze. I sat down by her as she reached up and turned off the lamp. "Oh, my sweet Lord," I'm thinking, "all this just because of well-placed salt." From that night on, we rarely spent another day apart over the next thirteen years. She was the air I breathed and the joy of my life.

When the fairy dust settled and I was able to see beyond the stars in my eyes, I was suddenly faced with my deepest fear. What would God think about all this—my being gay, being in love, and acting on my love? Does there always have to be a catch? Damn it! The question was my constant companion, what does God think? It would take me five more years to understand the blending of my sexuality and spirituality, two of the most powerful forces in our human nature. In the process, I would read, study, pray, plead, rant, and rave until, finally, I gave up—and in so doing could hear the soft still voice heard by the prophets before me. And there was peace. It was a long time in coming.

Carolyn and I moved in together after about three months of seeing each other daily. We never planned it that way or talked about it, but it just happened that for one reason or another, we could not let a day go by without seeing each other. Once we moved in together, I could not wait to get home to her after work. At the same time, the drive home each afternoon was always torturous. That same little rat bastard party pooper was always on my shoulder, whispering in my ear. He never stopped his bantering. On and on he droned about the evil of homosexuality, but every night, as soon as I opened the door and saw her smile, he vanished into thin air. Unfortunately, he'd always come back.

Carolyn never seemed to experience this theological crisis. Once when I asked her about it, she said, "I don't think my sex life is any of God's business!" So there you have it. Wish it could have been that easy for me, but then with the chaos comes creation. I was about creating a life with her, so I suppose a little chaos could be expected considering our cultural setting and my religious upbringing in the South. My "tor-tell-ah" was indeed upside down, inside out, and all askew, God love me.

Sr. Virginia Smith, OP, was my spiritual director at the time. We had had many meetings and retreat work together when I was discerning a vowed religious life. She was also a very dear friend. So I decided I would "come out" to Virginia and see what she had to say about it. Because I had had some practice with Ginny, it wasn't too hard. Besides, I thought Virginia was very close to God and probably had a direct line to Jesus. She ranked right up there with Sr. Peggy. Had I painted the last supper, they would have had the seats at the right and left hand of the Savior.

I was living with Carolyn at the time and called Virginia to ask for a meeting. I came in and sat down with her. Her office was at the convent Holy Rosary, where she lived with about eight other Dominicans. The room where we met was small, probably not unlike that of any counselor/therapist, maybe a bit more modest, complete with couch and easy chair. I stared for a moment at the Bible lying on the coffee table in front of me. Then I looked up and said, "Virginia, you know that time on my first retreat when I had such a terrible struggle in the prayer?"

"Yes," she said.

"Well, do you remember at the end of the retreat when I was crying and saying over and over, 'I don't want to be gay, I don't want to be gay,' and you said, 'Well, you're not!'" There was a brief pause. I looked up at her and stated, "Well, I am."

Virginia started to laugh. "Did I say that, that you were not gay?"

"Yes," I said emphatically, "you did."

"Well," she said, "don't ever tell anyone I said that. I should have never told you, you were not gay."

"Well, regardless, you were wrong because I am."

Then we both laughed.

"Cindy," Virginia said, "I don't think God cares if you're gay or if you're straight."

I looked back at her in questioning disbelief because, obviously, she was wrong once before.

Again, there was a deep healing just as there was when I told Ginny I was gay and she responded with the same kind of "so what" response. Then Virginia looked at me with deep love and said, "Did you tell God you were gay?"

"Yes, yes I did," came my reply.

"And what did God say?" Virginia asked.

"I don't know. I just said I'm gay! Then I ran like hell."

I think Virginia got a stitch in her side after that round of laughter. Then softly, in all seriousness, she said, "Well, maybe you might want to tell God again. And this time, wait for a response."

I listened to all that she said and knew she was right. It would never matter how many voices or people told me my sexuality was right or wrong. I would only know the answer if the words came from God. So I would ask—but not just yet, because if God said my relationship with Carolyn was wrong, that would mean I would have to give up the love of my life. I was not ready for that possibility.

Days turned into weeks, turned into months, turned into years of happiness. Carolyn and I settled into life and into St. William's Parish. We called it the island of misfit toys. There were other gay couples, divorced couples whose second marriage was not recognized by the church, priests and religious who had left religious life, and a whole parcel of radical left-wingers. We were young and old, black and white, straight and gay—but we all had this in common. We fought for justice, and we disagreed with about everything Rome insisted we believe—with the exception of Eucharist, which we found not just in the Host but within each other. The bishop turned a blind eye at our liturgies, which were not exactly in line with those proscribed by the Holy Father. We liked to color outside the lines, and we did so with great abandon.

I continued my work at St. John's with the homeless. It was my custom to walk around the corner and down the block to another Catholic church, sometimes for Mass and sometimes just to pray during my lunch hour. The old Catholic churches in Louisville are quite awesome with their cathedral ceilings and grand stained-glass windows. In this particular church, the window behind the altar captured the scene of Isaac and Abraham. I kept being drawn back to this window where I sat many days during my lunch hour only to look up at the scene that haunted me beyond knowing. There was something there that I could not put my finger on, but it kept pulling at me until the insight made its way into my consciousness.

Abraham could give up his son; could I give up Carolyn? It was time for me to face my Mount Moriah. I would never have peace without knowing. Although my love for her was so great that I believed I would risk hell in exchange for this lifetime with her, I was not willing to take that same risk with her soul. At that point in my formation, I still believed in the fires of hell and the all-seeing, wrathful, punishing God. I sat with Carolyn and told her about the window and about my struggle, which never stopped. She knew I had to do this; I had to go on retreat. I had to ask the question, and this time I had to wait for the response. She looked at me with tears rolling down her cheeks when I left for Chicago that February to meet with my spiritual director. We both knew that I would not return to her if God said our love was sinful. Oh, let me say that over one more time, love was sinful. Really? You would think I could have bought a vowel and got a clue at that point, but no.

I called my current spiritual director, Rita Petrusa OP, and made the arrangements for the retreat. I would be staying in a convent for seven to ten days observing silence, not far from Chicago's North Shore. I would meet with Rita once a day for an hour as was the Jesuit custom for this type of retreat work. I always thought Sr. Virginia would be the one to visit this question with me, but we lost her tragically in an auto accident. She was hit head-on by a driver out of control. She was fifty-one years old. It was an incredibly painful loss for us all. Eventually, I came to believe releasing this incarnation would allow her to do more on the other side; otherwise, I could make no sense of the tragedy. To my fortune, after her death, Rita stepped in and remained my spiritual companion for several years, which is major for an extrovert. We need to run things past someone else when we are trying to understand the greater questions, even the smaller questions, for that matter.

I was not excited about this retreat; I did not want to go. Good sign. When you don't want to go, you know you are supposed to be there. Sr. Peggy was right. If I showed up, God would show up. That's just how it works. I took my Bible and guitar and drove to Chicago where Rita lived. I spent the first night with Rita and Mel (Mary Ellen Riley). Mel was a vowed Religious from another order. She and Rita shared community in a flat on Chicago's North Side. They were both dear friends. Carolyn and I spent many Thanksgivings at their table, bathed in their love. We had a very deep connection. In my picture of the last super, Rita and Mel would also be painted as disciples sitting in His presence. They gave all to follow.

I love Chicago, always loved going there, but on this visit, I was less than happy. I was not at all sure of my outcome and was preparing for the worst. That evening before the retreat, we watched a movie made for TV, and in the scene, a mother actually sits on her screaming, flaying child and says, "It's OK to be afraid, it's OK to be angry, but it's not OK to run away!" Well, the retreat was supposed to start the next day; obviously, the prayer was starting now.

Morning came on the first day, and Rita drove me to the convent. I knew I was scared, and I knew I was angry. I also knew I could not run away. My fear was the possibility that I would be asked to give up Carolyn. My anger grew from the thought that God would ask me to give up something I loved so dearly, not unlike Abraham's love for Isaac. Yet I knew I would do it. If asked, I would pick up a knife and sever the relationship. If God asked this of me, then I knew in his perfect love and wisdom it would be for the best—not only for me, but for Carolyn. I came to this place as much for her as for myself.

On the second day, the fear really set in and I was sick with dread. I could thump a Bible with the best of them. My born-again fundamentalist background reared its ugly head. I knew every scripture and verse that could be twisted into condemnation for every same-sex relationship on the planet including my own, no matter how holy I thought it was. I didn't need to pick up my Bible, but if I did and let it fall open without turning a page, it was jumping out at me. I was paralyzed with fear; I could not pray at all. I struggled through the day and evening, but by nightfall, I had had it. I lost every bit of courage I had mustered, and I was ready to get the hell out of Dodge. I called Carolyn over and over to tell her to cancel her plane ticket. I was coming home. Our plan included her coming to Chicago at the end of the retreat. I never reached her. The only thing that kept me there and prevented me from packing the car was "It's OK to be afraid, it's OK to be angry, but it's not OK to run away." I lay in my room despondent, without hope, but I stayed and fell into a deep sleep.

I met with Rita the next day. I told her about the movement of the prayer. Her response was compassionate and direct. She told me I had to deal with all my fears before I could get beyond them and hear the still voice of God that was deep within me. This was the first good news I had had since I arrived and probably gave me the hope I needed to continue. She said, "You think you know what God is going to say, but you don't. Ask for the grace to shut out the other voices and listen to what God has to say about the whole thing." So I did.

I had had about enough of my room, and although it was colder than kraut outside, as my mother would say, I needed to get out into the sunshine and fresh air—which is frigid, I'm telling you, at that time of year in Chicago. I walked down the sidewalks of the busy city, noticing all that I loved about the city. The scent of hot pizza being pulled from the oven, the sounds of the city, and the marvelous diversity one can witness on the streets of downtown. It was about four or five blocks to the lake, and so I decided to go there. It might be the best place to enter into the quiet and hear the voice of my Creator, I thought. Still a bit gun-shy after the last two days, I walked to the North Shore and sat down to listen.

The lake was beautiful. I was alone with the city at my back and nothing but horizon and water in front of me. It is a perfect place to induce a trance-like state, stopping all the noise of the city and, most importantly, the noise inside my head. I became mesmerized while watching a single seagull fly above my head. His movement was fluid and repetitive as his flight pattern outlined the figure eight, the sign of infinity. This continued for what seemed like a very long time. At first I thought, he must be looking for a fish below and soon he will dive into the waters and snatch up his prey. But no, he just kept flying the same pattern over and over again. I'm thinking why he is doing this; surely he would be getting tired by now.

In the silence created in that moment, I heard the voice, and it said, "He is flying for the pure joy of flying, doing what he is created to do… and you were created to love women, and that is what you do best."

Well, I almost laughed out loud. It seemed so simple and humorous. Doing what I do best, which is loving women. OK, so who said that? I wasn't convinced. Was that God? Was that voice just something I made up, something I wanted to hear? I had no idea, not really. My butt was falling asleep now and was half frozen to the concrete wall I was perched on, so I decided to walk back.

As I retraced my steps toward the convent, I notice a zoo. I was tired of working so hard at the prayer so decided, what the heck, I'll just take a detour. I need a little recess. What I didn't know was, it was not a detour at all. I was being guided right into the Living Word. My God was walking with me, each step bringing with it a new lesson. My lesson. Near the entrance of the zoo was a planetarium. It was warm, so obviously, my choice for first stop.

Outside this place, all was frozen, covered in ice and snow. The planetarium provided a warm, moist tropical environment with thousands of plush green living plants. They were thriving in the protection of the space provided. I walked silently, surrounded by the beauty of the plants and flowers that filled the rooms.

The voice came again, "Do you see how these plants thrive and grow even in this hostile frigid place? I care for them here. I care for you. Your world is a hostile place because you are a homosexual in a heterosexual world. Still I create for you a loving warm environment of friends, gay like you, so you can continue to thrive and grow."

I was silenced now; I stopped arguing. I walked without the noise of my head through the rest of the planetarium and out the door into the zoo. I didn't see any animals at first. Of course, they were all smarter than I was, taking refuge inside the buildings. Then suddenly, I heard splashing. Splashing. It was cheek-stinging, butt-numbing cold outside; who was swimming? I walked up the path following the sounds I heard, and there she was, a great white polar bear diving into the water with total joy. She dove in, swam a figure eight, climbed back up on the rocks, and repeated the process. Over and over. I stood awestruck and watched her movement mirror the figure of infinity, just like her brother the seagull.

The voice said, "You certainly wouldn't want to do this, nor could you, but she is doing what she was created to do. No voice tells her she should not do what she is created to do."

I stood, silently watching; my heart was full.

Soon I continued my divinely guided tour. The weight was lifted now; it was gone. I was open, and there were no dark voices badgering me. The light had exposed and burned away the darkness. I continued walking, down the paths and through the buildings. Each turn brought with it another very unusual animal. I never knew these creatures existed; they were so far outside my experience. All of them, in all their oddity, appeared joyfully going about their day. All created differently, each one bringing their own unique gift, all living out who they were created to be. How perfect.

I walked back to the convent, so full I could do nothing but sit in silence. I was overwhelmed with love. I met with Rita the following morning on the fourth day. I told her of all that happened and, in so doing, realized the retreat was over. The prayer unfolded in a way I could never have anticipated. So unusual from my past experiences, during this retreat, it was nature rather than scripture that brought profound peace. Retreats in the past had been much longer, but I guess five years of struggle is long enough.

While living in Buckhorn, I read the story of Jonathan Livingston Seagull. The scripture "You shall know the truth, and the truth will set you free" was tied to this book for me. Peggy and I had many conversations over that one phrase, but I knew I was not free. Now I was finally free. No voice would ever come again to shatter my resolve. The voices would come, those that wound and strip away the skin from your back, but they would never again destroy my faith in love.

I packed my bags and went home with Sr. Rita. I called Carolyn and, the next morning, went to pick her up at the airport. She was glad to hear my voice, to know it was over. She sat at home and waited for me to work through my fears. When she saw me at the airport, she threw her arms around me and then leaned back and said, "You really are free now."

I took Carolyn to the zoo as I babbled on and on about the retreat, the prayer, and what transpired during those three short, very long days before my resurrection. For me, it was like reliving the prayer, each scene in the zoo bringing back the insights and the still voice I heard there as God walked with me through the mist into the clearing. I thought the retreat was over, but just as it started before I planned, it also continued beyond my plan.

Carolyn and I returned to Rita's and Mel's for the weekend. In an effort to entertain us, they suggested we go to a play. They knew very little about the production, but the play company had a good reputation, and the title was intriguing, "Just One World." As it turned out, our seats were on the front row. The set was modern, very beautiful but very different, not what you might expect. When the play began, it was as if the writer had attended my retreat with me and wrote this play from my experience.

To this point, the prayer had been soft and gentle. Now it was as if a tidal wave had broken through the wounding of the past, and the voice, God's voice, would have its say. There were no human characters in the play; all were animals. Each animal was cast to portray its unique difference in the world. As the characters of the animals were introduced, so were their unique gifts. Each gift brought with it balance to our world. The play was a reflection of all that I had been shown in the prayer. I could not speak; tears ran down my face. There was a huge aching knot in my throat as I worked to hold back the sobbing release that made its way up to the surface. I turned to Rita to see if she understood what was so clear to me now. She nodded and smiled back at me. If there were any room for doubt, it vanished with the grand finale. In a beautiful blending of voice and characters, the last musical number spoke clearly of being who we are created to be. I could not speak when we left the play; all of us were profoundly moved by what we experienced. We traveled home in silence.

The following night, we went out to dinner. Rita raised her glass to make the first toast of the evening, "Here's to love, procreation, and polar bears." The dance of the polar bear and the dance of infinity are not so different. Love brings light and joy to our world, expressing itself in many forms. We are procreators with our God. Our dance goes on, no matter how different or odd it may seem to another. The beauty of the dance is known when we embrace who we are created to be and allow our creation to transform the darkness into light.

In the spring of the same year, on the day of our fifth anniversary, we invited our friends and family to join us for the celebration of our vows. It was a bittersweet day for me, my family was not there, and many invited would not come to celebrate, although it was one of the happiest days of my life. They could not see the gift we were embracing; it was far too different. Although we would publicly celebrate our love, there were many dear to me who could not join us. The "don't ask, don't tell" policy reaches far beyond the military. There are so many who would prefer to pretend we don't exist. They would ask us to keep our love for one another cloaked, hidden, and tucked neatly away where no one could see.

Carolyn's family came and many of our friends, about a hundred in all.

A small, semiformal traditional wedding was held in the Unitarian Church and presided over by our parish priest. What the bishop and the Pope didn't know couldn't hurt us. As the sun set over Louisville, we walked hand in hand through the candlelit sanctuary, looked into each other's eyes, and made promises of love and shared life for one another, for our community, and for our world. Our relationship was to be about more than the love we held for each other but what we would bring to our world through that love. We kept those promises for the years we shared together. Our love spilled out from our home to all those whose path we crossed and, most assuredly, to others we never met. We stood at the altar and joined in what I thought was going to be a lifetime together. Many happy years followed, but a lifetime was not meant to be for the two of us. Our contract ended eight years later after thirteen years of joy and life together.

CHAPTER 10

When all that you know and understand of this life is taken from you, when you stand stripped bare of all you've loved, there dawns a darkness of such magnitude and emptiness it can only be compared to a black hole discovered in deep space. From this place and this place alone the specter of the past is released and creation is born of new light.

LEAVING

"HOW MUCH DO YOU LOVE me?"

"Ever so much!"

Over thirteen years together, we playfully spoke these words to each other, sometimes while giggling when life was good, and sometimes with solemn fortitude when life was hard. They were words of promise, a vow of commitment that helped me feel safe, filled me with joy and called me to a deeper level of living one with another. Connected on such a deep level, without filters, without safety nets, just raw pure love; this was ours to have for a time. Our rings were engraved with these three words, "Ever So Much." Words that for me reflected my heart's knowing, an understanding that cannot be spoken, not truly, an unending, undying love expressed in three words. They make movies about it, of happy endings and joy beyond knowing. As with so many blessings in my life, I never knew how fortunate I was until I looked around and realized we all don't have loving families or loving partners. I never knew how fortunate I was, until one day it was gone. The love I expected to last a lifetime ripped away from me, unexpected and unexplainable. I could not breathe.

I walked through the house for the last time. Totally empty now, everything gone—"broom clean," as they say in real estate. The new owners had our keys, and it was hard to get my head around strangers living in the place we built together. My red Toyota truck with new Lear topper was parked in the driveway outside, packed from top to bottom. Wagon train of one was ready to make the trip west. There really wasn't much left. Most everything we built or owned sold in an estate sale. Appropriate, I suppose, as our relationship was dead and I felt like I was dying. I wasn't very happy about being left with a truck as my only mode of transportation. It was so cliché for a lesbian to be driving a truck, and I hated the thought of becoming the cliché. I bought the Toyota for gardening. Now without garden, home, or partner, I would have preferred a little red sports coupe. I never dreamed the truck would one day be transformed from my gardening vehicle to a moving van. I had been about hauling plants and topsoil for the garden I was creating on the little plot of land in our new subdivision. Bringing in soil was necessary if you were going to grow anything. They rape the land when they build a house, scraping off all the best and leaving hard clay. I was feeling like the clay, raped of all that gave life. The truck no longer filled with the makings of a beautiful garden, instead only fragments of the past as I headed west to Utah.

It is hard to describe the devastation I was experiencing. It felt as though everything was lost, including myself. Home, friends, family, and career: all that I loved was simply gone. I walked away from a job that was my life's work. Providing health care for the homeless wasn't a job, it was a calling. The clinic was a part of me. I was known throughout the state as an expert in homeless health care. I served on the governor's Commission for the Homeless. I was the one looked to for the coordination of volunteers and staff while, at the same time, providing care for those we served. I knew from the moment I walked into the shelter, this was my place to make a difference. Working with these men was what I was to be about. This became a way of life over the eighteen years I worked there.

Now, suddenly, I was homeless like the people I served. All that I owned, all that was left, was in the back of a truck. I had no home. Giving up the home I helped to design and watched built was hard, but harder still was walking away from my gardens. Countless hours were spent in the flower beds, as the earth allowed me to lose myself, tempering the challenge of my daily work with the broken and wounded who came to us for solace. Now I was the broken one. My community was in Louisville, friends of over twenty years. In Western Kentucky, my family would all be left behind as well as I stepped through a portal that would take me to another world. All lost, yet nothing compared or came close to touching the pain I felt around Carolyn's leaving.

I must have appeared a bit like the living dead. I lost forty pounds in the three months that followed her announcement. It was an announcement; there was no discussion. I never saw it coming. I had yet to touch the rage smoldering deep within but had obviously internalized the anger, dangerously close to imploding. On this day I walked through the motions, felt almost nothing, not unlike the hard clay. It was the only way I could remain upright and do what I knew I had to do, rather than collapsing into the loss. I could not escape the pain, but I could keep moving. Moving was almost like a form of artificial respiration; it kept me breathing. No longer confident, no longer sure of myself, I felt for the first time the fragility of being.

I stood in the corner of what was once our bedroom. The place where Carolyn rolled over in bed and told me she was leaving. November 14, 2000, my parents' wedding anniversary, this was my "Night of Broken Glass," when everything would change forever. Unlike my Jewish brothers and sisters whose Night of Broken Glass came in November of 1943. They would lose everything they had known and loved to be imprisoned and tortured by the madness of a deranged sociopath. I too would lose everything, but my torture and imprisonment would be inflicted through self-hatred.

I was just starting to get my feet back under me after a very long depression. Carolyn truly suffered through the depression as much or more than me, I suppose. My mother died the year before. I lost her slowly to dementia, macular degeneration, and then finally a massive stroke. It was a very hard loss as she was my best friend, my greatest ally, and my most enthusiastic cheerleader. Between the stress at work and the five years of watching Mom's decline, the depression was probably inevitable.

On this night, I settled into the place that had been my cradle for thirteen years. Without fail, over those years as we went to bed, I molded myself into her back, hips, and thighs with my arms tucked in snugly around her. This night was no different in my mind, but it was to be the last night I would ever feel this place of being one with another. I announced, "Honey, I think I'm going to be OK. I have an appointment with a counselor tomorrow, and this new medication seems to be working. I can feel it. If you can just hang in there with me a little longer, I know things are going to get better." There was no response, only silence, and I felt confused by what was not happening. I kept waiting to hear "ever so much," which was our code for how much we loved each other or "I'll always be here for you, baby," which is what I expected throughout the rest of our life. The words I anticipated never filled the space between us. Instead, after a very long pause, she said, "Well, I have been thinking about leaving." I could not believe what I was hearing; surely she didn't say what I thought she said. Everything within me recoiled. I pulled away and sat up, asking her to repeat herself, and waited to hear the words again. The moment was surreal. I could not speak; this could not be happening. It was and it did. And before the night was over, as we lay in bed talking, I found out she was not just thinking about leaving, she was leaving, and leaving to be with one of our best friends.

Three months later, I stood silently looking around the same room. The place where I was filled with joy and held by love was now only a reminder of betrayal. As I stood there looking at the emptiness, trying to understand how this could have happened, Carolyn walked into the room. It was time for final good-byes; her new partner, Rita, remained outside. She walked over slowly; I could see the pain on her face. She wrapped me in her arms and kissed me one last time. The kiss lasted far too long and was far too tender. Was she still in love with me? No, Rita was just outside the door waiting in the car. As I was preparing to drive west, leaving everything behind, they were to remain here together, with our friends, not displaced, not homeless, but starting a new life. Suddenly the kiss felt more like pity, and the silent rage I could not feel grew even stronger. She walked out the door and got into the car with her new partner; they drove away into their sunset, I suppose. I called Baxter and Tess; we got into the truck and drove away as well. Our sunset was far from here and closer to the sun, in the Rocky Mountains.

Baxter was barely a year old and Tess was turning two. It was February, dead of winter, and I was driving a pickup truck with two almost-puppies across the mountains. We would be in the truck together for two days, driving about twelve hours each day on roads I had never traveled. Tess had a reputation of being terribly carsick; she could look at the car throw up. I figured I would be one ripe sight by the time we got there, with her puking down the back of my neck for 1,200 miles. Honestly, I could put her in the car and, before I started the engine, she would vomit, conditioned response. This didn't happen now and then, it happened every time she had to take a ride. So I was ready with rags in hand when we pulled out of the driveway.

My first miracle, my first sign God was with me. We drove into Louisville and no incident; across the bridge into Indiana, nothing; and still in St. Louis Tess was wagging her tail and looking out the window. I could not believe it, but I offered up a halleluiah and amen. At least, I wouldn't have to deal with her offering of recycled Alpo in my ears as she rode with her head next to mine for most of the trip.

Tess was my furry soul mate. Looking back, I know she came into my life at just the right moment and, from the beginning, shouldered more pain than most animals are asked to bear In the two years since I found her on the street and brought her home, my mother died, one of my best friends and spiritual mentors died of bone cancer, my father came very close to death from grief and starvation, Carolyn left, and now this cross-country exodus. Tess is what one friend called a "working dog." Totally in touch with others, my little white empath was always in tune and watching, caring for her pack. She was quick to curl up her lip if she didn't like someone's energy or intent. Even as a puppy, she could change from hell on wheels, tearing through the house, dragging a rug in her teeth to quietly walking over and laying her head on a foot or a lap if someone needed her attention. She was always working the room. As a result, she has always been a pensive little soul, very serious. This is why I suppose we were given Baxter, our court jester. He was always working the room too, but for a cookie. He had very clear intent, feed me and let's play! Tess was regal, graceful, and had beautiful soft white fur. She carried with her a set decorum inherited from her ancestors the wolves, I assume, very polite. For all her seriousness, steadfast monitoring, and guarded weariness, Baxter was more like a rodeo clown. He exploded into our life burping and farting, looking for the party. There was no decorum, and he certainly wasn't polite. My boy loved everyone, had no idea there could be a villain in the mix. A wire-haired black terrier of some sort, he looked a little like a black fireplug with legs, stocky. He chewed up every pair of shoes I owned in the first year, his dog bed, our down comforter, and my glasses. And that was just for starters. He survived, and no one killed the little bastard because he was so damn cute. They were yin and yang, black and white, night and day—my Fu dogs. They kept me alive during those first years when I spent many days and nights thinking of other options.

Traveling across country with the pups was not too challenging. They did very well, really, for being cramped into their little space between my seat and the Beverly Hillbillies' load I carried in the back. I'm sure we looked the part; you could see an ironing board through the topper windows, boxes, TV, and computer equipment. A curious mix of odds and ends that really didn't even make sense, I often wondered what I was thinking when I made the decision to keep one thing and throw another away or sell it in the "estate" sale. People came in like locusts, swarmed the place, and left nothing behind. I avoided being there; it was just too sad to see everything go. We had beautiful things, and the buzzards came through and walked away without paying a fraction of their item's worth. I didn't care. I was numb and just wanted to get the hell out of Dodge. I didn't feel bitter about it until later when I started buying back the items I sold so I could furnish a home again.

The first day across country was fine—better than fine, really, when you consider my condition. I was afraid and dreaded the trip, which was atypical for me. I felt weak, weak on many levels and that was atypical too. I was held by the universe on this trip and knew I was not alone. This became very obvious as I looked out the window to see hawk after hawk lining the sides of the road. Not one or two but twenty or more, countless, really. At one point, I saw one after another after another lining the highway on either side of the road for miles and miles, like stoic guardians urging me on. It felt like a rite of passage as I saw them there, and indeed it was just that. I felt held and knew this as sure sign I was heading in the right direction. The hawk had come to me as my power animal two years earlier. When I look back, I know I was being prepared, and all was falling into place for this horrible, wonderful metamorphosis I was now undergoing. I was to enter into the chrysalis to become a new being. Beautiful metaphor but I felt like a branch ripped from the tree and stripped of all its bark, vulnerable, exposed and naked. With nothing left to identify who I once was, I was to create myself anew. There was no other choice. At the time, I had no idea it was indeed my choice.

I listened to Carolyn Myss's tapes as we traveled from state to state. A very dear friend loaned them to me for my cross-country tour. She was one of the first of many Avatars I would come to study with over the next eight years of metaphysical graduate school. No, it wasn't a formal education, but it was an education. Myss is a prominent medical intuitive, mystic, theologian, and teacher. A sassy small woman with quick wit and great wisdom—I needed wisdom, and I definitely needed to laugh. As she spoke, I was amazed, clinging to every word. I needed to understand why and how my life had fallen apart. I wanted to make sense of it. I wanted to believe there was a reason and that I could survive it all and come out alive. As I listened, every word, all that she said, seemed to be written for me. She talked about the angels ripping the rug out from under you if you didn't follow your path in a timely fashion.

Well, that's me, I thought. The rug is definitely gone: the rug, the room, etc. She mentioned having to leave your tribe (family) and step outside their boundaries to find your own path. Well 1,200 miles away, that's a step. Then she went on to say everyone will experience a great betrayal during this period of growth, a betrayal of great magnitude, not unlike the betrayal of Christ. Yep, me and JC, Rita and Judas, I could see the plot unfolding. I had to believe there was a plan greater than my understanding that was going to lead me to a deeper expression of who I was to become. I had to find God in the chaos and believe this was all for a greater good and not a punishment, which is what I felt the last time my life fell apart.

We made many stops as we continued on our excursion. The dogs needed to stretch and pee, and I needed to stretch and pee. We hit as many fast-food places as one dared; Tess and Baxter started to bark and wag their tails every time they saw the golden arches. They were fast becoming McDonald's french-fry junkies, having never had anything but dog food before this trip. When my world collapsed, so did their diets. I just kept driving and poking fries back at them from over the seat. It kept them entertained in between naps.

Griff helped me find a motel that allowed dogs before I left, and I was relieved to find it. I worried a little about someone breaking into the back of the camper and stealing what was left of my world. I guess the ironing board helped because no one seemed interested in my little treasures; it was still there in the morning. The dogs flew into the motel room and jumped on the beds, happy to be out of the truck. I turned on the TV and started looking for the Weather Channel, still concerned about the condition of the road for the next leg of the trip. Our stay was pretty short as the forecast called for snow and ice. I woke up at 4:00 a.m. and decided to get back on the road and try and beat the impending storm. It was starting to snow, and I was starting to get really nervous about the next segment of our trip.

My dad cautioned me to keep my gas tank filled, worried I would run out of gas. I thought, "Good grief, Poppa, I'm not that stupid." Well, I ran out of gas. Between herding the dogs from the room to the truck, watching the snow coming down hard now, I never thought about gas. Besides, there are usually gas stations every whip stitch on interstate highways. However, we were not on just any interstate. We were in Kansas, where the road goes on forever and there is nothing in sight for as far as you can see, just endless horizon. At the time I could not, for the life of me, understand why Dorothy was so anxious to get back home. All was going well for a while. The truck only slipped a couple times, and there weren't many people on the road at this hour of the morning. Then I looked down and saw the needle pointing to less than a quarter of a tank. I gasped, looked back up at the freezing roads and black abyss we were driving in, and proceeded to freak the fuck right out. I started talking out loud to the dogs, telling them we could be in serious trouble. It was freezing cold, we were in the middle of nowhere, and I had let us take off in a semi-blizzard without gas. Right, pooches! Your human is an idiot. They didn't seem to be interested. They were looking out the windows for McDonald's signs, I'm sure of it. Then to top it all off and make matters worse, now I had to poop.

I started talking to myself as talking to the dogs was no help at all; they never get wrapped up in the drama. I was getting absolutely no sympathy from them. I rambled off a litany of self-soothing scenarios and tried to slow my breathing down. It will be daylight soon. Someone will stop and help us. We won't freeze. This is just a temporary setback. On the list went as the gas gauge continued to drop when, suddenly, I saw a small light in the distance about the same time as the small light on the dash began to flash. I grew excited, hoping it was the gas station we so desperately needed because now the needle was on empty.

Yes! It was a gas station, a very small rundown station, but who cared? There were two pumps; I just needed one to work. I turned on the exit ramp, breathing more easily now. As I pulled up to the gas pumps, my heart sank. CLOSED said the paper neon-colored sign in the window. Still looking for light at the end of the tunnel, I thought, well at least we are off the icy roads, and surely, someone will come to open the station soon. My relief was short-lived as I was suddenly made aware again of the building pressure in my sigmoid colon.

It was freezing cold, dark, and incredibly quiet as the snow covered my windshield. The dogs could not understand what was happening. What, no fries? Why would I stop here? You could see confusion written all over their faces as sweat was popping out on mine. I could not believe this, what a mess I had us in. And a bigger mess was on its way if the gas station attendant didn't come soon. I sat quietly, trying to convince my body I was in control. Suddenly running out of gas seemed inconsequential, and I understood the order of the universe. Funny how bodily functions can bring everything into perspective. When you "gotta go"—especially in this form of expression—nothing else matters.

Well, I was long past the sitting quietly now. The mix of coffee and anxiety made for one sure and certain outcome, Mount Vesuvius was getting ready to blow. I had no choice. I found my last well-worn McDonald's napkin, and out the truck I bounded. I tried the bathroom door one more time and wondered if you could be thrown in jail for breaking and entering into a toilet. No matter, I could not get the door open. Thank God it's still dark, and thank God I am in Kansas and there is no one here or within miles of the place, and oh my god, I hope the gas station guy doesn't show up in the middle of this process.

I was in a trot, now tearing around the back of the station hoping there would be something to get behind or give me some sort of albeit false assurance of privacy, but no, nothing, not a tree, a bush, or a shrub. Lady Bird had obviously not impressed the people of Kansas with her campaign for beautifying our great nation. My impending contribution for the station's landscape was obviously not what she had in mind either. Sorry, Lady Bird. So there I was, squatting on the plains of Kansas, icy wind whipping up my ass and feeling like I was playing a scene in some really bad Mel Brooks movie. Could things get any worse?

I walked back to the truck in my humiliation, wondering. What if they are not open today? What if the guy doesn't come? I have no idea why I wasn't crying, but as I said, hard clay has its attributes. Fears were soon relieved as I watched an old beat-up truck drive down the road and into the station. The attendant had arrived. Dawn was breaking over the Kansas horizon, and my recent trauma gave way to awe as I watched the reflection of light cross the plains of new-fallen snow and ice. A beautiful landscape unfolded with pristine illumination as man had yet to touch the virgin portrait—well, with the exception of my touch around back. Fitting, I suppose, the analogy. In the midst of all this beauty fallen from the hand of the Creator, my creation was symbolic of my life at the moment. No longer wholly capable of designing and manifesting more beauty in the world, my past decisions and misguided thoughts brought me to this place of disempowered collapse. My friends in Salt Lake had no idea what a mess I had become, but when they did understand, they still stood by me. Not only old friends but new friends came to stand with me, strangers drawn into my life that held me up and called me out of the darkness. I came to call them my Angel Brigade, as it took a brigade of the holy to help me find my way again.

Tank full of gas, I pulled back out on the interstate and made my way across the Rockies to Salt Lake. Griff wrote the directions for my drive, and they were quite simple. Although Salt Lake is large in number of people across the valley, the city proper seemed more like a small town than big city, and so there was no problem driving to her house. It was late afternoon as I pulled into the small driveway and stepped out of the truck. My legs began shaking badly. I suppose now that it was okay to collapse, my body was thinking seriously about doing just that. As my friends walked out of their house, I could see the shock on their faces as they looked at me. Between forty pounds of weight loss and the deadening energy of suppressed rage, I was not the Bo they knew and had seen just six months earlier. The person they saw now was a stranger to them, much older and forever changed. At one point, Griff turned her head, and I could tell she was fighting back the tears as her partner Jo reached out and wrapped an arm around her, silently transferring the strength she needed to get through the moment. Swallowing hard and impaled by the pain between us, Jo never stopped looking into my eyes. In that moment, she held us both with the strength and love born of a woman whose roots reach back to the Kentucky Hills of Appalachia. These women are fierce and strong beings who let nothing come between them and their family. And on this day, I became family. As hard and as strong as the gaze directed at me through Jo's steel-blue eyes, our union was forged. In silence and with deep knowing, a bond was sealed, never to be broken.

Griff moved to Salt Lake fifteen years prior to my coming here. Carolyn and I visited many times to hike, camp, and ski. Utah is a wonderland for outdoor recreation, which fit me like a glove. I was also acquainted with many of her friends that made it much easier with regard to my newfound loneliness. Jo moved to Salt Lake the year before, she and her three children came to make their home with Griff. The two of them in love since college, life sent them in separate directions and it took a while before their paths converged again, this time allowing for the expression of their love in all its fullness. As with all loves that are true, their happiness spilled out to their friends and community. From their love, they were able to move beyond themselves to give to others. I was to be one of their first challenges, and they would have to call on "all the king's soldiers and all the king's men." Humpty Dumpty had nothing on me; at least, he fell broken off the wall. I was broken behind the wall, and it was quite the fortress.

I walked into their home, and there I was held and cared for until I found a job and moved out three months later. During this time, I continued to study the modern-day prophets. Books, guides, angels, experiences, teachers, and prophets all came to me, one after another. It was as if I was connected to the high-speed Internet of the Akashic Records, the mystic's Library of Congress. As each new insight and step unfolded, I continued to ask and, as promised, the answers continued to unfold. Authors Caroline Myss, Eckhardt Tolle, Wayne Dyer, and Gregg Braden all became my closest companions. I read and studied all I could lay my hands on while searching for understanding. I needed to find myself again, to create myself anew. I was totally lost. The year was 2001; I was forty-five years old. This was the first time in my life that I didn't have a job. It was the first time in my life to know the pain of betrayal. It was the first time in my life to feel homeless. Despite the love and concern of the Angel Brigade, I remained enveloped in an unquieted, horrid loneliness. This unresolved grief would continue to follow me for years to come, but in this space of molten fire, the coal was being transformed into crystalline light.

CHAPTER 11

Life is never stagnant; it is constantly unfolding like the lotus flower. Opening to the next mystery, our daily routine is never routine. We are creating, giving birth, and being guided more deeply into the unknown until, eventually, we remember why we are here and what it is we intended for creation.

HAPPY STREET

I WAS JUST ABOUT READY to panic with the house searching. It's one thing to sell your house, but then it's quite another to find just the right new house to call home. When I moved to Salt Lake, my sticker shock was terrible. I had a perfect picture in my mind with regard to what type of house I would buy and how much I could spend. I knew I would have to downsize, I didn't know I would have to transform myself into a hobbit to fit the size of my new dwelling. Reality hit, and I was hard-pressed to find anything I thought I could live with. My agent was patient. We went online and looked at dozens of homes, all altered with Photoshop. I'm sure of it because what was online described as "charming," "picturesque," "dream home," and "newly remodeled" looked like "shabby," "hard to look at," "nightmarish," and "needs more work." I really loved the signs in the yard that said, "MUST SEE INSIDE!" This is right. You must see inside because the outside looks like hell.

My favorite experience of house shopping was the day my agent, Mark, took me out to look at a bungalow, of which there are many in Salt Lake. We had culled out countless nightmarish "needs more work" models online. This was our third time out, and I was starting to feel badly for Mark. I like bungalows in general. I wasn't crazy about this one, but I was thinking, not too bad, I could live with this. The interior needed a major face-lift. They didn't have one of those "Must See Inside" signs on this place as both indoor and outdoor versions looked the same, mediocre. We did our walk-though as I started trying to imagine the place with new paint and carpet. Completing our short inspection, we walked back out to the front porch. I was feeling like maybe I could live here, and then I met the neighbors, indirectly.

I looked over my shoulder to see another "charming" bungalow right next door. Hanging from the porch was not five or ten but at least fifty wind chimes, neatly aligned in rows of ten, all sizes and all description of wind chime you could ever imagine. The entire ceiling of the porch was covered in them. On the door, a large sign read, "THE WITCH IS IN." Now I love characters more than anyone, I'm a kindred spirit of sorts, but at the time and in my fragile state, that one just about pushed me over the edge. Unfortunately, we never met the witch, but I knew with certainty I didn't want to live next door to her. What's that they say, "You have to kiss a lot of frogs before you find your prince?" I was beginning to feel a bit warty.

So we continued to look, and it was probably only a few days later that we drove up Happy Street to what was to be my new home on Browning

Avenue. After all the frogs, I was starting to think everything looked a bit more "picturesque." Like a forty-year-old pole-vaulter returning to his high school playing field, I had to face up to the fact that the bar had to be dropped. I wasn't going to have what I had before. I didn't have the resources as my income was literally cut in half. I had to add to the equation home prices in Salt Lake. In addition, I was certain I was starting to smell like that three-day-old fish they equate to guests who have outstayed their welcome after living three months with Griff and Jo. They never complained, but they didn't take me to raise, as my Poppa would say. It was time to move on.

The house was only blocks from my friends, right down the street from my future place of employment, literally a short stroll due south. I did not know I would work there in the future, but they did—those guides and angels who were blazing my path. With bar lowered, I thought I could live with this one. I actually thought it was picturesque and charming. I always wanted a Tudor. I loved the high steep gables and the interest of the architecture. These houses offered so much more to the eyes than the cookie-cutter Ritz cracker boxes that were the norm of my childhood in rural Kentucky. There, everything was either a square or a rectangle with a low pitched roof and very little landscaping. I am not one to think about function, it's all about pretty. Carolyn helped balance me in this area, but without her there, I was on my own. And so I bought it.

When I found this little, and *little* would be the operative word, Tudor on Browning Avenue I, like the Mormons before me, declared, "This is the place." I loved it. Standing outside, the house looked like an English cottage of sorts. The lot was big, comparatively, and the yard was fenced in for the most part, so that would work for the dogs. There was a huge garden plot out back with a very old apple tree standing alone in the corner. In addition, my most favorite part of the property was this most incredibly huge tree just outside the door on the other side of the driveway. Its branches so long I felt like they were reaching out to hold me as we walked into what was to be my new home. Large trees are rare in the high desert, and this little place with its big tree definitely struck a chord for me. I think I was a druid in another lifetime, and to be honest, I suppose I still am a druid of sorts. I held my breath as we walked inside. As we all know, you can't judge a book by its cover. I was hard-pressed not to jump up and down. There were arched doorways, a sunken living room with a barrel ceiling, hardwood floors, and best of all, no witch next door. No color on the walls, which bores me, but that was OK because there were no holes in the walls either. The front door had a little hinged shutter you could open to see the person standing outside. It reminded me of *The Wizard of Oz*. I've always loved that masterpiece of illusion, fantasy, and deep wisdom. I thought to myself, "This must be a sign!" People would knock, and I would playfully open the little shutter and say "The Wizard will see you now!" or "The Wizard will not see you, not now not ever!" depending on my mood.

The honeymoon was pretty short because it was not too long before I started feeling really claustrophobic. The new home we built in Kentucky had an open floor plan with over 2,500 square feet on the ground floor and that much again in the basement. This little place was about 800 square feet and seemed to be a hundred years old in my mind. When I stood in the hallway, I felt like I could reach out and touch every wall in every room without moving from the spot. The kitchen was so small, you couldn't realistically cook more than a can of Campbell's soup because there was no counter space to prepare anything. No place for dinner parties, no dining room—and on went the litany of disappointment. It was old, musty, drafty, and small.

Was it really that bad? Well, of course not. But as the anger and grief began to bubble up, I could not focus on what I had, just on what I had lost. Until now, I had only felt the pain of losing Carolyn; the reality of everything else was just beginning to come into focus. It doesn't hit you all at once. It comes piece by piece. It seemed I was waking up out of a walking coma. I lay in bed one morning gazing at the white ceiling of my eight-foot-by-eight-foot bedroom thinking, "I have moved from the Starship Enterprise into the shuttlecraft." Oh, but it was my little shuttlecraft, and it would take me to worlds never dreamed of, hoped for, or imagined.

Like walking into Sr. Peggy's clinic in Buckhorn some twenty years before, I was totally unaware of what I was stepping into or how it would alter my life. Spirituality is never stagnant. It is ever changing. If the living, transforming, breathing expression of faith becomes stagnant, begin to look around because someone has probably snipped your lifeline. It's the vine-and-branches analogy; we are a part of something living. In this place, my faith would be challenged and all safety nets torn away. The work of transformation is never experienced through ease. It's a wild ride. Throw away the oars because if you think you are guiding your little canoe on these waters, you are sadly mistaken.

Of all the neighborhoods in all of Salt Lake, I just happened upon this one. It was perfect in all too many ways. I have come to believe nothing is just happening; all is unfolding for our highest good. I do not believe we are pawns moved about on a celestial chessboard, but instead believe we are fully participating in our evolution. We may be, but usually are not, fully conscious of our decisions. However, we are, on some level, the major player and creator of our becoming. To our credit, we do not always choose the way that is easy. We choose instead that which brings us into alignment with our purpose of being, given there will be a few detours along the way.

Browning Avenue was to be the set and stage for the beginning of my healing and an explosion of my spirituality. As the play unfolded, I was introduced to character after character. They filed in one by one and, occasionally, in pairs. I soaked up all they brought, both gift and challenge. I was to be held in this place, as if in my mother's arms, while being spoon-fed by the angels. These kindred souls, my Angel Brigade, provided for my intensive care. I was unaccustomed to being the one being cared for, and although comforting, it felt strangely odd and was difficult to embrace.

During my first year in Salt Lake, I was at my nadir. One could not be more broken. This was the first time I had to deal with this depth of "dark night." It was always my intention to heal, to avoid the bitterness that can sneak in behind such loss and betrayal, robbing you of life force, this force the ultimate expression of clear vibration and loving light. My greatest fear was being lost in the darkness. They were there, like stars charting my path through the abyss, guiding me patiently, gently—sometimes without words, sometimes with great discourse. I was fractured, shattered, and unrecognizable even to myself. I was soon to learn there was a gift in this shattering. The depth of this fracture created a passageway into a part of me never explored. They would be my guides, walking with me, holding the light for what was to be the birth of a new consciousness.

Location, location, location. I was within walking distance of my greatest supports. Griff and Jo lived about nine blocks southwest, with Amy and Charise about equidistance northwest; how perfect is that in the world of probability? The shaman teaches, the South is where we shed our past, the West where we face our greatest fears, and the North heralds our stepping into the future. Browning Street corners Fifth East. In numerology, five signals change, and the East is in keeping with seeing the divinity of the whole. Looking back, it is amazing to watch the unfolding of all these "coincidences," knowing now, there are no coincidences. Those first months were incredibly hard. The challenge came in living alone again after thirteen years partnered, our home a hub for the gathering of friends and family, in a place I'd lived for twenty-five years. All this gave way like a cave-in; when the dust settled, it left in its place a deafening silence.

It was very difficult for me to stay home, to sit in an empty house. I knew I needed to give Griff and Jo a break after 24-7 of my unhappy ass for three months; it's a wonder they didn't open a vein. So Amy and Charise moved to front and center to keep me breathing while Griff and Jo caught their breath. Almost like, "Do you know CPR?" "Yes!" "Well, take over: one one thousand, two one thousand, switch."

I met Charise years earlier on a trip to Salt Lake; a group of us were setting out to hike the Grand Canyon under Griff's tutelage. She came to the send-off party we had before driving to Arizona for our big trek. Charise is probably one of the most intelligent, witty, big-hearted people I have ever met. Standing about five foot six, with shining brown eyes, she had the most incredible dimples. Dimples that transformed her smile into an impish overture of mischievous playfulness. I just love that in a woman.

Charise had a profound weakness for the wounded. I've seen her melt into tears under a bird's nest as, try as she might, she failed to return the winged creature to its home. The little guy kept wiggling its way out of safety, falling helplessly to the ground. She was also known for feeding every feral cat that found its way to her front porch. She kept ample food and water there, much to her neighbors' chagrin. So I fit right in with the nestless birds and the stray cats who staggered up to her front-door stoop. Charise chatted away, trying to ignite any glimmer of hope, her purpose now to resurrect even a tiny bit of hopefulness in me. She was one of the angels who came with great discourse. She was a philosopher and great thinker—a genius, in fact, by measure of her IQ scores. She continually outlined ways to be joyful and things to be thankful for in the grand scheme of things. We would stand for hours, out on what we called the smoking porch, waxing prophetically about all manner of things. I listened, for the most part, while Charise waxed. My most favorite piece of advice still makes me laugh, which was the point. She said, "Bo, I want you to get some colorful boxer shorts, a purple boa, and red socks. Put them on, and nothing else. Then turn on the Supremes. Crank it up as loud as the neighbors can stand, and dance in your living room until you start to feel better." Eventually, I did just that, and it worked famously. I think everyone should try it.

Amy, Charise's partner, was more the silent type. Without question, she matched up with the divine heart I found in Charise. *Gentle* would be the word I would use to describe Amy. She was a listener, wise beyond her years, and a lover of all that is good in the world. She was grounding for the two of them, the homemaker. She called me Bobo and instituted Pot Roast Thursdays, when she would cook and invite friends over. I wonder now if she created the end of the week holiday just for me. No matter, most evenings I seemed to show up on their front porch at about suppertime. Like God, invited or uninvited, I was always there. It became a source of embarrassment after a bit, but need outweighed my humiliation. Most nights found me at the front door knocking, me and the feral cats.

Charise and Amy knew what happened. Griff had filled them in through tears on the night I called to tell her Carolyn had left. The rupture of a long-term relationship is wounding for the gay community, because we hope beyond all odds we will be able to sustain relationships in a world hostile to our unions. Relationships are challenging enough without this caveat, but it is ours to have until the world changes, and I don't see that coming anytime soon. With the knowledge of at least part of my history, they were beyond gentle with me. In retrospect, I see their interactions with me mirroring their efforts of trying to put the baby bird back into its nest. Every time I fell out, feathers flying, they would gently scoop me up and set me right again.

In keeping with my passion and theirs, the conversation always came around to spirituality. My box was still very narrow and very full. I thought I was incredibly enlightened, having no idea what lay ahead. I evolved from the cookbook religion of a fundamentalist evangelical Christian to the deeply symbolic mysticism of the Catholic Church. I experienced visions, communicated with the Almighty through symbol and scripture, and was quite frankly pretty smug about it all. Imagine that, a smug religious zealot. Seems the two go hand in hand somehow. So in my mind, I had it all figured out but, on the other hand, I was still searching. The still small voice within was always there, urging me forward, calling me to step further into the mysteries of what was yet unknown. Although at the time, it was only a faint whisper, drowned out by the racket of my howling self-pity.

Amy and Charise were trying to lighten me up a bit. I mean, for pity's sake, snap out of it. They were to introduce me to yet another side of spirituality. It was not aligned with organized religion—it was aligned with the divinity they found within themselves, the cosmos, and all of creation. This was to be a major paradigm shift of consciousness for me. I used to accuse the Catholics of having "God in a box," referring to the host in the tabernacle of their churches. Then when I was Catholic, I would accuse the fundamentalists of putting "God in a box," referring to their rigid rules and Bible thumping. In reality, I was always putting "God in a box," but each time I did, I was introduced to yet another facet of the Source of all being. As a result, my box would be blown apart. My understanding continued to grow outside the boundaries of comfort. Morphing and changing like light seen through a kaleidoscope. Nothing was black and white anymore, and nothing was static.

My first baby steps out of these boxes always presents like a waddling, hesitant toddler. I liked my box. It is safe, and I understand it. Yet I am always peeking outside to see if anyone else has a better box than me. The still small voice urged me to move beyond my well-established boundaries, whispering, "There is more, come and see." Have you ever watched a two-year-old climb down from their mother's lap to explore the room? They venture out but soon return to home base, if only to touch her skirt, and then they launch out again for another short adventure around the room. This is the dance for me, the pattern of my evolution. I move farther away from the comfort of my box, but when I am scared or wounded, I tend to run back, jump in ,and pull up the flaps, enclosing myself in what I know, what is safe. Before too long, I start to peek out again and gradually realign with the path. It is a process.

I have come to believe God is ever expanding, ever evolving. We follow a living God who is not stagnant. The minute we create these boxes, we have stepped away from our Source. The boxes, these religions, may have served us well in the past, but no longer. In truth, they create pain and separation from our Creator, from our own divinity, and from each other. They are divisive and have been the underlying cause of countless wars and terrible, needless suffering. When enough people understand this and embrace the new energy generated by this understanding, the Kingdom Jesus spoke of so often will come. As he tried to point out, through the unfolding of his short life, it is here now, not in some distant place, but within. Stepping outside the box requires faith and courage. This new information shared by my friends and their challenge to once again blow up my box meant I would be walking into a new world. I felt like I stepped from the black-and-white scenes of Kansas in *The Wizard of Oz* to the Technicolor brilliance of Munchkinland. Like Dorothy, I was blown away by this well-timed tornado and a little disoriented.

Through Amy and Charise, I met Shawn. Amy called him "Shawn of God." Shawn was psychic and wise. Like me, he was commonly a guest at Pot Roast Thursdays. Shawn has his struggles, for he is as attuned to other dimensions as he is to the third dimension we all live in here on the planet. He walks, like many of us, with a foot in both worlds, the seen and the unseen. The unseen was taking a pretty good plug out of his day. This is a challenging place for those who are this open. He has a big energy; of course, this makes sense. He was hanging out with us, and even though my energy was drained, I could probably still fill a room with my presence. We matched up, in other words. Shawn channeled some of the energy and connection with the unseen through tarot readings. This sparked my interest, tarot readings. Amy added to my curiosity while giving a description of her own reading, so I asked Shawn to do a reading for me.

He carried his cards in an old faded scarf. Laying the cards in the center of the cloth, he would bring the four corners together, tying the ends in a knot in ceremonial fashion. We sat on the bed together in order to have more privacy. He pulled the well-worn scarf out of his backpack, laid it on the bed, and began to untie the knot to reveal his cards within. Symbolic, I thought, as he was helping me to untie or unravel the chaos.

Shawn asked me to pull the cards with intent for a better understanding of what was unfolding in my present and future. What I can remember from the reading was pulling not one, not two, but three death cards in addition to the tower card. Even Shawn shuttered a bit, and the shocked look on his face was not the least bit comforting as he turned the cards over. He understood and explained my world was falling apart, being dismantled. As the symbols were explained to me, I wasn't surprised. I was living it. I think he felt a little sorry for me, although he knew it was only a transition and, obviously, a transition I needed. The death cards represent the death of something in your life, an ending. I had three, which made perfect sense: relationship, job, and home. All had ended. The tower card signaled the toppling of my past spirituality. How's that for change?

Amy and Charise lived on Williams Avenue. I called it St. Williams because we always had such deep, heady conversations about spirituality. One day, as I was reeling from all the changes and swimming hard to keep up, Amy looked over at me and said, "BoBo, keep your feet up, your butt down, stay in the flow and keep it holy."

I laughed, wondering what the heck she was talking about.

Seeing my confusion, she said, "Have you ever gone white-water rafting and fallen out of the boat?"

"Oh! Yes, I certainly have fallen out of the boat. I was scared to death."

My mind drifted back to the day when Carolyn and I joined a group of friends to raft the Upper Gauley in West Virginia. This is not "kiddy ride," the rapids are graded class 4 and class 5 when the dam is opened. Lucky me, the dam was open.

The rafting guides told us, several times, if you fall out of the raft, you could be in really big trouble—dead, in other words. They went into great detail about getting caught up in one of the eddies they called "The Washing

Machine." These fellows seemed to love to strike terror into the hearts of their passengers. I sat wide-eyed and tachycardic as they talked about being pulled under the water to the bottom of the river, only to be released to the top and pulled down again. If you're lucky, they said, when you pass out and relax, the river will kick you out on the other side. Then with downcast eyes and a small voice, he murmured, "The last lady wasn't so lucky." Awesome! This sounds like real fun, I thought. Our explicit instructions were, if you fall out, turn in the water, float on your back with your feet up and look for the boat. When we see you looking at us and we make eye contact, we will throw you the rope and pull you back to safety.

So we enter the first rapid. I think I peed a little bit, but other than that, things went well. Then we hit the next rapid, which was probably up around a class five. That's when I went overboard. It happened so quickly. Just before it happened, I was thinking, no way am I going to fall out of this boat. Even if they hold a pistol to my head, I would rather be shot than take a chance on meeting up with the "Washing Machine." Unbeknownst to me, I wasn't alone in the water. Another lady had fallen out too, and she was the one in trouble because they threw her the rope or maybe they just liked her better. Anyway, I didn't know I wasn't in trouble and was facing the boat trying to stare them down, wondering when are they going to throw the fucking rope! Fear makes me talk ugly. I didn't know they were on the other side of the boat trying to pull in another white-water flunk out. I knew Carolyn loved me because she was looking right at me, but she didn't have the rope, so it was of little help. What I didn't know was she was stifling back laughter as she thought I looked just like a woman in labor, wide eyed with dread, huffing and puffing as if in the middle of transition. "Well hell," I said, "I was expecting the 'Washing Machine' to swallow me up at any moment. I wanted to get as much air on board as I could before I went down for the count."

I could not understand why Carolyn was not as upset as I was with my cold-water plunge, but then suddenly, I could see fear spread across her face. That wasn't a good sign. As instructed, I was floating on my back with my feet up. But my face was pointed upstream toward the boat; my demise lay down stream. I was looking for the flipping rope, that wasn't coming my way. They all started yelling in unison, "Turn around! Turn around, there's a rock!" I'm thinking, "Oh shit, now what do I do? If I turn around, those bastards won't throw me the rope." I'm such a hopeless rule follower. Their screams became more frantic, so I flapped my arms against the current as best I could in my super deluxe life jacket, just in time to meet the rock they had all so kindly and emphatically told me about. I had a split second to react, drawing my knees up to push off the rock with my feet, letting the current safely move me into open water. I was surprised at how easy it was once I turned, allowing the current to take me where it would—feet up, butt down. So yes, now it made perfect sense.

The current I was riding now was the rapid incoming flow of Divine energy and information. The changes were coming faster than I could manage gracefully; it absolutely carried me with the force of white water. Grace or no grace, I was not getting out of this water. I had no idea where the current was taking me, but to fight against the current would only lead to being bashed against the rocks. I'd had my fill of rocks to date, and I wasn't the least bit interested in being bashed, not one more time! So the best advice Amy could give was, point your feet downstream. Stop looking back for the old boat that no longer serves you. The lifeline is not coming, it's up to you to navigate these waters and make your way safely back to shore. You are in the water now, relax and go with it. "Feet up, butt down. And keep it holy." What a ride.

Day-to-day life was becoming pretty rote. I was working at the VA, which was a short drive up the mountain to the foothills. I didn't really have a job because, God bless them, the unit wasn't even open yet. I found this posting online for the VA when I was in Kentucky, looking for jobs in Utah. The job was posted for a nurse-practitioner (NP) to work in and help open an inpatient substance abuse center. It was perfect, I thought. I had been on the street with the homeless for eighteen years and was intimately acquainted with substance abuse and substance abuse therapy. I had worked for the VA before briefly in Louisville. They assured me I would have a good chance at the position and so I applied and then I waited. When I came to Salt Lake, I started looking for work immediately, but there was just nothing out there for nurse-practitioners, which I found odd. I couldn't move out of Griff and Jo's place until I found a job, and we were heading into month three now.

I'm sure the operators at the VA thought I was stalking someone due to the frequency of my phone calls. I was finally able to reach the chief of psychiatry who relented and got the ball rolling for my hiring. Soon I would learn the program was still in the planning stages, and at the VA, that could mean another three years to its inception. He hired me anyway, probably because he was concerned I would take another job, and I was a perfect candidate for what they had in mind. Truth be known, the reality probably had something to do with the angels working overtime. I was in no condition to take care of anyone, not even myself when I arrived at the VA.

I had grand ideas. I knew what we needed and how to set up what I needed to do my job. I rapidly came up with a list and presented it to the chief of psychiatry, thinking, OK they will get these things together this afternoon, then in the morning I can set up and start working on the treatment plans and scheduling. Oh, I was so naive. There were a few problems with my plan. The building that was being remodeled for the grand opening of this center was still under construction. I was given the tour. Not only was it not quite ready, they were nowhere near completion. I walked into the space and stood looking at drywall dust and naked metal studs outlining what was to be a clinic. I found a kinship with the steel studs. They reflected an image of my soul at that point: naked, cold, hard, and silently holding space for what was yet to be. So, now what?

Well, not much. They found a narrow dark room off in the corner of an isolated building that was to be my office. No windows, no frills, no sound and did I say narrow? And we all know by now how fond I am of small, tight spaces. I went back to the chief and asked if there was any other place they might find. I really needed light and people. I'm sure he had had about enough of me at this point. Nothing available, I would have to make do. So I made do, by just not going in there.

They came up with a schedule for me, which included doing rounds with the psych team and meeting with the other nurse-practitioners weekly. That was it; that filled up about two or three hours of an eight-hour workday. I met an extremely nice NP who had worked for the VA for years. She befriended me, took me under her wing, and told me she would be glad for me to use her office when she wasn't there. This was often as her schedule, unlike mine, was busy. I thought that a fabulous idea and, from there, learned rather quickly how to office hop, totally avoiding my sarcophagus altogether. I had hours of downtime. They found bits and pieces of this and that for me to do over the months I worked there, but still, we're talking hours. I would use the time to read authors I thought would help me find myself again; Wayne Dyer and I became good buddies at the VA.

I continued in my semi-nonexistent job for about five months. There was an unspeakable grace in being given that job at this time in my life, which is the purpose of telling you the story. Had I been in a busy practice that required direct patient care, I truly don't think the patients would have been well cared for on any level. My brain had shut down, my memory and ability to concentrate severely impaired. Standing in a checkout line, it took several moments for me to remember how to use my ATM card, never mind the code.

I could never remember it. Sometimes I would just turn and silently walk out of the store, leaving my items with the now-confused grocery clerk.

Each afternoon when I returned home from work, I would open the tailgate of the little Toyota, call the dogs, and head into the mountains to hike. I was getting some better, and able to spend more time alone in short increments anyway. The mountains surrounding Salt Lake provide for endless hiking. Alone on the trail, hiking up mountains, I was able to escape the endless mind chatter for a while. The energy of the mountain brought solace. The earth, the Mother, was working her magic. With each hike, I was getting stronger, imperceptible, but happening all the same.

Baxter and Tess were still very young. The dog trainer told me in puppy school they don't really grow a brain until they are three. Baxter was one and Tess two, so they were brainless with lots of heart and even more energy. On the trail, I could let them off their leads where they would run until the seemingly endless energy could be at least semi-depleted. This made for better, well-behaved dogs at home. After being exhausted from hiking two to three hours, I would bring them back to our ample yard. Here they would run a little more while I sat on my backdoor steps, watching in amazement. When I wasn't able to take them to the mountains, we would walk around the neighborhood. I used retractable leads hoping to simulate some of the freedom they experienced on the trail. I could never understand the people who want their dogs to heal right by their side. What fun is that? Unaccustomed to the leads and crazed with their desire to run in every direction, this was probably not a wise idea on my part—a bit brainless, like my dogs. It was like flying kites in a windstorm as they ran right and left and up and down behind me, beside me, in front of me while I was dancing around swinging the leads wildly over my head and between my legs to keep from being totally roped. It was no easy feat keeping up with those two hellions. Add to that equation poop sacks. So I'm juggling poop sacks and the leads and the dogs; inevitably flogging myself about the head and shoulders with the "to go" bags. It just wasn't pretty.

On one particularly challenging day when I was ready to crate them both up and ship them off to a Vietnamese hot dog stand, I looked up to see Jamie standing there smiling, extending her hand to introduce herself. Watching from across the street, which was her custom, she saw her opportunity, as I was "all tied up" and had stopped for a moment. I didn't see her until she was standing right in front of me; that's how it is with gifts from the universe. Sometimes they almost have to hit you in the head before you wake up and realize, oh, standing right in front of me all along. Of course, I would have preferred to be hit in the head with something besides poop bags. I said hello, but I was totally distracted by the fear I might have dog shit on my face from my most recent flogging.

Jamie lived directly across the street with her partner Isabel. They moved to Salt Lake from California while Jamie was working on her PhD in exercise physiology. I immediately felt Jamie's kindness; there was and still is something "fairy-esque" about Jamie. I would learn, as our relationship unfolded, that she was quite psychic and would become a channel and watch guard for me. She and Isabel were excited about my moving in across the street. I was unaware they were watching my comings and goings, particularly when I bought the house. On the day I brought friends over to see the house I was buying, Jamie called to Isabel from the living room window, "Come quick, a whole carload of lesbians just piled out of that car across the street!" We homosexuals all have "Gaydar" you know. It's an evolutionary thing, keeps us from making the sometimes, literally deadly, mistake of hitting on the straight people.

Jamie and Isabel were to become the third couple to continue my CPR, giving Charise and Amy a well-deserved break—"four one thousand, five one thousand… SWITCH." We became great friends, the three of us. They watched me like a hawk out that living room window. It was through Jamie and Isabel that I met all the other neighbors on the street. I was soon to find out that there was another lesbian couple down the way and a single gay man. I felt like I landed in the Castro District of Salt Lake City. I mean, what are the odds of even finding a Democrat in this town, let alone a street full of queers? There was also a straight couple and a single woman living on their side of the street who were not homophobic and became a part of our little block party. That's where Browning Avenue got its nickname. Elise and Lisa sent a card during the holidays, signing it "Welcome to Happy Street." It was a happy street, welcoming on all levels and, I was soon to find out, on all dimensions.

Then there was Earl. Out my kitchen door, on the other side of my beloved big tree, was a small rental that housed my soon-to-be new teacher and friend. Earl was quite the character and was to be my next introduction into the strange and bizarre new world I found myself entering. I am still unsure if he was "of this world" when I think back about our meeting. Earl was older than me by about twelve or fifteen years, putting him in his late fifties or early sixties. He looked like a distinguished college professor, intellectual type with beard and graying hair. He rode a bicycle quite a bit, which I found a little odd, rare to see a guy that age ride a bike where I came from, for that matter rare to see anyone ride a bike in Kentucky. People are just not very biker friendly there.

When I finally met Earl, after several brief encounters accented by the smiles and head nods exchanged in our passings, I was to find out he was a college professor. I think a college professor incognito, his real passion lay far from the classroom.

My encounters with Earl grew longer and longer. He was a very friendly guy, a bit of a Don Juan really. Jamie got a kick out of that and proceeded to tease me about a tryst with Earl while watching his frequent trips to my backdoor. I am pretty sure that was not Earl's intent. He had a girlfriend in Paris, which he was soon to join, or that is how the story went. Again, I'm not certain Earl moved to Paris when he left Happy Street. Regardless, right now he was planted next door to me, soon to be a part of my education. What he was to teach and share with me was not contained in an English book.

Earl was a philosopher, a theologian, and a student of the universe. He invited me next door to see his library. The space was very small and filled with books. I was still trying to figure out how a guy this intelligent landed in a little run down rental property at this stage in his life. Divorce is the short answer to that long story. She took everything. He wasn't bitter, not even bothered it seemed. Loss was not his focus. That in itself was a big lesson for me to digest at the moment.

Little by little, he tested the waters with first one bit of information and then the next, as if titillating my curiosity into the unknown. He dangled the bait; and I took it hook, line, and sinker. I was hungry for the unknown, I wanted to know all, everything, no matter how foreign or unbelievable. I met the right guy for that bit of news. Earl was the "King of Strange."

Everyone's life story is interesting if you take the time to listen. Earl's was beyond interesting. It was fantastic, over the edge, hard to believe, out there. His first lesson for me was about channeling. While introducing me to his library, he began telling me about the book *Urantia*. I knew little to nothing about channeling and was hard-pressed to open my mind to believe entities, angels, spirits, or other out-of-body guides would or could talk to us directly through another person. It was just a bit much for me. I listened to every word spilling out of Earl's mouth with total wonder and a bit of disbelief. I was hard-pressed not to exclaim, with the innocence of Gomer Pyle, "Shazam!"

According to Earl, *The Urantia Book* was channeled by a group of people living in Chicago. I don't remember all the details. The story goes, when they were first contacted, the words for the book *Urantia* appeared on paper without anyone on the other side of the pen. Initially, a small group of "seekers" were meeting to wrestle with unanswered questions. So "ask and you shall receive," the universe responded through these entities from "the other side." The first time they were contacted, I suppose they were pretty shocked, as one might assume given these spirits out of body were coming through from the other side to have a little chat. This was not the group's intent, to leave the room and come back in to find a letter written by extraterrestrials on the topics of their concerns. Who would? Can you imagine?

The Urantia Book is 2,097 pages long, published the year before I was born in 1955. This expansive composite of information, channeled from "celestial beings," integrates science, philosophy, and religion in addition to unveiling explicit new details about the life of Jesus. There is scientific information in this book about genetic coding undiscovered by scientists until years later. With this, Earl had my undivided attention. Science and Jesus all in one book; I ran right out and bought one.

I was soon disheartened by the patriarchal content of the book, referring always to "God the Father" and the "Sons of Man." I don't know where these "celestial beings" hailed from, but in my mind, they couldn't be too enlightened with this kind of language. In looking back, perhaps referring to God as Creator, Source, or Mother of us all might have been a stretch for 1955. I guess it didn't bother Earl because the cradle of his religious background began in the bosom of the Mormon Church. I thought the Catholic Church was bad, with the exception of the Muslims, the Mormons take the cake on doctrine of male superiority.

The next lesson was even harder to get my head around, which, of course is, the problem. To understand the infinite, or spirit, one cannot use the intellect. We may be able to catch a glimpse of the overall game plan, but our minds are finite. So trying to "get your head around" the infinite is probably the epitome of an exercise in futility, don't you think? Regardless, I guess we all still try. "Faith seeks understanding," Sr. Peggy always says. Spirit is spirit—timeless, existing in nothing and in everything. So following the yellow brick road that Spirit was laying in front of me meant leaving my brain behind, like the Scarecrow. There are times when brainless is a good thing.

I was still wrestling with the notion of channeling when Earl introduced lesson number 2: "walk-ins" According to Earl, "walk-ins" are soul exchanges. The person embodied here becomes weary of this place, longing to go home. The soul yet to be incarnate makes an agreement to take their place. One soul walks out and the other walks in, easy as that. Earl told me of meeting a "walk in" who had memory of his soul exchange. Imagine your soul just changing clothes, putting on a new skin. That's how it was explained to me. I didn't know what I thought about channeling, but I suppose my take was "guess it could happen, why not?" Walk-ins on the other hand, well, that was a far stretch for my vanilla experience of spirituality. It was more in line with the flavor tootie fruity, if you know what I mean.

I sat listening to Earl as he explained he had met a "walk in" many years prior. My mind at that point was running on several different channels. One was tuned in to what he was saying, one was thinking "this guy is Looney Tunes," and the third channel was questioning, "is he really from this planet?" I still ask that question. I mean, is this guy really an English professor? To this very day, I wonder if Earl was far more than he appeared in his human form. An angel perhaps, or a member of another race from another solar system disguised in human form? I had far more questions than answers. Which brings us to lesson 3: star nations was next on the agenda.

This was not a stretch for me at all, this notion of extraterrestrials. I give Shirley McClain five stars for having the courage to state the obvious. I have always believed there are beings in other galaxies and solar systems—some behind us in their evolution and some far more advanced. It only made sense to me; to think anything else seems either arrogant, ignorant, or maybe a little of both. I feel comfortable with the notion that they come and go from our galaxy as easily as we make a trip to the Wal-Mart. However, I did not know they intervened on occasion to keep us from destroying our planet.

According to Earl, this has happened many times. He told me Mikhail Gorbachev was counseled by these beings during the fall of the Berlin Wall. They were responsible for keeping the peace during this very difficult transition. Mikhail would never have been able to lead the country through those turbulent times without their counsel. He went on to say the star nations have intervened throughout our history working with leaders all over the world, including our own. I'm sitting on the other side of all this information thinking, I wonder what normal people do to pass their time on Saturday nights?

Earl became a good friend. He was always showing up; sometimes I felt like I could not get a moment alone on my back porch. If he saw me, he came out for a chat, and we would have a lesson. I wasn't so bothered by the visits; I needed that close contact. I needed Jamie, watching from across the street, and Earl covering my flank. Their watchful eyes helped me feel supported and safe.

"It was the best of times, it was the worst of times," those days on Happy Street. One of the most challenging periods of my life, on so many levels, opened doors I didn't realize I had knocked on. I was in the flow and determined to keep it holy. I would be held, challenged, and recreated by strangers—*strange* being the operative word here. What I have come to know and believe, there are no strangers. *Strange* is just a word that holds the mystery of things yet to be understood.

CHAPTER 12

"Hear the Angels whisper.... The road is not far, the light's behind the stars, the shadow never was and home is here. The Fire Burns within, this love that never ends, the Spirit calls your name and home is here."

"Hear the Angels Whisper"

The Hot Coal Cha-Cha

NO MATTER HOW HAPPY HAPPY Street was, or how interesting the characters, it was month three now for me and the shuttlecraft and month six in Utah. The new was wearing off, which brought with it a whole new set of feelings. I was questioning my decision to move to Salt Lake. My nonexistent job at the VA was becoming more boring by the day, and the unit no closer to opening. The urge to move was overwhelming. When you are dancing on hot coals, it's best to move. And this is what it felt like: dancing on hot coals. I was in pain. I could not escape the pain, and I wanted it to stop. When I left Kentucky, all I could feel was my loss of Carolyn. But now I was beginning to feel the loss of my roots, my home, and all that goes with it. The Southern drawls, the humidity, the river, and that little coffee shop I visited every day on the way to work. I missed the green, all fifty-two shades of it. I missed the trees and the flowers. Never mind that I was surrounded by some of the most beautiful mountains in the world, there's just no place like home. In short, I was now homesick on top of everything else.

I stayed in close contact with my past medical director in Louisville; we became fast friends when she was hired by family health centers. I felt her immediate support. Lisa was a remarkably intelligent woman with multiple degrees and incredible leadership abilities. Her talents far exceeded her predecessors who attempted to lead our motley crew. She was not ego centered but driven by an inner force that demanded she make a difference in the world, which she did. I had great respect for Lisa, and somehow it seemed the feeling was mutual. I e-mailed her on a regular basis and began to turn over the idea of going home. I felt foolish in even entertaining the notion of returning to Kentucky, but I finally said it out loud.

Lisa swiftly replied in the next e-mail, "Are you serious?"

"Yes," I wrote back, "I want to come home. This was a mistake."

"Well, then come," she said.

Lisa needed a nurse-practitioner for a clinic out on the south end of town. It was a very different population than I had served previously, but it was a job. I took it and started making preparations to leave. Cha-cha-cha!

I e-mailed dear friends of mine who lived in Southern Indiana. They had a small apartment above their home, so I asked if I could live there at least initially. "Yes," they said, "it was available." It was all falling together. Piece by piece, it was as easy as falling off a log. It's a sign! If it's this easy, it must be the right move. It was the right move, eventually, but not for the reasons I imagined.

I was in counseling as all these plans unfolded and was advised this would not be the best time to make any major life decisions, like moving across country. I nixed that bit of advice, plugging up my ears while signing the "lalalalala" song. When I told Griff and Jo about my decision, they became deathly silent. Griff walked out on the front porch and began to cry but didn't tell me what to do.

Other friends, Maggie and Peggy, dropped by and did try to tell me what to do. They stood outside my kitchen door while I sat on my back stoop telling them about my plans. They listened to all my reasoning. Peg tried to help me see the other side of the coin, while Maggie silently pulled weeds out of my dry-as-a-bone flower bed, where nothing seemed to grow. The little bed seemed to match the inner landscape I was supporting in those days. Others in the Angel Brigade didn't say much; however, their silence was very loud. I could feel their sadness, but I forged on. At this point, although I was unaware, I did not have my feet up or my butt down, and I was soon to be knocked ass over teakettle against the rocks.

There was this incredible relief that came with my decision. Like struggling in a tug-of-war with a whole group of bullies much bigger than me on the other end of the rope, I let go. I simply let go of my end and watched them fall. Struggle over. Have a nice day, boys. I gave my notice at the VA and called the moving company. I was embarrassed but called Mark and Tyler, my realtors, to put the shuttlecraft up for sale. As you know, finding a place was not an easy feat, and now I was selling it just shy of the dust settling from my arrival. Mark was terribly kind and never let on that he thought I was off my rocker, because, of course, I was off my rocker. At this point, I couldn't even find my rocker. I'm sure I was matching right up there with the "Witch Is In" nutcase on the other side of the hood. But just wait, it gets better.

Relief lasted for about a day, and then I could hear it. That tiny little nagging voice of sanity on the other side of the closed door was now screaming at me. Did you know, if you stay busy enough, you can avoid hearing that voice altogether? Well, you can. I was doing a pretty good job of it too, but anytime I got even close to quiet, the calm solvent droning began to seep in, making it hard to maintain my resolve regarding making the right decision. I started to feel myself teeter-totter. If there had been a teeter-totter event in the Olympics being held in Salt Lake that next year, I would have entered and won gold because I was fast becoming an Olympic champion of the seesaw. Even when

I was successful in avoiding the Voice, I could feel a deep, intuitive, primal "dis-ease" about this move. Still, I tucked my head down and forged ahead.

Moving day came around quickly, and the uneasiness and questioning voices never stopped. When the movers arrived, I wanted to say, "Sorry, boys. I've made a big mistake. I won't be needing you." Then the seesaw would swing, and I would think, "You quit your job, you have another one waiting in Kentucky, you have to go." Each loaded box placed on the back of the truck brought me face-to-face with the reality of my decision. I thought, well as soon as I get in my truck and head for Kentucky, this will get better. The movers pulled out of the driveway as I stood in the front yard with my friends. I spent that night on Amy and Charise's couch, Baxter and Tess by my side looking very confused and bewildered. A great sadness descended as I lay there, trying unsuccessfully to sleep. Bad move. There was silence, and I was silent. The Voice had its say, "YOU ARE MAKING A BIG MISTAKE!" I rolled over and ignored reason as if it were a bad dream. The next morning, Baxter, Tess, and I pulled out of the driveway. The back of the little red Toyota truck was packed to capacity again with our Hillbilly load. We left silent, troubled friends in our wake as we retraced our route back to Kentucky. They stood as reflections of what I was feeling but would not own.

I was frantic to find some kind of affirmation that my angst was unfounded. There was none to be found, quite the opposite, really. First of all, my assumption that I would feel better once headed down the road was dead wrong. I felt more anxious and much worse. My second clue was Tess. She went into a deep funk, which got deeper the farther we drove away from the mountains she loved. The animal kingdom was having its say, Tess in her silence and the absence of my power animal, the hawk. On the way out west, they lined the route like highway markers. On the road back to Kentucky, there were no hawks. Not one. No blessing, totem, or guardian would greet us for this journey. The spirit world was as silent as my friends had been. This was the final and most profound sign. Still, I clung to the hope that as soon as I crossed the state line, my ole Kentucky home would make all things better. Well, not so in this fairy tale.

As you may have guessed by now, the state line came but I wasn't feeling better. I was in tears. Suddenly I remembered why I left Kentucky and what I had found in Utah. I called Griff on my cell, and she listened while I blubbered on about what a mistake this was. What was I going to do? I wanted to turn the truck around and come right back home. Except, I really didn't have a home. I didn't feel at home anywhere, and this trip brought that understanding to an exclamation point. No matter, I was going to go back to Utah. The question now became when.

My quick loop through Louisville confirmed the state line brought no healing balm. I drove back over into Indiana where I was supposed to live. By the time I got to Pat and Sharon's about fifteen minutes later, I had convinced myself the best thing to do would be to give it a try. I had a job, and Lisa, my medical director, was counting on me for the clinic out in the south end of town. I didn't have a job in Salt Lake now, and it was no easy feat finding the first one. I drove up to the entrance, opened the gate, and headed around back to park.

Sharon and Pat were happy to greet me and, of course, I was glad to see them. The stairs were narrow and steep, but Pat helped me haul everything up to the empty apartment waiting above. My load included an old forty-inch TV that was extremely heavy and hard to move, along with my computer and all the boxes of this and that. My furniture had not arrived, so I slept that night on the floor. The next morning, I woke up and told Pat and Sharon I was going to move back to Salt Lake. Pat helped me move everything back down the stairs, only to help me move it all back up the stairs in the morning when I changed my mind again. Sharon watched silently with great concern. And that is how it went—seesaw, seesaw. Poor guy, he had no idea he signed up for moving calisthenics when he offered to help. Pat never complained. Both my friends were totally befuddled, probably wondering who had stolen the real Bo while totally avoiding the topic of my loose screw.

My furniture arrived, and my good friend Ginny came over with her sister Cathy to help me unpack the boxes. I did not mention my ambivalence or the cha-cha; at this point, I didn't trust anything I thought or felt. Ginny was glad to have me home. Our friendship reached back over twenty years, and we were very close. They stayed long enough to get me settled and then drove back over the river to Louisville. I looked around the room and suddenly realized how very alone I was now. No triad of friends surrounding my flanks in my quaint little neighborhood, no characters to soften my days and call me to mysteries and adventure—just me and the pups alone, facing the repercussions of my deaf and dumb decision.

The place and the apartment were very nice. Pat and Sharon lived not in a neighborhood but a business district in the little town of Jeffersonville across the river from Louisville. The property was gated and surrounded by a ten-foot chain-link fence. The yard was very large and manicured to perfection. Despite the perfection and security, I felt like I was living in a compound, more alone than ever and now caged in to boot. I tried to busy myself with the usual moving-in chores, but this time, busy or quiet, I was hounded by the realization that I really screwed up.

I decided the only thing I could do was to stay for a while, at least until Lisa could find another nurse-practitioner so I didn't hang her out on the line to dry. She hired a crazy woman, she knew it now, but I didn't want the rest of the administration to know. She trusted me, and now my insanity was going to make her look bad with her superiors. I didn't want that. So I spoke to Lisa about what was happening in my head and showed up to work again for Family Health Centers on my appointed start date. At some point I called Mark and told him to pull the sign and take my house off the market. I figured I would drive back out before the first snow fall if I was lucky. It was late summer and I was hoping she could find another NP before October.

My days in the compound were numbered. I could have knocked on Pat and Sharon's door anytime but embarrassed by my behavior and trying hard to be invisible, I pretty much stayed to myself. Before too long, I just couldn't take living alone anymore. I found myself pacing back and forth like a caged animal at the zoo. I could not find comfort, only unrelenting agitation. I called my friend Norah for comfort and described the shape I was in as if reciting the litany of the damned. She was used to it. Norah's background in social work and caring for our mentally ill homeless patients came in handy. I suppose she thought, one more nut, what the heck! She said, pack your things, bring the dogs and come on over. You can live here with me. She did not have to ask twice. I packed my suitcase and we moved again. Pat and Sharon, again remaining politely quiet. Still bewildered by my behavior, they said nothing but offered to babysit my furniture for the next several months until the moving van came back to load up again.

I went through the motions of daily life, but I had lost all confidence in myself and in any decision I made. I was still looking for signs, for any clues. Hell, what I would have given for just one scrawny hawk—but nothing. I wanted someone else to say "OK, this is what you need to do with the rest of your life. This is where you should live. God wants you here in this place doing this job and following this path. Here it is outlined and wrapped up with a bow." Isn't it funny how it never works quite like that in discernment? You are always left with the final say, and my say was obviously quite broken.

Days turned into weeks as I waited for Lisa to find another nurse-practitioner, releasing me from my obligations. Living with Norah was healing and provided for the best situation I could hope for in my current condition.

We were compatible and on the same wavelength on almost every level. Probably had something to do with our Aquarian natures, born on the same day, February 13, ten years apart. Still, I would always refer to us as Lady and the Tramp. I was a bit shabby in my jeans and dress khakis next to Norah who always looked like she walked out of *Vogue* complete with stilettos. The apartment was lovely but small, and I was concerned about the dogs and how Norah would adjust, having never had a dog in her house. Baxter and Tess were still waiting for that brain they were supposed to grow at age three, wild as March hares. Fortunately, for some reason they were relatively well behaved, working their magic on Norah. In short order, she was in love.

Norah had this maternal thing going for her. She was a wonderful mother. With both her children grown and living their separate lives, she had no one left to mother, and the grandchildren had not arrived yet. The dogs became her next best substitute. Everything they did charmed her, and soon she had them eating out of her hand, literally. Prior to this, my dogs were on a "down stay" when I went to the table and, with the exception of our cross-country McDonald's french fries, they got dog food, not people food. Well, that was "all over but the shouting."

One day I came home from work, and as we finished eating dinner, Norah said, "Can they lick my plate?"

"No!" I said in disbelief. "No!"

To which Norah replied empathically, "Well, why not? You're a bitch!" This was followed by a brief pause while she glared at me. Then the Southern belle charm kicked in as I watched her morph before my eyes. Looking coy, her head cocked to the side, with lilting voice she said, "When you're not here, I let them lick the cake bowl. They love it!"

Daftly I just shook my head. "OK," I said, "so much for my perfect well-behaved children."

In addition to cake batter and dinner plates, she made them popcorn every night, hand feeding them a piece at a time. They sat adoringly at her feet, looking up lovingly into her eyes. She smiled, giggling from the toes up. "They just love this," she said.

In addition to the cramped quarters of apartment living, there was very little room to maneuver my "screaming Mimis" outside either. In the middle of the busiest commercial/residential district in Louisville, like it or not, they were city dogs now. They adjusted far better than me, it seemed, even though I had to keep them on their leads at all times. To make things more interesting, the apartment complex was surrounded by those tall Kentucky trees I am so fond of, and these trees were full of squirrels. These little furry rodents drove my brainless mutts into a psychotic frenzy the minute, and every time, we walked outside the apartment doors. The fact that Norah was feeding her substitute four-legged grandchildren sugar-enriched cake batter probably didn't help the problem. I had this recurring vision of myself tied securely with the retractable leads to one of the trees, squirrel on my head, with dogs barking wildly at my feet. It never happened, but it was totally within the realm of possibility.

Still waiting, still looking for clues, each day turned into a quest to find the truth about my next step. Praying for some sign, some direction, something that would assure me moving back to Utah was the right thing to do. As has been the case for my entire life and relationship with my God, things began to unfold, but not in the manner I would have expected or anticipated. Certainly not as quickly as I would have liked because, remember, I was doing the cha-cha, and avoiding pain was key. Divine providence had a different plan and, among other things, this trip back to Kentucky was to help me let go of the past and move forward. I left running away from the pain I could not face. This trip brought me back to center: face-to-face with all that I was to leave, to grieve for, and to release. This was a necessary process, enabling the new plan for my life to unfold. I still felt like a naked tree branch, stripped of leaves and bark, exposed to the elements and left to die. I would learn another part of me had to die for the resurrection of what was to be.

In an effort to speed up the process, I went to a local Barnes and Noble to play bookstore roulette. Like Bible roulette, where you ask God for guidance and then open the Bible and read the first verse your eyes fall on for inspiration and direction. It works—works for me, anyway. It's all about intent. So on this day, I stood in the bookstore and said, "Help me find what I need to read. Show me." Simple prayer, profound effects would follow. I walked over to the shelves, and in keeping with how the game is played, I picked up the very first book my eyes fell upon. It was called *Bringers of the Dawn* by Barbara Marciniak. I thought my friend Earl was out there, he could not hold a candle to Barbara. However, in hindsight, he set the stage and planted the seeds for this next step.

Barbara Marciniak is an internationally acclaimed channel for the Pleiadians. Yes, friends, we are talking about the star nation of the seven sisters of the Pleiades. I know; me too. I had no idea. She has published four books and is editor for the quarterly newsletter *The Pleiadian Times*. Now this is a bit much for a backwoods kid from Kentucky to entertain. I drove back to Norah's, opened the book, and began to read. One chapter into the book or maybe two, I closed the book and thought, this lady is crazier than I could ever hope to be. I was so shocked by some of her writing, I almost threw the book away, but then there was that little voice again, reminding me how I came to find the book in the first place. So I just quietly packed it away. Right now, I was nowhere near ready for this information. I suppose, although the ground was broken, it wasn't quite ready for these seeds to be planted, or maybe they just needed to lie dormant for a time. Regardless, I was going to acquire the information one way or another. It wasn't long before the next door opened.

Norah grew up in Kentucky. She was the epitome of a Southern belle. Her social circles formed by the country club set, she was quite the lady. Raised as a Southern Baptist, she seemed to feel pretty safe and at home in her beliefs and really didn't question them. However, Norah was a bit of a chameleon; she would adjust and change to just about anything. I witnessed this initially when I watched her while we worked with the homeless those fifteen years. In addition to her big heart that was totally open, she also had an open mind and could at least listen to whatever one had to say, carefully considering another's view without judgment or fear. I was amazed, and the more I got to know her, the more I realized the depth of her multidimensional persona. She was as comfortable, literally, picking a drunk up out of the gutter in her stilettos as she was sipping cocktails at the club with her friends. She could charm the socks off any of our elected officials while trying to persuade them to support the folks living on the street and, in the next scene, light up a cigarette with one of her homeless boys, listening intently to their deepest, darkest scenarios without even flinching. So as like energy attracts, her friends were just as multidimensional, just as colorful, but not exactly carbon copies, particularly when it came to the expression of spirituality. Enter Margie, stage left. We are talking way stage left.

Margie and Norah had been friends for many years, far longer than the twenty years Norah and I could boast. A part of that Southern belle, country club set, Margie had another side, which wasn't exposed for all the world to see. This was not out of fear, but wisdom. You "don't cast your pearls before swine" unless you are a bit masochistic. Margie played for the same team as the internationally acclaimed Barbara Marciniak. In short, she was and still is a great mystic. Although she would probably never boast of this gift, I would soon learn it was quite real. Although Margie was not in conversation with Barbara's friends, the Pleiadians, she was given to conversation with her good friend Merlin. That would be Merlin the Magician, counsel to King Arthur.

Margie talks to Merlin as easily as you or I might talk to the milkman, if there were still a milkman. In this case, it doesn't matter that he no longer exists in this realm. Unlike the milkman, he pops in for a chat when Margie needs direction or assistance. Margie is not a channel, or a person whose personality can be set aside to let another being or entity come through from the other side. She does, however, have access to the guidance of Merlin who has been her friend, companion, and guide for many years.

When Norah first introduced me to Margie, I had no idea. Norah probably had no idea either—well, not at that time. Margie was wise and humble. One could boast of such a gift; she did not. One could try to convert the nonbelievers; she did not. This was not hers to do. She went about her work through the guidance of the unseen with incredible, unquestioning faith. Her work was performed without fanfare. It was hers to do, and nothing she did made much sense on a third-dimensional level. So no need to share this information as people would tend to think you are a kook. However, as Merlin was a guide for Margie, Margie was to become a guide for me. Little by little, she began to share her mysteries, life's study, and work. First on the agenda was helping me to find the yellow brick road again so I could go home.

Norah invited Margie to go out to dinner with us. We sat together chatting. I was listening more than chatting when Margie casually mentioned something that piqued my curiosity. I think I knew on some level, which was not totally conscious, Margie was going to help me. So I shared with her my plight, my return to Kentucky, my short stay in Utah, and my desire but fear to return there again. Margie listened smiling with the proverbial twinkle in her eye exuding, "I've got a secret." I could see her genuine concern and, at the same time, a very calm reassurance that all was well and a part of a plan that I could not at this point grasp even faintly. Years later, I was introduced to another mystic who said to me, "It's all good. It's all God."

I had not grasped this concept yet. I had no idea there was anything holy being born within the context of the mess I had made of my life. I could not see through the fog, which cast a deep shadow over everything, leaving me blaming myself for my failures. There are no failures, but I didn't know that at the time and was busy flagellating myself, in keeping with good Catholic tradition. Through Margie's light and direction, I would soon have the fog blown away, finding myself standing on a great precipice. Soon I would step out into the great void and experience my faith on a whole new level.

On that night, Norah introduced two of her very dear friends to each other and then stepped aside to allow the magic to unfold as it would. Sadly, seven years later, Norah left us and the planet, dying in her mid-sixties of a rare lung disease. As all Bible scholars know, seven is a sacred number, holding within its energy an imposed symbol of deeper, more expanded meaning. This revelation was saved for those who would study the mysteries. Norah, for her part, held such energy, although I do not think she wielded this energy consciously, even though it was, in part, why she came to the planet. Although unaware and unimposing, she had a part in igniting the fire that would bring to pass a mystic union—a union meant to hold space for the dawning of a new age. Aquarian, at her finest, she would be one of the alchemists assigned to change the consciousness of creation. Margie and I are still amazed at our paths intertwining and Norah's part in that woven fabric. She was a good Southern Baptist; her perception of the Divine was not unlike my own. We were by the book, the "Good Book," and had a very limited understanding of those writings. Yet she was introducing two people who were called together to bring a gift that would bridge the old with the new, a necessity for the world's ascension into the "Kingdom Come."

As the night continued and I told Margie my story, Norah sat patiently listening to it again, God love her. Margie sat quietly listening on every level and in between the lines. I could feel her feel what I had been through and then felt her reach through the camouflage and drama to create an opening for the truth to emerge. Clearly she saw beyond this dimension. Even before she shared that little piece of information with me, I knew.

After a few moments of silence, she looked across the table into my eyes and began to break bread—not literally, but symbolically. She began to share with me what was the most sacred in her life. I was getting the Cliff's Notes version, but still this was the information I was waiting for and knew was coming. The unveiling was heralded by an underlying current of energy. It was palpable at the moment of our introduction. For a moment, I started to feel my position change—feet up-butt down, picked up by the current, not fighting it anymore. The gears of the universe shifted once again, and I could feel myself slide into my assigned cog instead of being sheared by the grinding force of a misguided step. Margie told me briefly and gently about the metaphysical community of which she was a part, as if to test the waters and see if it was safe to share what was her sacred path. At the same time, she guarded the information, wielding great care not to shock Norah or make her uncomfortable.

"There is a young woman who is just coming into her gifts as a psychic," she said. "She is really very good, and I think she will be able to help you." She gave me the woman's name and number and told me she would call her friend so she would know to expect my call.

I felt hopeful and disappointed at the same time. There was a part of me that felt Margie was going to be a direct key to my understanding the next step. Well, she was, but not in the way I expected and not at that moment in time. Her role would come later when I was a bit more naked and far more ready to embrace information beyond the outlandish and certainly beyond my comfort zone. It takes a lot of skinning to get the layers off so we can see a deeper truth. I thought I was about as raw as one could get, but I was wrong. There was more to come. It is beyond amazing how many layers we can dawn in such a short lifetime.

I was hesitant, for a minute. My fundamentalist background came seeping to the surface, taunting me with the threat of hellfire. This mumbo-jumbo stuff was "of the devil!" said the old well-worn tapes. Fortunately, logic prevailed and my mind snapped back into alignment with my own wisdom. Since I wasn't choosing that path "of the devil," I need not be bothered by these old tapes anymore, and so it ended. It was that easy, like taking your finger and flicking off that little guy who sits on our shoulder, bedeviling you about every move you make. I thumped the little bastard into the next county. I'd had enough and I was taking the next step, and this was obviously my next step. There is more to faith than what we know and believe; that's why they call it faith.

I called Margie's friend, arrangements were made, and she gave me directions to her home. I was to have "my reading" there. I knew absolutely nothing about psychics or their gifts. I had never had a reading. This was all new, and despite my resolve to step forward, I was moving with great caution, given to backsliding into my homegrown fears.

Psychics see into your energy field, picking up on images that help you unravel mysteries or find direction. Typically, this information is seen through images symbolic in their representation of your life and, sometimes, on a deeper level, your soul. At least, that is how it works with some. If they are wise and are able to step outside their ego, they know that what they see is about potential possibilities. Nothing is set in stone because, as the quantum physics people will tell you, the flap of a butterfly's wing on the other side of the world sets into motion an energy that will land in your lap sooner or later. At the time, I knew none of this and was sure this lady was going to give me a play-by-play plan of what to do next.

This psychic lived in a section of Louisville called Germantown, settled by German immigrants soon after Louisville first made the map. The place had a charm all its own, with small clapboard houses aligned in rows of symmetry and finite conformity. I thought it a bit of an oxymoron for a psychic who was neither a German nor a conformist. In addition, there was nothing finite about her gifts. I drove up to the assigned row house, clearly the right place because the house number matched the address. Otherwise, the houses truly all looked the same in the dim streetlights. I stepped out of the car and, with anticipation, walked toward the house. The little bastard had found his way back to my shoulder and was raising three kinds of hell when she opened the door.

The house was quiet and dimly lit. There was no crystal ball sitting on a table in the center of the room like you see in the movies. Just a coffee table with knickknacks, worn furniture, and pictures of family scattered about the walls. Very much like any modest Kentucky home. In keeping with Southern hospitality, I was invited to sit down as she spoke to me in soft, gentle tones. She told me she had started her meditation and trance before I arrived, and so she would like to begin, which was fine by me.

After a few moments of silence, she began to speak in the same soft, gentle tones. I guess I thought she might have a different voice when she began, but no, it was just the same. The only thing that seemed a little odd was her very flat affect. I listened carefully while she told me what she saw into my past, present, and into my future. She began to tell me of past lifetimes, things that I really had rather not known about myself. Beginning with a lifetime as a wicked demanding warlock whose evil sent fear and trembling into the village surrounding his castle. Sounded like something out of a bad mystery novel. They were fearful for good reason, she told me as I listened in shock and disbelief. You were very powerful during this lifetime and extremely cruel, using your power not for good but for selfish gains. Then she said, "They"—referring to her guides—"are showing me this because they want you to know you still have this power, but in this lifetime, you will use it for good."

The reading lasted an hour, and toward the end, she began to talk about my future. It seemed so ill-defined, nothing as concrete as I had hoped for when I arrived.

"They are showing me a top hat." She sat for a moment in confusion, then she said, "You are getting ready to do something entirely new, and you will be very successful at it." Then the session was over, leaving me uncertain if going back to Utah was right or wrong.

I didn't know if I believed in what I had just heard. I had always wondered about reincarnation, but to layer reincarnation with being a warlock in a previous lifetime was rocking my world a bit. All the while, Shorty was still on my shoulder, jumping up and down now, screaming "I told you so!" Once again I gave him the finger, flipping him off the screen. That boy was like bad interference, static on my universal receiver. Thank God I had at least that much insight into his role. My discernment was starting to improve. There was nothing in her reading that told me going back to Utah was good or bad, nothing. However, after we met, I started to feel confident that going back out West was what I wanted, plain and simple. This was truly progress.

The weeks continued to drag by as I waited for my replacement who was obviously going to be a no-show. It was the first of September now, September 11, 2001. I was in the back of the clinic waiting for my next patient. Suddenly I was aware of an eerie silence. I walked out of my office to find no one in the clinic area, which was typically swarming with medical assistants, secretaries, and patients. It felt like I had been transported into the Twilight Zone. I hurried out into the waiting room, and it was just as deathly quiet there, but I found them all. They stood in a semicircle around a television screen, which was now showing the second plane crash into the World Trade Towers. No one said a word. There were only muffled moans as the realization soaked into our awareness. We were watching an unspeakable act as it was channeled live across the airwaves in real time. It did not feel real—it was surreal, leaving us all feeling as shattered as the concrete we saw crumble to the ground.

We went back to work, going through the motions, as we saw our patients in the wake of this disaster. Within what seemed like moments, Lisa called. As medical director, she was doing all she knew how to do to support us as we supported our patients. She was on her way, making her rounds of all the clinics. Lisa tried to present like a rock standing strong in the midst of all the confusion, but I knew her better than some. She was visibly shaken when she arrived. She spoke to each staff member and, at the end of her rounds, walked into my office where she closed the door to speak with me.

Lisa looked as much in shock as the rest of us, but it grew worse as she listened to me turn the conversation from what was to become known as 9/11 to my own self-proclaimed tragedy. She looked utterly disillusioned when I think back on the moment. I think, in that brief conversation, she lost all respect for the woman she had placed on a pedestal. I fell off. In retrospect, I feel like Vivi, that sad character in *The Divine Secrets of the Ya-Ya Sisterhood*. When trying to explain her incomprehensible behavior, she could not and simply stated, "I dropped my basket."

I was no longer able to feel the pain of another, not even a tragedy of this magnitude. Something hollow remained. I think it was very sad for Lisa, as if she had lost a comrade in her fight for social justice and greater acts of love in the world. I was not the woman she once knew. Soon after that day, I called

Lisa and told her I couldn't wait any longer, giving my two weeks' notice. It was all too embarrassing, and yet there was nothing I could do about it, at least, not at that time. More healing would be needed and would come.

I started making arrangements, called the movers, told Norah and the others of my plans, and counted down the days until I was to be on the road back to Utah. My last day at the clinic came; they seemed sad to see me go even though I had not been there long. So I must have salvaged something to offer even though I could not see it. The end of the day came, and I climbed in my truck. I paused for a moment in the driveway looking back at the clinic, thinking quietly about my time there and the people I had met. Then I turned my head back to face forward in what was to be my first step in closing this chapter and moving back to Utah. As I did, I saw a familiar sight. High above my head, there on the electric wires, perched a huge solitary hawk looking down and straight into my eyes. Finally, as soon as I was headed in the right direction, my power animal returned as if to punctuate the final decision and the first step. Not a moment sooner or later, but in perfect timing he appeared above me. I knew, in this moment, I was making the right decision.

Each day was necessary during those short months of returned stay in Kentucky. There was more I needed to release, more layers to shed, more to grieve. There were also new lessons to learn and people to meet who would be intricate in what was to be my new work. All this was necessary to place me firmly back on my path. You can never really explain to others why it is all necessary, or why things evolve the way they do. That it wasn't really a mistake but a necessity for growth. So rather than trying to explain when I crossed back over into Utah, I just told folks, "I took my furniture on vacation. I'm back home now." The "light behind the star" would be far too difficult to explain.

CHAPTER 13

Into this place one walks in concert with the energy of the spheres, for the cosmos knows this quickening. It is only through trust in the Divine and in creation that we are able to see through the mists surrounding us to observe clearly our Avalon. Enlightenment brings us to the ultimate expression, the new birth of conscious living.

Crystals, Obelisks, and Energy

WHEN ONE PORTAL CLOSES, ANOTHER one opens. I know the analogy is "when one door closes, another one opens," but that doesn't seem adequate to describe the next leap. Portal jumping seems to be more appropriate. When a door opens and you walk through the threshold, it may be different but it's recognizable and usually comfortable. When you jump through portals, it's like Star Trek's warp drive. The transition leaves you loopy and disoriented for a while, but also full of wonder. In retrospect, I would have to say I felt like Dorothy when she walked out of the house having arrived in Munchkinland. That is a perfect example of portal jumping.

As I traveled across country, back to Utah, the hawks returned. They were on every post and pillar, lining my way, calling me back to my path. They were almost as good as the new navigation systems they're installing in cars now. If I didn't see a hawk after a few miles, I started to question if I was still on the right road, "recalculating." Tess was wagging her tail and smiling; my previously carsick mutt was now queen of the road. The closer we came to Utah, the happier she became. Baxter, on the other hand, was always happy, and that's just the name of his tune. As for me, either I was picking up on their energy or I too was relieved to be returning to the West. When we came to the first gas station and someone said "You bet 'cha," I knew I was very close to home. There are several standard lines used in Utah that I find totally endearing, and they are "You bet 'cha," "Preciate 'cha," and "Oh, my heck." If they are really out there on the edge, they say "Oh my hell"—but never in mixed company and only when emotions run high.

As easy as putting on a well-worn shoe, I slipped back into place. Seems this is always how it goes when you are walking the path intended by your core essence, the universe supports you on all sides. Nothing changed really, but suddenly I didn't mind my little shuttlecraft. It was plenty big for now. It didn't matter that I was unemployed; I would find a job. Best of all, my friends eased back into my life as though we never missed a beat from the four months of my absence. The healing continued. Their presence acted like a medicinal balm pouring over me, filling up the fissures and fractures left from the past. It was a bit like the cracked china doll's face, with the right skill and enough love, it can be filled in and repaired, almost as good as new. Of course, it's never the same; but on the surface, it looks like it was just unpacked from its shipping crate, whole and without blemish.

I was never so glad to be back in my little house and in my neighborhood.

The house wasn't so thrilling, but having Jamie and Isabel back right across the street, and all my other friends within blocks of my home made it seem like Nirvana. My furniture arrived before me, and my friends unpacked everything as a surprise. When I turned the key and walked in, it looked like I never left. The only thing different was my kitchen was better organized and I couldn't find my underwear drawer. That was easily rectified; I just called Griff and Jo. They thought it was pretty funny that I had to call them to find my panties. Good friends, what would we do without them?

First on the agenda was finding a job, and I have to say I was a little nervous about it. Nurse-practitioners are usually afforded more mobility, but finding a job in Salt Lake was not exactly easy. There seemed to be a glut of NPs. Nothing online really, nothing that I was interested in or felt accomplished at doing. So I had another couple months of unemployment. I didn't enjoy my time off as much as one might hope because I could not allow myself to trust in the unfolding of the game plan. I was too busy trying to make it happen. I had very few skills and absolutely no knowledge of the law of attraction or my ability to create my life. I was still in victim mode, but the anger was starting to surface, bubbling up in little ways. And that was a good thing. Anger may be uncomfortable, but I would find out it is a great emotion to help shift stuck energy. I was up to my armpits in the immoveable force. Like quicksand, it sucks you farther down to the bottom of the swamp unless somebody throws you a rope.

Many ropes in many forms came my way. Margie's psychic encouraged me to meditate every day; she told me this would be extremely important for my healing. Well, I seemed to have plenty of time for meditating, and I was dead serious about healing. *Dead serious* being the operative word—too serious, which can be deadening in itself. I needed to lighten up. That would take some work and time, but this too would come.

I began my daily meditation and journal entries as soon as I returned to Browning Avenue as was encouraged by my psychic friend. As I sat in my living room, I became more adept at quieting my mind. I noticed a recurring visual; a deep indigo light would appear during my trips to "the gap," or place of stillness, between the worlds. The light would be reflected at about the level of the sixth chakra. The third eye marks this sacred energy wheel and is found where our Hindu friends adorn their foreheads with the ornamental tribute called the bindi, traditionally a red dot between the eyes. However, as I said, the color I could see was not red but deep indigo blue. The color presented as a small triangle, point inverted and top curved like a dome. Later I would discover this was the color of the sixth chakra, the third eye. At the time, I knew very little about chakras and certainly didn't know there was a color associated with each vortex of energy. I saw the light frequently, noticing with curiosity but not understanding why it appeared or what it meant. I've come to peace with unusual happenings in my life, understanding I may never comprehend the experiences or be able to explain them with mental language. At the same time, I have learned to accept the unknown with gratitude, appreciating each mystery as gift.

I fell into a routine of meditating and hiking, interspersed with trips to my friends' houses. I was far more grateful now, experiencing a brief separation helped me know how gifted I was in this place. Like the old tune "Big Yellow Taxi" by Joni Mitchell ("Don't know what you've got 'til it's gone. Paved paradise and put up a parking lot.")—I was living in paradise, but it would take a few years to be in touch with this understanding. Paradise was unfolding for me on all levels. The old was falling away, and the new was blowing my socks off! There would be no parking lot for me. Far to the contrary, I was on the move.

My work with meditation was opening the door to a new world, the world of energy and energy work. I had friends in Kentucky who talked to me about these things, but I just wasn't quite sure about it all. That's how I approached anything I could not see, hear, or feel. Maybe it was so, maybe it was possible, but I was more like the apostle Thomas. I needed to see it to believe it. I found it all interesting but never really understood it fully. However, when I started seeing and feeling energy, it was no longer a matter of faith or abstract possibility, it was becoming a part of my experience. And so belief quickly followed. In the past, I was more like my partner Carolyn, who was far more logical and concrete than I. The difference between us was this: I was fascinated by anything that had to do with spirituality or mysticism. She, on the other hand, was not. In fact, she was perceptibly uncomfortable talking about anything that had to do with spirituality or the unknown, particularly if it was outside her comfort zone. Her zone was pretty narrow, outlined by the Catholic Church.

I was a stretch for Carolyn, and so were my friends Mary Jo and Ginny. Mary Jo, or MJ as we called her, was an extreme challenge for Carolyn because she didn't have any filters. If she did have filters, she didn't care to use them. She was a free-spirited wildass from the sixties, the epitome of ole hippie chic. Ginny, on the other hand, was gentler in sharing the wealth of her knowledge, knowing when to speak and when to be silent.

Mary Jo gave me my first crystal, a beautiful purple amethyst geode. I knew nothing about crystals. Mary Jo and Ginny both understood energy and spoke about it freely, like I might talk about the weather. We felt a kinship to one another in those early years and still now. MJ calls us "soul sistas." My friends were probably pivotal in planting the seeds or, at the very least, getting the ground ready to plant the seeds. It's a slow and gradual process, changing one's core beliefs. I was extremely conventional in those days, as was Carolyn, making for a good match at the time. However, I was open to their more radical, free form of thinking and spirituality. I thrived on our conversations, but they made Carolyn nervous. At the very least, I think she thought we were a bit off our nut. This was totally proven out for her on the night of the Judy Collins concert.

Typically, Carolyn would steer clear of my visits with Ginny and Mary Jo. Carolyn was not so comfortable with our trio, always appearing a bit on edge and hoping to change the conversation to something a bit less esoteric. On this night it was just Mary Jo, Carolyn, and I. We were on our way to hear Judy Collins perform with the Louisville Orchestra in Bernheim Forest. This was an incredibly beautiful setting, magical in itself, setting the stage for more than Judy's performance. As usual, Carolyn was a little nervous around us. Mary Jo was far from nervous, as she was communing with the universe. The parking for the venue was limited. We were instructed to park some distance away where we were bused in for the concert with strangers. I could tell Carolyn was just about ready to jump out of her skin because she never knew what we might say, in public, no less.

It was a beautiful summer night complete with full moon. We stepped off the bus, to be ushered toward the concert with the other Judy Collins fans in the soft glow of Kentucky moonlight. You know what they say about the effects of the full moon. Well, MJ was affected, wound up, excited, and bursting with the joy of being. Suddenly, without warning, she whipped out a small crystal from her pocket, threw her head back, and slapped the stone squarely on her forehead. Flinging her arms out in full extension, she narrowly missed whacking a woman walking next to us. Palms turned up to the light, balancing the crystal on her third eye, she shouted to the moon, "Energize me, baby!" I laughed out loud, and Carolyn put her head down, walked faster, and acted like she didn't know us. I could not stop laughing, and MJ could not stop being MJ, so Carolyn was just out of luck on this night. We were having the fullness of the moment and all the magic it brought with it.

I never took it very seriously and never discounted it totally, this understanding of being bathed in energy. An unseen force that controls our universe while at the same time is the universe, connecting all that is seen and unseen. In its entire specter, energy is the underlying force of creation and what has yet to be created. There was energy before there was form, making its star, pun intended, appearance initially through the vibration of sound and light. That's a big concept when you think about it. Added to this understanding was another new concept, energy can be manipulated by us for healing and for creating our life. Being introduced to this notion resulted in my "Jesus chip" kicking in, causing me to question its legitimacy. If things don't line up with my Christocentric background, I have a tendency to follow Carolyn's lead. I put my head down, walk faster, and pretend I don't hear a thing. It took a little time, but then I understood and it all began to make sense.

When Jesus said "you will do far greater things than these," referring to his miracles and healing work, he meant it. As my mother would say, he "wasn't talking to hear his head roar." He spoke the truth, lived the truth, and provided us with a living example of alignment with source and work with energy. It became more and more obvious to me; my past understanding held only a fraction of the message being presented. As was my fortune, I kept knocking, and so the doors kept opening, as was promised.

Living in Salt Lake may not seem like an obvious place to delve into the metaphysical, but, honey, it is the hotbed of the outlandishly absurd for a fundamentalist kid from Kentucky. The Mormons may have found it first, but the "woo woo" contingent followed rapidly on their heels. *Woo woo* is a term used endearingly to describe the metaphysical, what cannot be seen or explained by science or empirical evidence, at least, not yet—although quantum physics is giving it a good shot, exposing the cord of connection between science and the spiritual realm. Salt Lake has more than its fair share of these practitioners. Like moths drawn to the light, they seem to come from the four corners of the universe to find their home here. Consolidated centers of energy exist on the planet. Salt Lake is named as one of these spaces, referred to as a City of Light. This energy setting makes it a perfect place to shift old energy that no longer serves. This was perfect because I wanted to make sense of what had happened and move beyond it. The other choice, staying stuck and imploding into jaded bitterness, was just not acceptable.

I continued to read numerous books written by modern prophets, scientist, mystics, and theologians. I attended conferences, classes, channelings, and online seminars. Knowledge is a good thing. Meditation was also helping to lay the foundation for my next steps. Study, prayer, and meditation were all a great combo, but more was needed. Energy work would be required to break free of the past. Conventional measures were not working very well. I was seeing a counselor, using the traditional methods for addressing my general state of total confusion, fear and loss—and it was really no help at all. Our sessions resulted in my crying and blowing snot bubbles while bemoaning my loss, and that's about as far as it went. I could see no progress.

My poppa would say, "Charge it to the dust, and let the rain settle it." In other words, let it go. That wasn't working either. I was in a place that felt terrible, and I wanted out of it! Not at some unknown time in the future, I wanted out yesterday. So, more briefly put, I was ready to move beyond my understanding and take the next step. Drastic measures for drastic times. Bring on the "Woo woo!"

During my first year in Salt Lake, I was introduced to Peggy and Maggie who would become, for me, great friends, healers, and teachers. Unfortunately, our introduction came through a mutual friend's battle with ovarian cancer. We met in the preoperative holding area before Vicki's surgery. They came in smiling, their energy was light and clear. They were able to shift Vicki's attention away from the moment, which was, to say the least, extremely unpleasant and frightfully scary. Maggie and Peggy were both energy workers. Peggy was a physician, a radiologist, and a shaman. Maggie was trained in EMF work, Electromagnetic Field Balancing work. I would become intimately acquainted with each form of healing practice in the days and months ahead.

Energy workers learn to manipulate and work with energy in a way that is therapeutic, essentially bringing one back into balance. When you work with these forces with intent, you can shift the energy of a room just by walking into it. Come to think of it, you can shift the energy of a room without walking into it, for that matter. Healers emanate a higher vibration, a tone. Like striking a chord on a guitar; if it is a strong clear stroke, the other strings will begin to vibrate along with it, having never been touched physically.

Vicki's prognosis was very poor; the cancer was not diagnosed until it was deemed terminal. The surgery was meant to give the chemotherapy a chance to keep her alive for a bit longer, and of course, we all hoped for a miracle. Energy work provides us with the opportunity for miracles, defined as a shift or change in energy that cannot be explained by science. Unfortunately, we only seem to be willing to work in this realm when all other avenues have been exhausted. I dream of a world that will allow the marriage of empirical science practiced by medicine and the metaphysical skills of the true healers. We are not there yet, but we will be, maybe sooner than we dare dream.

Vicki was relatively comfortable with energy work. A Southerner from Tennessee, she was not introduced to the power of manipulating energy until she moved to Salt Lake. She settled here after attending college at Brigham Young University. Her major was dance, which she loved with all her being. She was the first person I ever met whose soul was so obviously fed by the rhythm of movement. She was sensual to the core, and she expressed that sensuality through dance. A deeply spiritual being who found the world a difficult place to call home, both her spirituality and sexuality were not in alignment with the accepted status quo. Frankly, I think the world was just too mediocre for her.

Vicki often told me she thought she must be from the constellation Alpha Centauri, alluding to the fact that she just didn't fit in anywhere on this planet. Most homosexuals feel this way. Vicki had the double whammy: she was gay and conscious, a guaranteed recipe for being ostracized from the pack. Alpha Centauri is one of a binary star system. Alpha and Beta Centauri are referred to as the "Southern Pointers" showing the way to the constellation of the Southern Cross. How appropriate that this Southern woman would point the way to a crossroads, my portal of entry.

Vicki was the first person to teach me how to feel energy. We would talk about energy, and she would discuss being able to feel energy. I had heard others talk about this, but it had not been my experience. Her attempts to show how to feel energy in the past were not successful, although she kept patiently trying. Returning from a woman's festival, she called my house all excited about a gift she bought for me there. I invited her over, and as she walked through the door, I knew the gift was far from ordinary. I could tell by the look on her face. Her expression reflected excitement, anticipation, and "I'm going to teach you a thing or two." She had me sit down and handed me the small package. Tearing the paper away, I found two crystals, again beautiful amethyst. MJ's crystal was a raw geode, broken open to expose the treasure inside. Vicki's amethysts were highly polished geometric forms. They were shaped like obelisks—a pillar- like structure, columnar topped with a pyramid. Each crystal was about three inches tall. She placed one in each of my hands and asked me to feel their energy. The crystals served as amplifiers, opening wide the aperture of my palm chakras. These miniature obelisks sealed the deal; no way could one not feel the energy. I was shocked—totally, speechlessly shocked as I felt the vibration of energy buzzing in my hands. I sat there wide eyed looking back at her, trying to catch my breath as she giggled her "I told you so." The Egyptians placed pairs of obelisks at the entrance to their temples. This moment was an entrance into a sacred space within me. It was always there, but like many sacred sites, the entry is not always easily found.

And so she journeyed on, my friend, to her own crossroads. There would be no miracle for her in this lifetime, but she stayed long enough to introduce me to Maggie and Peggy before she left. The web of life leaves me speechless in its magical weaving. As Vicki transitioned out of my life, my new friends transitioned in. Maggie would be my first energy practitioner, and I would learn firsthand about energetic healing on her table. No more blowing snot bubbles while droning on in hours of therapy; this was the real deal, energy work. Let the healing begin.

At some point during Vicki's first hospitalization, I had time to meet with Maggie in the hallway and ask her about EMF. I knew about energy, but I never heard of electromagnetic field balancing. Maggie began to help me understand more about her work. The technique helps to organize and strengthen the body's universal calibration lattice. OK, now that you are totally confused, what the hell is a universal calibration lattice, you ask? I asked the same thing.

Everything is made of energy. The organization of these energy frequencies creates our experience of form. In addition, energy is not held in time or space but is infinite. So there are those who believe we exist on multiple dimensions at all times. The quantum theorist can explain this far better than I, but the bottom line is what you experience with your five senses in your daily existence is a bit like the proverbial tip of the iceberg. There is far more to our life force and the expression of who we are than can be seen. Energy is not random. To create form, it becomes organized. The universal calibration lattice (UCL) is a part of this organization. As we think of our physical anatomy and organization of flesh and bones, the UCL is the energetic organization of our energy anatomy.

Traditionally, the ancients of Eastern cultures knew our energy system through the organization of chakras. Understood by ancient Indian practitioners, chakras are energy centers that lie within our bodies, as well as above and below, connecting us to the planet and to the cosmos. The word *chakra* is derived from ancient Sanskrit and translates as "wheel turning." These practitioners understood our well-being is dependent on the healthy ebb and flow of these energy centers. This wisdom is over two thousand years old, and yet until very recently, those in the Western hemisphere were for the most part unaware. This is due in part to the industrial age, which is quite mechanistic. Healers were burned at the stake, and we began worshiping at the feet of the empirical scientist. If it doesn't exist here on this physical plane, then it doesn't exist. How limiting. We truly threw out the baby with the bathwater.

I am still so caught in this limited expression, the empirical scientist. Trained as a nurse-practitioner in traditional medicine, I was pulled into the realm of energetic healers by necessity, yet I remain torn. This internal struggle is best described by a dream I had several years ago. In the dream, there was a beautiful African American woman, her face aged by time but her body a chiseled reflection of perfect form and heath. She was an extremely wise woman and an obvious archetype for the goddess. She was a famous dancer, respected by all the world and master of her art form. This master of art and health had a granddaughter who was also very beautiful and talented. I was the observer in the dream for some time. I watched from a distance in awe of their beauty and talent. The child of nine playing freely, dancing about her world stage on a grass covered field. I was so excited for her, understanding what great talent and potential she possessed, apparent from my observations and the knowledge of her genetic heritage. Finally I could not contain myself, I ran up to the child embracing her and said, "Oh, do you know how very lucky you are? You are such an artist and you can be an incredible dancer just like your grandmother." The child quickly jerked out of my arms, her energy shifting from playful joy to deadening rigidity. Whirling around, her glare cut through me, piercing my good intent, as she emphatically stated, "I am a Christian and a scientist!"

This is the jump, the leap. To trust and step out into the abyss, no more ground under feet. Just like stepping off the cliff into thin air, not unlike Jesus' invitation for his disciples to step out of the boat and walk across the water. It can't be done, it doesn't make sense, it is not logical, we reason. Well, true. It is not logical or reasonable because it is not scientific. It is spiritual. It is, for now, a matter of faith. I know it is possible, healing with energy and consciousness. I have witnessed it and experienced it firsthand. Yet I am tied by past religion, culture, and scientific training as surely as those poor souls were tied to the stake where they burned. What the hell? The atrocities we create with our limited understanding, when will it stop?

The understanding of chakras does not come from scientific evidence, and yet these vortexes of energy within and around our bodies have been used for millennia in healing work. More recently, in 1989, Peggy Phoenix Dubro identified, some say channeled, the universal calibration lattice and relayed the technique of electromagnetic field balancing. It was only recently discovered because it just became activated in our energy system, a part of our evolution and ascension process. The lattice is a composite of energy and light fibers that are connected to the chakras. The EMF worker believes these fibers of light "contain a record of all that our spirit has ever experienced as well as our heredity patterns." In EMF, the practitioner works with the client to release all that does not serve and support that which strengthens healthy energetic expression. Sign me up!

I worked with Maggie until I completed all the phases the technique offered. She suggested I learn the technique myself, but I did not feel a significant pull in that direction, and so I did not proceed with the training. However, Maggie and Peggy became invaluable friends and remain so to this day. Maggie felt I could use some bodywork to coincide with the energetic piece she was helping me with, so she referred me to Kristen Dalzen. Kristen, what an angel of light. Another portal opened, and I met my second energy practitioner.

Kristen was a Reiki master but was also trained in massage therapy. A profoundly psychic woman, she was in tune on many levels. Maggie sent me to Kristen for massage, understanding touch and bodywork would also be key in bringing me back to health. However, that's not exactly what happened. Per my usual in those days, it did not matter what I thought was going to happen. My intent was to heal, how that manifested in the physical plan was never quite what I envisioned. My vision was too limited, and so I got a little help. The autopilot was obviously calling the shots. Thank God for that, as my skills in decision making were a bit askew.

I called Kristen and set up an appointment. She lived and worked out of her small studio apartment above a modest home in the Sugarhouse area. Sugarhouse, isn't that just the best name? It is a hamlet within greater Salt Lake made up of small houses built in the thirties and forties. I lived in Sugarhouse; my home was located almost right around the corner from Kristen's place. What a coincidence. If you still believe in coincidence, good luck with that. Her location was a very good thing because anytime I tried to move beyond my little village, I would get lost and my anxiety level would shoot through the roof. This was not like me, but I was changing, and so I just accepted it for what it was and kept stepping to the tune I heard playing.

I knew Reiki was about energy, similar in my mind with healing touch, but that's about all I knew. I had experienced the benefits of massage while living in Louisville and knew Maggie was right. I needed touch. When you live alone, there isn't much of that going around. The day of my appointment finally came, and I had no trouble finding Kristen's place. I parked behind the house as instructed and looked for the stairs on the side of the house. An easy find, they were covered in living plants, flowers, and crystals. The entrance felt incredibly inviting, and my energy shifted as soon as I placed my foot on the first step of my ascent to Kristen's studio. I felt held, even before I knocked on the door.

I knocked, and the door opened. Kristen stood there with the most incredible smile, stretched out her arms, and said, "Welcome." To say she is a beautiful woman would be an understatement. I had never known such beauty in another; it was tangible and it was spiritual. There was something goddess like about Kristen. With little imagination, I could see her in another realm, part of a temple guardian sect. Perhaps she was serving the sun goddess Eos while dressed in the long white robes of servitude. The image was so clear. As soon as she opened the door, perhaps before, I could feel the vast soulfulness of her being and her energy. It was huge, do you hear me, Big! Such an energy and presence, I was a bit star struck and a whole lot nervous.

As I stepped into her home, the same energy found on the stairway spilled out into the house. It was clear and alive, comforting on all levels. We walked over to a sitting area, which was a very small womb-like alcove, appropriate for the work we were to do. Kristen sat down across from me. Sunlight was filtering through the dormer, spilling out on her face, which was soft and openly waiting. We began to talk at her invitation. She was not hurried, there was no judgment. She just listened as I told her everything about my past and my losses and how I found my way to her door.

We talked for what seemed like a very long time, and I was conscious about being in her space and taking up too much time, but she didn't seem to have the same concern. So I was more at ease. I was stilted in the telling of the story, never shedding a tear and trying hard not to touch the pain and lose control. I gave all the details like a seasoned reporter, devoid of emotion. "Just the facts, ma'am." I had a very hard time losing my shit in front of a stranger, so I was holding myself together with all the strength I could muster. When the story was told, I was spent but lighter, and we still had not started what I thought I had come to do, which was have a massage.

It was Kristen's turn now as she began to tell me more about her gifts and what she could offer. I really knew close to nothing about Reiki, and so she explained the technique. Again, I found myself learning about another form of energy work. The Reiki practitioner acts as a conduit for chi, a healing energy, which is passed through their palms to the client.

A Japanese Buddhist, Mikao Usui, mastered the technique in 1922. While on retreat, Mr. Usui was given this tool through what he called a mystical revelation. It came from God, in other words; that's how we would define it in Kentucky. Others might say it came from a distant galaxy or another dimension. We don't know, do we? Well, I don't, but I do believe it came in a mystical revelation just like the guy said it did, so not from this physical dimension anyway. One cannot just learn the technique, but instead, the power of Reiki is passed on through being attuned by a Reiki master. Reiki would be mastered and used by thousands of healing practitioners, including my Reiki master Kristen.

I listened intently as always and decided it was not massage that I needed at this moment; it was Reiki. Kristen agreed. I walked over to her massage table and lay down. I really had no expectations but trusted I would receive what I needed, whatever that might be. Kristen's cat was very interested in the whole process and, despite Kristen's objection, jumped up to share my space. Animals seem to be drawn to these spaces and are really little energy whores. They love it. I reassured Kristen I didn't mind sharing my space, and so the kitty was allowed to stay on the table with me.

I closed my eyes and began to relax as Kristen cleared the space and started her work. She began at my head and worked her way down my body, stopping at each chakra. I was instructed I could receive all or as little energy as I wanted. I was a bit like the kitty, also an energy whore. I soaked it up as I felt my body become more and more relaxed. It was pleasant and soothing. All was going well, and then she came to the second chakra. The second chakra is our emotional center. This is where we experience our sexual and sensual energy. Suddenly and without warning, the dam broke. I had no power over anything; so much for stilted control. The tears began to flow uncontrollably, and before I knew it, my body was shaking in violent sobs of release. I could not stop heaving as I tried to catch my breath between my convulsing. Up until this point, Kristen was working for the most part above my body; very little touch was involved in this transference of energy. I felt a slight break in connection as she laid her hand gently on my leg, bringing me back to center. My breath returned and I was able to compose myself, sliding once again into the present moment, now in control of my emotions. Kristen completed the session, and I got off the table changed. It was another first step, another experience that could not be explained with the logical mind. Step, step, step; I'm dancing now.

If you look up the term *Reiki* in Wikipedia, it will tell you there is no empirical evidence to suggest Reiki does anything to promote healing. The American Nurses Association recognizes this healing art and actually provides continuing education credits for those who take classes in Reiki. Interesting.

Last month, I spoke with a psychologist at the University of Utah. She is a friend and a sister of the ODTs (that would be the Order of the Doubting Thomas). It is easy for me to recognize these members because I belong to the order too. The psychologist, who was a personal friend, was given a gift certificate on her birthday to see Kristen and receive a Reiki session. Every time we see Cindy, we ask her about the gift, only to find out that, well no, she hasn't gone in for her session yet. However, her curiosity seems to be piqued a bit. As coincidence, again, if you believe in coincidence, would have it, she recently attended a meeting where a researcher presented her study on Reiki. Cindy is the dean of the school of psychology, so she is very much aware of good versus bad research, and she was very impressed with not only the study but the findings.

The woman doing the study is working with cancer patients who are undergoing chemotherapy. She had three study groups: a control group, a group who received Reiki, and a group who received massage. I would go into more detail about study design to help all the rest of you ODTs, but it bores me to death and so I won't. I'll just cut to the chase. All of these patients were undergoing chemotherapy, which is a killer of not only cancer cells but also the patient's immune system. Blood levels were drawn to measure the number of these killer white cells, the body's defense against invaders of all sorts, including cancer. Once chemo begins, these cells are rapidly destroyed. To the researcher's surprise, the cell count dropped dramatically in two of the groups, but the group receiving Reiki maintained their pre-chemo levels. Again I say, interesting.

Science will eventually catch up. Until that time, I think I will continue to choose to trust in the universe for providing what I need when I need it, with or without empirical evidence. Healing will and does occur without scientific design or discourse. There is a place for science and a place for what we cannot explain scientifically. Crystals, obelisks, and energy seem as good a place to start as any. And so the journey continues.

CHAPTER 14

There is within each of us a shaman, mystic, master. The healer, the seer, the enlightened one is found in our awakening. As our consciousness evolves, we will begin to look within for guidance, and there it will be found.

"Living JoyUs"

PANIC WAS STARTING TO SET in when I finally found my new job online. A local group of physicians was looking for a nurse-practitioner. I knew nothing about their subspecialty but, to my favor, no other NP knew anything about it either. I brought my baseline knowledge and skills from which to build upon. From there, it became totally on the job training. I was hired by three men, two MDs and one PhD; I far prefer working with men. I know that sounds odd coming from a lesbian, but I like men. I just don't want one to keep.

Utah was far behind Kentucky, and the rest of the nation for that matter, with regard to their understanding of nurse-practitioners as health-care providers. The fact that most NPs are women does not help our visibility. I think this is due, in part, to a cultural lag enhanced by a religion that places the sexes in a hierarchical order. The order of women in Utah is, shall we say, not at the top of the list. I felt like I'd been catapulted back into the forties, or perhaps even further, and began to feel a kinship with the suffragettes. Of course, medicine has its own hierarchical arrangement, brought to a defining point for me when I heard one of the docs refer to me as the "scut monkey." No offense intended but, decidedly, I was offended.

Numerous research studies prove the excellence of care provided by nurse-practitioners. My new group was unaware the NP provides comparable care, and in some cases, our outcomes are better than that of the physician. Understand, this means within our scope of practice. I am not suggesting we get rid of any physicians. Although I have met a few in years past who would better serve their patients in another profession. Please also understand, this group I joined fast became a fan of my work, and I theirs. The physicians were totally supportive. It just took a little time for us to understand one another and define our work together.

Not in a million years would I dream of working in a subspecialty I knew nothing about. Not in a million years would I dream I would be living in the West. Not in a million years did I ever think I would walk in the world without Carolyn. Not in a million years would I envision walking between the worlds. There were so many of those "not in a million years" events that it was hard to keep track. So I settled into believing this must be the new theme for my life, and so it was. I applied for the job and was hired. As it turned out, the office was three blocks away from the shuttlecraft. I could walk to work if I wanted to, perfect since my gyroscope was still off. Close was definitely better for calming my inner state of panic whenever I found myself too far from my safety net. It was a slow start, but as soon as I became more confident in my management skills in this specialty, it was a perfect fit. Unlike my years with the homeless, it was easy and stress free. The job was ideal. The stress of the past was just that, in the past. What was unfolding now was another incredible unthought-of thread in the tapestry. Without my knowing, I was creating my new life. The relative ease of this new position left me with enough energy to begin my new vocation.

My new vocation would be about healing, but not in the traditional form it had taken in the past. Coming to Salt Lake meant leaving behind my life's work with the homeless. I know what "life's work" feels like, and this was not it. There was something more that I was supposed to be doing; I could feel it. Let me interject here. I learned from my experience in Buckhorn, God does not move us around like pawns. In fact, to think that God really needs us to do anything seems a bit arrogant when you look at the whole picture. When I say "supposed to be doing," I mean something deep within me wanted to find expression in a work aligned with my purpose for living on this life plane, in this lifetime. There was something more, I just didn't know what.

At first, I thought seriously about going back to graduate school to complete another specialty as a psychiatric nurse-practitioner. I applied and was accepted and then decided this was just not the right path. Something did not sit well with me; it didn't line up. There was something I was supposed to be doing, to be learning; I felt certain about that but what then? Trying to see my purpose then was like trying to learn to drive a car without the car, the epitome of futility. Feet up, butt down: that was the theme, and it would take me a bit to get the hang of being in the flow and allowing the universe to guide me down the river. Keep it holy.

All was well with my world, but I was still terribly lonely. Some folks are good loners; I'm not one of those folks. It used to chap my ass when friends would pontificate about loving yourself and enjoying time alone. Of course, the ones best at this were the ones living with their partners in conjugal bliss. I do enjoy time alone, but not 24-7 alone; I don't enjoy that in the least. I never have, and I'm quite certain I never will. Doesn't mean I can't survive it. I can and I have, but it would not be a preference.

I was sitting on the front steps outside my small tutor home, having one of those joyfully alone moments, when Jamie walked across the street with a booklet in her hand. "Whatcha doin', BoBo?"

This greeting always made me smile. Jamie just made me smile, period. What a light, incredible spirit. "Just hanging out," I said, trying to appear cheerful when what I really wanted to do was slit my wrists. I find it's better to try to be cheerful when you want to make friends and keep them; the "sucking pit of need" thing seems to repel folks after a bit.

Jamie went on to chat about this and that, and then she said, "Why don't you think about taking a class, BoBo? Look at this."

She handed me the booklet. I took the paper flier from her hand and started scanning the pages. "Well, maybe I will. That might be a good idea," I said, trying to be positive. At least, Jamie was giving me some direction instead of telling me I should enjoy my miserable state of aloneness.

I thumbed through the pages as we talked. They were the typical classes for adult education: photography, pottery, basket weaving, foreign languages. Nothing jumped out at me until I looked down to see a class on shamanism. I said, "Hey, I might like this class. *Shay-manism*," I said.

Jamie giggled. "Well, if you are going to take it, BoBo, maybe you better learn how to pronounce it. It's *shah-manism*."

"Oh," I said, feeling a little embarrassed. I sat the book down.

Jamie was very wise, intuitive, and psychic. She shared this side of herself, the psychic, with very few people, almost as if she was afraid of her gift. A scientist, she was just finishing her doctorate in exercise physiology. An incredibly brilliant woman with a heart to match the brains, one doesn't always see both gifts so well developed in one being. Although I was fascinated by her psychic abilities and saw them as a great gift, Jamie seemed to wish this gift would go away. I suppose it haunted her, sometimes literally.

Jamie's ability to see brought her face-to-face with entities she had not invited to the party, if you know what I mean. She first experienced these beings while living in her home in California. Playing with the tarot, she was pretty good at reading the cards. However, when she came home to find the cards laid out in a totally different fashion than where she left them in her locked apartment, the experience frightened the "begeebees" out of her. So she closed down and tried to avoid connecting or dabbling in the occult thereafter. However, it really mattered very little about liking or disliking her gift; it was hers. She was obviously a clairvoyant, which became even clearer to me later in our relationship.

Terribly interesting character, my friend. She commanded many gifts: a PhD in exercise physiology, scuba diver, fantastic cook, hunter and gatherer, fisherwoman, researcher, and teacher. Oh yes, and she sees spooks and receives messages from other dimensions on a fairly regular bases. This is the woman you want living next door if suddenly you had to learn how to live off the land, or as in my case, you were learning to live again, period. Jamie has a way of nurturing without enabling. For me, it felt as though I was given an incredible gift from the universe in her being. She was like a spiritual midwife helping me through a very painful transition into my new birth. The class in "shay-manism" would also be key in that birthing.

Jamie has this incredibly cute way in which she cocks her head to one side, smiling up at you with twinkling eyes. She supports this very mischievous look that says "come play with me." She always made me feel better just by being in her presence. God knows I needed to play. God knows, and Jamie knew. I think her inner child is alive and well in addition to her inner elf, her inner fairy, and her inner leprechaun. There is something just magical and mystical about her. However, of all her gifts, the one I treasure the most is her ability to see goodness or "god-ness" in every person. There seems to be no duality in her understanding; she connects in a way that leaves you feeling loved and cared for during every encounter.

Case in point, it was not uncommon for Jamie and her partner Isabel to have houseguests. They lived across the street from me, and I watched their comings and goings as they watched mine. It was common for me to come home from work and look over to see Jamie sticking her head out the door calling, "Bobo! Want a come over for a little?" Then she would hold her hand up with her thumb tipping toward her mouth and pinkie finger extended toward the sky. Tilting the hand ever so slightly as if holding an imaginary bottle of hooch, she would give a couple of short, shrill whistles that coincided with her hand gestures. This was my invitation to happy hour, and I certainly needed all the happy hour I could get. Don't we all?

One particular weekend, I noticed two men staying with my friends across the street. I'm watching these guys and wondering why Jamie and Isabel would have men spending the weekend with them. They looked straighter than an arrow, without the usual qualities of gay men, pretty butch, in fact. If you are not familiar with that term, it means they were quite masculine. So that in itself seemed a bit odd. Why would straight men be staying with lesbians?

After the weekend was over, I wandered over to talk to Jamie about her guests. I was right about their being straight. They were old friends, traveling through town. The one guy was active and held an office in the National Rifle Association. That was the first little stretch for me with regard to their hanging out with lesbians. Republican lesbians might have made it easier to appreciate, but they were neither Republican nor conservative. The greater stretch came when I learned the other guy was a leader in the Ku Klux Klan.

"Jesus, Mary, and Joseph. The KKK," I said, as I saw visions of a cross burning on my front gay lawn. Jamie just smiled.

Without judgment, Jamie met each person where they were, observing them quietly and offering them whatever hospitality they might need at the time. I thought I was the queen of hospitality coming from the South and all, but then something like this happens. Suddenly I'm aware of my lack of charity and my quickness to judge. I have no trouble extending my hand to just about anyone in need, but "buddying up" with the KKK? Let's say it gave me pause, just to keep it more polite.

Living in the South and living in Louisville with many African American friends left me with a near hatred of the KKK. White male supremacists and bigotry in all its forms did not sit well with me. The vile expressions of bigotry became very real for me through the eyes of my African American friends' experiences and stories. I came to know its sting firsthand after coming out as a homosexual. My first reaction was just that, a reaction. How could Jamie be friends with these people?

My Christian background taught me to avoid judging anyone. However, how does one avoid judging an organization like the KKK? This was a hard one. But I'm telling you, Jamie lived in what seemed to be non-judgment. Her lists of friends looked like a who's who from the Rainbow Coalition. There was plenty of color in her world; she was not middling about anything. So it was not about being unaware. She could get angry and indignant anytime she noticed injustice or watched someone be unkind. It was not at all unusual to hear her refer to someone as an asshole when witnessing asshole-like behavior. That would be anyone hurting another or acting in a way that was not in accordance with her code of ethics. It's just that she never seemed to hold a grudge, at least not for too long. There was so much she would teach me during our brief time together. She was one of many of my teachers, but one of the best and most interesting was yet to come.

As discussed, I was very naive and a virgin of sorts when it came to understanding there was more in the universe than what we could see and touch. My spirituality was one-dimensional. My perceptual framework was more than limited by religion and culture. I had yet to even come close to the infinite, although I was always on the quest to experience another piece of it. Still very black and white in my understanding, I was totally chained to the physical; the third dimension was home, but the forces that be kept giving me a not-so-gentle nudge, pushing me outside my lines. Our physical world provides for a great playground for learning, but it is not the "end all, be all" we think it is, far from it. There is so much more. We understand this better as children, but then we get lost in the shuffle of life and forget there is a level of reality beyond what we can experience with our five senses.

I had not a clue that other dimensions existed. I mean, I watched *The Twilight Zone* as a kid, but that was about the extent of it. I did not know it was possible to travel between the dimensions or have a communion space with beings outside our physical world. It gives "I believe in the communion of the saints" a whole new meaning. We live and breathe and have our being in God, and let me just say, God is not one dimensional, and neither are we. We just aren't conscious of our multidimensional living. I would come to learn that not only can I travel in between the worlds, there are many other beings doing the same thing. In other words, there are many around us and even taking up residence with us. Our experience of these beings does not come through our senses, well, at least not the first five. I would soon be given the tools to experience the others that Jamie saw and experienced without training. This was her gift; I would have to work for the ability.

I decided I should take the class on shamanism, thinking it would be like an anthropology class. I knew very little about the shaman. The extent of my understanding was the shaman was the healer and priest of their tribe. I hold firm to the belief, a person can only be healed through body, mind, spirit, and emotion. The shaman's approach outlined the perfect framework for healing. Their inception predated Christianity. They were the original healers of the indigenous peoples, crossing all continents and cultures. This, I thought, was very cool.

The class was held on the University of Utah's campus. The buildings were a bit run-down and shabby. Well, what could you expect as an adult learner? I was excited. I can't help myself. I am always excited to go to any class and would probably be a professional student if someone would pay my way. I was attributing my excitement to my usual first day of class. This was a familiar emotion that could be traced back to my childhood. However, that was just the half of it. The excitement I was feeling was not so much about the past or past experiences. A whole new world was opening for me on this night. A part of me knew this, but it wasn't the conscious part. The conscious part of me didn't have a clue.

I arrived at the right building and the right classroom with notebook and pen in hand. As I walked through the door, I saw Joy, the instructor, and the others scattered about the room. If my memory serves me correctly, and sometimes it doesn't, there were about seven of us in the class. Joy was looking around the room, and when it was time for class to start, she said, "This room won't do. We are going to have to find another one."

Well, I was confused because there were plenty of desks, far more than our little group would need. The lighting was good. There was a chalkboard. The room filled all my expectations for class. Obviously, it didn't matter as we filed out behind Joy like a row of baby ducks following their momma to find a better pond. We walked down the hall and turned the corner to a much smaller room with far fewer desks. I was thinking, "Well, maybe she just likes a cozier classroom."

As we walked in and started to take our places, Joy smiled in the mysterious way she always smiled. A facial expression I would grow to love because it always accompanied some veiled, wonderful mystery that she was about to impart or not, sometimes just leaving you with the mystery. Magic of some sort almost always followed this look. She said, "Don't sit down in the desks, we are sitting on the ground."

Now I am really confused. This was not the traditional way I was accustomed to learning, and how was I going to take notes? Well, forget about the notes. The notebooks were to remain on the desks that we were now pushing into the back corners of the room.

Joy instructed us to sit down on the floor; our small group formed a circle in which she was included. Well, she definitely had my attention. Within a very short period of time, I would learn this was not an anthropology class, and the woman sitting in our circle was not here to teach us about the shaman. She was a shaman, and she was here to teach us to be shamans. Remember that shocked expression I told you about when I first held the obelisks in my hands? Well, imagine it again to the power of ten because, as they say in Kentucky, "I was got!" I did not sign up for this, at least not consciously.

As she talked to us about the class and we introduced ourselves to one another, I looked around the room to my other classmates. They did not seem so shocked; so maybe I was overreacting. I seem to have a tendency to do that, overreact. This is a tendency that has not served me well over the years. Reaction in combination with poor boundaries has, at times, resulted in tragic consequences that were never my intention. But I am drifting away from the subject—back to class. A part of me was thinking "I am definitely in the wrong course," and the other part of me was thinking "Oh my god, this is way cool!" The latter ended up being the reality.

Much of the first night of the course was devoted to a little housekeeping, a little history of the shaman, a little history of our teacher Joy, and a little shared history about each other. Joy introduced us to her website *LivingJoyus*, which would serve as a bulletin board for class announcements and other classes she offered. The website offered reflections and a little online education that included her philosophy. LivingJoyus was a perfect name for Joy's work and what she brought to the world. Her classes would teach us to live from this space, in her words: "Free to be living joy! Us."

It seems so odd to reflect back now and realize I cannot remember exactly who was in our class. It was so small. I remember there was only one guy and he always fell asleep anytime we did a closed eye meditation. I knew he was asleep as did everyone else, the snoring was a dead giveaway, making it hard for us to stay focused and avoid laughing. I can remember many of the people I studied with but I don't remember how they showed up; which class I met them in is a mystery. There were three courses taught by Joy at the University of Utah. I took all three and through the classes I was introduced to some of the most remarkable people I have ever known, some of whom would become cherished friends. The one person I do remember with great clarity in class 1 was Heidi. Heidi is the epitome of love and light, her spirit soars, gathering up everybody in the room with her on the ascent. We used to tease her about never having to buy new shoes. We were all quite sure she floated above ground rather than walking on the earth.

Heidi missed the first class making her entrance on the second week. We met once a week and each week we were given an outside assignment. I felt like I had been shot out of a cannon on that first night of class and now I could see the same look on Heidi's face. As she walked in and saw us all sitting on the floor, she looked a little like a deer in the headlights. To make matters worse she could not just slide into a chair on the side of the classroom unnoticed. In fact, she was to become the center of our attention for a moment. Joy told her to go back outside the building and find a stone that called to her. No, this was not a punishment for being late or missing the first class. It was the assignment, in abridged version, from the first week of class. We all laughed years later recalling the event because Joy was thinking, "I wonder if she will come back," and Heidi was thinking "I'm not sure I want to go back in there." But she did come back, and class two of course 101 on shamanism continued.

The week before, Joy asked us to take a nature walk and begin to feel a part of the earth we walked on. Being one with the planet is a huge piece for the shaman and one of the reasons we were asked to sit on the ground during class. Joy instructed us to walk very slowly, feeling the energy of the earth with each deliberate step. We were to pick up a stone that called to us, that we felt a connection with while walking our path. I'm thinking, "Now how might a stone call to me? Yo, lady! Hey, pick me up, doll!"

No, not exactly. But I did hear the call; all of us did. Each of us came back with our stone and the story of our walk. Not just the nature walk but our walk, our past and present journey. To our surprise and delight, there was much more out there than meets the eye. With this exercise, we were beginning to tap into this unseen presence that is always with us. It was just a peek, a tease, really; but there was so much promise in those early titillating moments. We all felt it. Joy had us in the palm of her hand, a place where I found gentle refuge for years to come.

Each week brought with it different exercises that took place in and outside of the classroom. Before long, Joy asked us to select a cloth for our mesas. The shaman is one with their mesa; it becomes an external reflection or their internal reality. Joy was simple and direct in her observations and guidance. I think she avoided a lot of explanation so we could experience the moment rather than getting too far into our head. The mind is a wonderful thing; of course, we all know that. But for the mystic, the master, the shaman—it only gets in the way. The Egyptians knew. They saved all the internal organs after death for the body's return, placing them carefully in earthen jars. They sucked out and threw away the brain. Who said "the mind is a terrible thing to waste"? Nobody told the Egyptians. There is an obvious message in this practice if you think about it.

Each of us chose our mesa cloth carefully. Everything we did felt important. Of course, everything we do is important but, most of the time, we just aren't aware. If we are aware, we understand everything we do has a consequence—not just for ourselves but for our world, the universe, the cosmos, and beyond. I chose a piece of white soft leather that was gifted to me by my friend Vickie. This was another extremely cool gift but even more precious to me now after her death. With each class, we began to collect objects from the earth to place in our mesa. Each object was sacred, symbol and reflection of an unseen part of our life that carried our magic. The mesa is not held by time or space, but is constantly evolving. It reflects an image of our life's unfolding. As with all symbolism, the objects revealed a deeper, sometimes unnamable, truth.

The first stone I collected on my nature walk assignment became the first stone of my mesa and the medicine wheel I would create there. This stone would carry the energy of the South. In the shaman's tradition, the four directions are sacred, holding an energy and framework from which we explore our seen and unseen worlds. The shaman calls to the four winds. Each direction is connected to an energy held by a guardian, a power animal who assists one on the path. In the South, we call on the energy of serpent. She sheds her skin easily, quickly, and without drama. The South asks us to release our past in much the same way she sheds her skin. The West is home of jaguar, the great black cat upon whose back we ride as she stalks the darkness, helping us discover our greatest fear and so know our greatest potential. The North is safeguarded by the hummingbird and is home to our ancestors, those who have walked before us "the rainbow path." It is the place and portal of all time and where we begin the first steps of our new journey. The East completes the circle of life with the power of the hawk, the eagle, the condor—all whose great vision help us see with infinite clarity the greater picture. In short, the medicine wheel reflects for us the circle of life. From this framework we release our past, face our fears, step into our new path, and see with clear vision the greater picture. We visit the four directions not once, but repeatedly, as we spiral through time in the great dance. Through this tradition, we become aware of our connection to the All in all: the four directions, the earth, one another, and our Creator.

Understanding this framework introduced us to a new way, like seeing through a new lens. Seeing our world through this lens awakened an understanding that lay dormant in us for many generations. At least, this is how I experienced these new, ancient teachings—new to me but ancient in our world. Many of the books I read before meeting the shamans explained how very important it would be to understand the teachings of the ancients, particularly now during this time in our evolution. The indigenous peoples understood through their culture and spirituality a vision of life and interconnectedness with the planet that we have lost in our Western traditions. I was being asked to return to this place of revelation, which enabled me to see the sacred web, the God in all. I was led to this place as certainly as I was led to the little altar at Trinity Methodist; it was to be a part of my path and spirituality. It was unfolding even before I came to Salt Lake, but I would not have a name for it until now.

We were taking our baby steps in this process of revelation. Each week learning one more thing, each new piece of knowledge building on the other as the practice developed its own rhythm. Our mesas were growing with our knowledge. Our hodgepodge collection would look pretty funny to an outsider. Sticks, stones, seeds, feathers, crystals, and small carved fetishes of power animals filled our mesas' belly on any given day. Pieces would move in and out and change positions in arrangement as deeper mysteries unfolded for us through the work. The placement of these items and the energies they carried would reveal for us unknown secrets within our psyche far more quickly than months and years of therapy. You soon understand the mesa is a living reflection of you. Wild, isn't it?

What was hysterical was watching us trying to fold our mesas and keep them intact. There is a special way to fold your mesa so it securely holds all your treasures. If packed correctly, the cloth is tightly gathered from the four directions and folded in on itself, hiding safely the sacred objects inside. If you don't get the fold right when you stand up to walk away, everything starts to fall out the sides, and it's a mad scramble to hold it all together—fetishes, stones, and feathers scattered to the four winds. Those first nights really were comical. We were all trying to follow the directions in our efforts to be cool novice shamans—at the very least, trying not to call attention to ourselves or appear like stooges while carrying our sacred bundle. Well, stooge like, not cool, would be the better description: symbolic probably for where we were in the process. Regardless, it is really funny to think about how clumsily we entered the shamanic world. Like a toddler's first steps, I suppose. Joy was so patient with our stumbling. I don't know how she kept from laughing at us, but she did, at least in our presence. Maybe her ride home from class was different. I suspect, at the very least, there was a huge smile on her face.

Every week, I looked forward to class; and every week, I followed Joy's directions for our homework. Beyond the four directions and the magic of the mesa, I learned of the shaman's ability to walk in both worlds and know the landscape of other dimensions. I touched the mystic's path through my previous directed retreats, but never at this level. I found myself blown out of the water on more than one occasion, but the best of all was the night of "eye-to-eye meditation."

It is difficult to stop the busy chatter of an unquieted mind. Everyone who has ever tried their hand at meditation has butted heads with "monkey mind." This is, in part, why many give up or tell others, "I'm just not so good at this." It is a practice that, for most, takes years. The exercise we were to use on this night required that we attain this quieting of the mind just to begin the process. Quieting my mind, a brain that runs like a rapper on crack, could take the whole night and into next week. So you might imagine, I felt a little like I was participating in an exercise of futility.

Sitting in our circle, Joy would teach us a new way and a new entry way into another dimension. The shaman has many tricks. Tricks used to distract the mind, and within that magic moment the leap is made from this dimension to another. Sometimes this is done through drumming, other practitioners use rattles, on this night we would use each other to transcend to another realm. A realm unknown to me, one I had never experienced in the past. This was all new to us and unbelievably powerful. I'm still not certain why or how novices could reach such a full blown state so quickly. State of what, you may be wondering. Me too, I'm still wondering what happened that night, I just remember how profound it was and how unbelievable. One could wonder about the practices of a shaman. Are they really real? Are there really other dimensions? Does the shaman really travel to other worlds? After this night, all the questions were put behind me. I was left without doubt.

Let me preface this by telling you, we never used the hallucinogens many shamans use to travel to the other dimensions, or other worlds. Depending on the culture and region, it is common practice for the shaman to use herbs—very powerful herbs, I might add. This was not Joy's way; she wanted us to find our way out and to track our way back. There was some control in our journeys other shamans did not experience. I cannot say one is better than the other. I can only tell you my experience of Joy's way.

We sat no longer in a circle but paired off two by two. In the candlelight that flickered between us, we could see into the eyes of our partners. The room was quieted now and Joy turned on a drumming tape that lulled our brains into a trance-like state. Each of us settling down into our own rhythm and the rhythm of our partners, as we were instructed to look into the left eye of the individual seated before us. We were given no other direction but were told before the start of the exercise, we would see them transformed before us.

Sitting across from my appointed partner I felt myself slowing down, lost in the rhythm of the drumming, taking me deeper into the trance. My vision softened and forms blurred as my mind entered the stillness. I was stepping into the shamanic.

Shamans are shape shifters, time travelers, visionaries, mystics but primarily healers. I witnessed the healing on many nights. I had been privy to it myself on more than one occasion. On this night I would witness shape shifting. As I looked into her left eye and she looked into mine, the soft glow of the candle light reflected her features dimly. My senses were melting into the earth, leaving me with only the raw energetic force between us. The silence now was beyond silence. I found myself in "the gap" and suddenly her face morphed and sitting 12 inches away from me was a lion. *A lion*, full mane, whose dark foreboding eyes looked back at me. I could all but feel his whiskers brush my face as his warm moist breath fell gently on my now pale skin. "SHIT!" I yelled loudly and found myself jerking violently backward away from the experience, panting

– heart pounding. Oh darn, " Sorry, sorry " I said sheepishly, embarrassed to have broken the trance not just for myself but for others. There were a few stifled giggles. I looked over at Joy to see if I was going to be reprimanded. Of course I wasn't, she smiled widely while continuing to arrange the pieces in her mesa, casting only a brief glance in my direction accompanied by a quick wink.

Later I reflected back on my experience and we all talked about the shape shifting, the changing morphing faces we experienced. I puzzled, "Well, so we can have hallucinations without drugs, what's the purpose?" Almost as quickly as these words left my lips, they were followed by, "Oh! The lion is about courage. I saw the lion because my message from Spirit is, Now is the time for you to draw on the courage of the lion." Yes, that was it but not only this realization. There was also an energetic imprint gifted to me at the same time. The king of the jungle just dropped in to share with me his magic.

Anytime I started one of the exercises, I always had a little fear or dread that I would not be able to see. Before long, it became the class joke, "I can't see." The joke was, I could see quite well, I just didn't know it. All of us had our insecurities and our epiphanies in these guided trips into the unknown. We began to know each other on very deep and intimate levels. The class would lend itself to nothing else. Our journeying together left us incredibly open to one another. There were no secrets, "our souls lay bared" as they say.

One of my most special classmates' name was Carolee. She was special to me in many ways; her gifts and her courage were unmatched in our group. Carolee was from Utah and was brought up within the strict confines of the Mormon faith. So even coming to this class was far more challenging for her than for the rest of us. She had a very strong motivation, her baby girl had been diagnosed with cancer. Theirs had been a long fight and they were running out of acceptable options. Suddenly the medical establishment and the Mormon Church were not enough.

Carolee was unassuming, extremely humble and wide eyed like the rest of us when it came to the information we were being presented. It was all new and it was all fantastic, in the mystical sense of the word, beyond our understanding would be an understatement. However, it was quite hard not to believe when you began to experience the all in all through the eyes of a shaman. The magic was revealed in such unexpected places and things, it left you reeling and without question.

On the first day of class, before we settled into "the work," Joy asked us why we came. Why were we here? Some of us rambled on about our search for truth, our own healing, because our neighbor thought we might want to take a class—which was you-know-who's lame response. Then it was Carolee's turn. Her face changed from gentle smile to grave resolve. "I want to heal my little girl." She went on to tell us about their struggle with the diagnosis and the, literally, deadly "cures" her child was subjected to in their efforts to stop the unstoppable. The room grew quiet, and suddenly we were taken to a whole new level of understanding. This was not for her a pastime or curiosity. It was for life, the life of her child.

We watched each other grow through that first class, but Carolee's experiences were always the most fascinating and truly awesome. I have come to believe when we call on Spirit and we show up, Spirit also shows up and in a big way. During one class, when we were getting ready to start and just discussing the weather or whatever trivia came to mind, Carolee told us she was having a heck of a time with the streetlight in front of her house. It kept blowing out. I noticed Joy's look as Carolee talked. It was the "I've got a secret" look, the "I'm going to share the secret" look. Joy was looking down at her mesa, moving and arranging the crystals, stones, and symbols of life into her special configurations and patterns. She sometimes seemed as though she was unengaged with our conversation. Of course she was engaged. She was always engaged with us and with the work.

"What do you think about that, Carolee?"

Suddenly our chatter stopped because when Joy spoke like this, we knew something big was coming.

"Well," said Carolee, "I guess it's bad luck or a faulty light."

"Really?" said Joy.

Now she had our attention; all of us were waiting for what was coming next.

"I think it is energy. Your energy."

Carolee looked back questioningly. "Energy," she said. "My energy?"

Joy smiled silently and waited for what would come next, which was always all our questions and all our reasoning behind our questions and disbelief. She would allow this to go on for a while, as was her custom, and then she spoke again. "Carolee, why don't you perform a little experiment? This week when you are out, I want you to look at another light and focus your energy there. See what happens."

"Well, OK," she said, smiling back uneasily.

The next week of class came, and Carolee looked unsettled. It's hard to describe, really. *Shocked* would be an understatement. She was excited, but *scared* might be a better term.

"Well," said Joy, "what happened?"

Carolee looked back, almost embarrassed, as she told us she had blown out most of the lights on her street and some of the lights downtown when she was out on an errand. Joy smiled silently. "And what do you think now?"

What did we think now? Carolee looked back blankly as if finding her power was almost too much for her to comprehend. A young Mormon mother was stepping into her power, the power of the Divine. No priest, no bishop, no man was a part of the equation. That in itself must have been a hard one to swallow after thirty-some odd years of a totally different paradigm.

During that very night, while journeying, Carolee brought yet another amazing piece back to class. As was our custom, we would journey with the drumming tape, and then afterward, we would share what we saw on our journeys. Carolee was strangely quiet. As our conversations traveled around the circle and back to her again, she sat staring into her mesa. Joy's gentle nudge followed. "What is it, Carolee? What did you see?"

After an uncomfortable pause, she slowly lifted her head and smiled sheepishly. "I don't want to say. It doesn't make any sense."

"Well, maybe it does." Joy smiled. "Try us."

It was obvious Carolee thought her vision made no sense at all and was even embarrassing to disclose to us, but at Joy's insistence, she said, "I saw eyes on my palms."

Joy's smile broadened.

"I looked into the palms of my hands, and there were eyes there."

We all looked back curiously, first at Carolee and then at Joy who was enjoying the pregnant pause. "Carolee," she said with the pride of a mother whose child had attained a great accomplishment, "what you saw was a very ancient symbol. The eyes you saw over the palm chakras symbolize 'Great Healer.'"

Carolee's journey never ceased to amaze us; I think even Joy was occasionally in awe of her dance with spirit. Carolee was probably the most astonished of all. One day, walking out into her garage, she was met by a bald eagle sitting on her daughter's bike. Yes, in Salt Lake, in the suburbs, a bald eagle. Our national bird, in all his grandeur, was sitting on the handlebars of her child's bike. You fill in the blanks. I was always amazed at my hawks who showed up to empower me with their magic, but a bald eagle in the garage, really? In the world of the shaman, this takes the prize.

Visions were not new to me. Connection with the divine was my life's passion, but the shamanic world provided a totally new experience that embraced the sacred in all of life, giving life a much broader definition. "Even the stones will call out to you." Who said that? Yes, right; it was the big JC. I think Jesus was the greatest shaman who ever lived. Don't let semantics, culture, or limited beliefs get in your way. He was the ultimate shaman, mystic, master.

Jesus walked the earth with consciousness, healed those who asked this of him (energetically, I might add), and in wisdom shared his knowledge of the sacred, ultimately journeying for the entire planet. Then he challenged us to do the same. We forget that part, don't we? So much easier to give up our power and pretend we are victims of human frailty or that we need another to step in and tell us what to do to win God's favor and find our place in the kingdom. Please, what a crock! We are connected and one with God and with each other. God is the epitome of love and wisdom. Tell me how that adds up to weak and pitiful. Lies, all lies, these modern-day fairy tales that would have us believe we are anything less than miraculous. *Sad* is the best term of description for this heritage of deceit that has kept us in fear and bondage all these years. The people of Israel were not the only ones who needed a Moses.

So this is the way with me. Although organized religions leave me with a bad taste in my mouth, I am a Jesus freak of the sixties. All that comes to me in this lifetime must come through the eye of the needle, the vision of Christology. Otherwise, it just doesn't measure up. I track my course with the compass of my true north. Light is light, there is no darkness. I would not call myself a Christian in the traditional understanding of this age and this culture. In fact, I see nothing Christ like about the traditions that teach from a framework of judgment born of fear. With great sadness I see this time and time again, the contortion of what was a message of great love, distorted by hatred and egocentricity. I see it even in my own family, the most painful vision of all.

I am a follower of the way, and for me, the way is always evolving, always changing, and always connected to the Christ energy. I fall short, I stumble and fall, I lose touch, I lose consciousness—but I always come back to the sacred through the Christ energy. An energy of purity and love that is infinite and knows no boundaries, it cannot be contained in a set of rules and regulations. I believe I totally understand what Gandhi meant when he said, "I am a Christian, a Hindu, a Muslim, and a Jew." Gandhi understood our connection. He honored the interface of all the created with their Creator without asking another to change their expression of faith and belief. Instead, he invited all to come to the table and bring their unique gifts with them for the betterment of the world. He understood the web of creation and embraced our diversity, turning away from duality in all its forms. He understood that diminishing another does not further one's cause or beliefs.

Coming to this space, sitting in this circle of other like souls while embracing an ancient tradition and spirituality, would act as a portal for seeing more clearly the interconnectedness of all life, all creation. To see with new eyes another world that you never knew existed is quite exciting. Class 2 was offered, and then Class 3. I was there. The classes continued for another seven years, and I was fortunate enough to be seated in the circle within the Circle of Life, "Living Joy Us" indeed!

CHAPTER 15

All that separates us shimmers in transparence, as thin as the last breath taken in our transition between the worlds.

Visitors on Dearborn

THE SHUTTLECRAFT HAD SERVED ITS purpose. I was held in this space between friends and strangers during a time when I was unsure of myself, afraid, and limping badly through my day. Enough healing had taken place through the shamanic classes and from the love of those surrounding me that I was finally able to touch the total loss. It was becoming clearer to me that those things I thought were not all that important were important and symbolic of what was taken from me unexpectedly and unjustly. When we have this kind of awakening, we come out swinging.

I was beginning to understand just how small the house was and how futile to think I could ever adjust to living there. Now a year out from Carolyn's leaving, I was able to look past the blinding loss of my heart's companion and begin to get in touch with my material losses. Until this point, I sat in abject defeat believing I would never have those things again. They were simply lost, and for that matter, I didn't care. Oh, but I did care. I cared very much, and now the next shift began to percolate. Up from the recesses of an unseen corner of my psyche, the voice was clear and the message distinct. This sucks! Thanks be to God for anger. It has an incredible way of moving energy that becomes stuck and recycles in a way that pulls you down the vortex of the great "oh, poor me" abyss.

I would rebuild my life and have the things I loved. I would do it one step at a time. The first step would be to sell the shuttlecraft and find a place to meet my needs and the needs of my partner. Oh, right, I didn't have a partner, a minor detail. I was planning on changing that too. I had no intention of living alone and no intention of living in a hobbit house. The confinement of my abode on Browning was cozy until it wasn't. Then it started to feel more like a straight jacket, a very austere straight jacket to boot. The decision was made and up went the sign for the second time in a year, "For Sale."

As with any next step, there isn't always a clear game plan. I just knew I needed more space, a larger house and a place to create a garden. After a year, I was starting to get a better understanding of where I might want to live. My first choice was The Cove. The Cove is a section of town that terraces the mountains bordering the east side. The houses in the area were designed in the sixties and seventies, not at all my favorite era of architecture. However, I was developing an appreciation for their form as I found what I thought was the perfect space. It was, by my standard, butt ugly on the outside and needed a major face-lift. However, the inside of the house revealed an open floor plan with surprising artistic design. The fireplace was built into a wall of curved stone, which separated formal living room from den in a soft arch of feminine strength. I could stand in the kitchen on the east side of the house and see through the dining and living room, which spilled out onto a deck on the west side. All of Salt Lake's valley could be viewed from the wall of windows, leaving me with the feeling of the proverbially "bird out of a cage." I could breathe in this space. The crowning glory of the property was the empty canvas waiting for the right gardener to arrive and weave a new masterpiece of living tapestry across the three levels of the property. I would see a waterfall of colorful foliage cascading down the gentle slopes of three plateaus, which fell across the yard from east to west. The Feng Shui of the place was incredible with mountains to the east and the open valley floor to the west. I was in love.

Well, it was not to be. My dream house was on the market for six months but on the day my house finally sold and I could make an offer, someone else beat me to it, not twenty-four hours before my closing. All my eggs were in one basket, and now I had thirty days to find another place and be out. To make it even more interesting, my realtors were playing softball in the Gay Olympics. They weren't just out of town, they were in another country and would not be back for two weeks. In doing the math, if I waited for them to come home, that would leave me with only two weeks to find a new house and close on it. I didn't know the city all that well and was thinking, as my brother would say, I am "screwby dobbie dooed."

There were plenty of beautiful homes for sale. Homes I could love, all of them at least $200,000 more than my budget allowed. I really missed the other half of my income that was provided by Carolyn; she left me with a wicked salary cut. This in addition to the housing prices in Kentucky verses the housing prices in Salt Lake left me standing back on the precipice of the "Oh, poor me pit." Thankfully, I was getting very good at side stepping that trap. I hit the streets and started looking.

I was dating Nicole at the time. I called her Coley. She was beautiful and sexy and about ten years younger than me. Who's the lucky girl? I will quote Grandpa Whitaker here, "Oh my." In the wisdom of Forrest Gump, "that's about all I need to say about that." Any more detail might be in poor taste.

We drove around a little aimlessly for a bit and then I asked Coley where she would want to live if she were the one looking for a house. She took me directly to Highland Park. I was still a bit disillusioned by my dream house evaporating out from under my nose, so it was a little hard to get excited about the gift of this neighborhood or the house we found. Nothing was matching up to the Cove. It would take a few years before I realized how fortunate I was that the other place fell through.

We drove up and down the tree-lined streets. Yes, tree-lined, an unusual feature in the high desert. I so missed the trees in Kentucky, and this was almost like being back home. Massive trees towered above both sides of the street. The homes were charming and a bit larger than the dwellings on Browning. The streetlights were designed to look like the old gas lamps that glowed above the avenues of the 1800s, yet another appealing touch. The lanes in Highland Park begin with "A," and each ascending street name started with the next letter for the alphabet. One street past Chadwick was Dearborn, onto which we turned and saw sitting there on the corner a modified Tudor, "For Sale by Owner." At the entrance of the driveway, a great Sycamore stood reaching its way into the heavens. A sign of nature's profound strength and creation, the tree stood at least five stories high. Next to the tree, in stark contrast, was one of the man-made streetlamps which, although insignificant in the shadow of the Sycamore, retained its own charm. Both introduced, in part, the entrance to the small property, which was in its own right sensually charismatic. The grandeur of creation reflected in the tree, and the light provided by the lamppost seems prophetic imagery in my mind now. There was to be, for me, a recreation of the house I found here and a recreation of myself.

The owner just happened to be outside the house doing yard work. I walked up to him and introduced myself, explaining my realtor was out of town. He agreed to open the house so we could walk through. I don't know why I love Tudors or what creates the magnetism between us, but it is just there. I probably had a high ole time in England in another life. Maybe that is the key. Who knows? When I bought the house, I had no reference for past lives, but that would change over the next few years during my in-house training.

As delightful as the exterior was on this old place, the interior held the opposite pole. I don't know what it is about Salt Lake and interior design, but someone obviously left that chip out of the gene pool. I cannot tell you how many houses and homes I toured and how dreadfully boring they were. This one was no different. The entire house was painted dirty beige. I mean not one drop of color anywhere. The kitchen and bathrooms were terribly dated. When one of my friends saw the bathroom, she said, in a state of shock, "Bo, what are you going to do with it?"

I said, "I am going to rip it out and start over, but until then, I am going to leave the lights off and feel my way to the potty."

In addition, what carpet there was in the house was industrial-grade, tightly woven office gray. How lovely. However, the price was right. I could afford the place. It was located in a great neighborhood, and what it lacked in interior design, it made up for in architecture, character, and space. The house had good bones; I was sure I could fix the rest. What I didn't know was that it came complete with a live-in community. Not a live community, mind you, but live-in. To put it more plainly, these visitors were not helping with the house payment.

There was much to do; I jumped in with both feet. As luck would have it, I moved right before Christmas and so had a break from work, which helped with time for unpacking and settling into the place. My little charmer was built in the 1930s, and no one had bothered to do much after that era. What they did do, God bless their hearts, wasn't an improvement.

I started with updating the electrical service. This was prompted by two things. First, every time the refrigerator or any other major appliance kicked on, the house groaned and all the lights dimmed. The second reason was more compelling. Standing in the basement bathtub, I reached up to adjust the shower head. My hand quickly recoiled. Damn, I thought, that is hot. My second thought was, "How can that be? I'm standing here right under the water and the water's not all that hot." So I touched it again, which resulted in the same hair-curling experience. I jerked my hand back. At this point, I was determined and a little pissed off at myself.

"Good grief, you big sissy," came my next thought, "take a holt of that thing, and get it where you want it." My Kentucky slang comes flying right out when I least expect it.

So I did, now I could feel the electricity running up my arm and exploding out my armpit. I jumped naked through the shower curtain while screaming, "SON OF A BITCH!" This was followed by thanking God I was still alive and calling the electrician. Someone had grounded the house on the wrong pipe; well, obviously, wrong pipe. In a positive light, I didn't have to shave that armpit for years thereafter.

Cosmetic changes started on the first floor. Of course, "presentation is everything"—gay boy influence, I suppose. New carpets, new paint, porcelain tiles, and refinishing of the hardwood were a must and just had to be done. In addition, I put up a beautiful crown molding, which was professionally painted with a glassy coat of oil-based paint. As time passed, I ended up remodeling the whole house, replacing not only the electrical but also the plumbing and the roof. Both bathrooms were gutted as promised and, finally, the kitchen was totally remodeled. I could feel the energy of the house rising.

When I hung my first alabaster light fixture, I began to realize I would have what I lost in my divorce. Come hell or high water, I would have it again. Unlike Scarlett O'Hara who swore to God "I will never be hungry again," I was swearing, "As God as my witness, I will never live in tacky gray beige and industrial carpet again!" The shuttlecrafts be damned! That was not my only promise to myself. I swore I would never again rely on another and be put in a position where I had to pack my suitcase and head down the road after creating my dream. If I packed my bag, it would be my decision. This time during my healing process was like an imbalanced cerebellar madness. Weaving back and forth between pitiful and "I am woman, hear me roar." Step at a time, step at a time, cha-cha-cha.

There was a reason for the house, this house. There were countless lessons that would come at me from all angles and dimensions. The hardest thing for me at that point was idle time. I hated to see the weekends come. I wanted to stay busy making this an excellent choice as it took me years to complete the restoration of the place. A good friend gave me a wonderful piece of advice that I didn't truly comprehend until I moved into this little house and began working on turning it into my home. When Carolyn left and I had fallen apart with grief, my friend Toby said, "Just go home and do your dishes, Bo." I looked back at him curiously while he explained. "There is nothing you can do with this pain. Just stay busy, and time will pass. One day you will wake up and the pain won't be so bad."

As the house was healed, I healed. Room by room, each project, each paint chip, each completed vision evolved right along with my interior healing. I was bringing color back into my life. The tones that now surrounded me were beautiful and warm. Not unlike the earth that surrounded me here. I filled the place with crystals, which provide a setting of higher vibration—along with symbols of resurrection, compassion, and peace. Some symbols were sacred geometry pieces created by a friend through beautiful beadwork. Others were statues of ancient enlightened beings. Quan Yin, the goddess of mercy, and her dragons were placed in the little alcove that greeted me each day when I walked through the backdoor. I was reminded of her passion and the alchemy of love she represented. Each project was put into motion with deliberate intent. Each altar in my home carried an energy of healing.

As I painted, I would chant mantras of love and intention. When I painted the front door, I repeated the mantra, "May the light of Christ bless all who walk through this door." When I painted my kitchen, which was the last room to be completed, my chant became "Heart of the home, heart of the home" with each gentle sweep of the paintbrush. On numerous occasions, people would walk through the front door and immediately comment on the peace they felt. One friend reported during a visit, "I feel held here." My best confirmation of healing intent came when Heidi walked into the kitchen and said, without provocation or knowledge of my mantra, "Wow, Bo, this room feels like a heart beating." Everyone loved it. Well, everyone except the spooks, and they were not all so happy about the changes or my presence.

Before Dearborn, I knew nothing about spirit out of body. I knew our spirits exist out of body. I just didn't know they could exist here with us on this dimension. I listened with schoolgirl simplicity to ghost stories around the campfire. I knew people who had encounters and talked about them, but I never had any up-close-and-personal exchange with any haunt. That was about to change, rather quickly, I might add. As soon as I moved into the house, they made their presence known. There was more than one; there were four and one ole boy who wasn't very nice at all.

Nicole had previous encounters with ghosts. She was a clairvoyant and knew when they were around and had, on occasion, seen their form. Before living with me, she had an experience of getting up in the middle of the night and watching one of the original Salt Lake City suffragettes floating across the kitchen to the table. She was arranging flowers there—the ghost, not Nicole. The reason Nicole believed she was a suffragette is because she found out the house was owned by a woman who was a leader in the movement, organizing a march for women's rights during her day. There was a newspaper article about her at the library. Nicole told me about the experience months before we moved into Dearborn together. My point is, she had experiences with the others, and she would be the first to point out that we had visitors.

As soon as I moved into Dearborn, weird things happened. Lights would turn on when I was in another room or on another floor. Appliances would turn on when I wasn't around. I would be on the first floor and hear the washer turn on downstairs, or be downstairs and hear the dishwasher turn on upstairs. Items would be hidden, like the stopper to the bathtub. I kept it on the side of the tub. I would finish my night of painting or plastering, walk to the bathroom to take a bath, and no stopper. I would look all over the bathroom and even walk upstairs and search counter spaces to see if I absentmindedly set it down somewhere else. When I gave up, I came back down to find it exactly where I placed it the night before, on the side of the tub. The other thing she loved to do was make the microwave bell ding by turning the oven's small light off and on. Nicole and I called her Mary. I didn't say anything to anyone about her at first because what do you say?

Friends were coming over to see the progress and the house. My friend Jamie visited and asked off-the-cuff, "How you liking your new house, BoBo?"

"Great," I said. "I really like it."

"Good," Jamie replied in a nervous sort of way, quickly following her first question with, "ready to go then?"

We had an invitation to a mutual friend's house. Dinner was served with pre-dinner cocktails, wine with dinner, and after-dinner drinks. We were both a little more than tipsy on the way home. There was a short lull in the conversation during our drive when Jamie blurted out, "BoBo, you got spooks in that house!"

"Really?" I said.

"Yep," Jamie stated empathically. "I saw her downstairs. She was standing in your bedroom, looking into the closet at the dresses."

"Hell, Jamie, I don't have any dresses in my closet." I laughed.

"Well, she had dresses in that closet when she lived there."

"Oh," I said, now listening more intently. I decided now was as good a time as any and told Jamie about the missing articles and the appliances turning on and off at will, somebody's will, not mine.

"Well, I saw her," she said.

"Well, we call her Mary," I said.

She just looked at me. I hoped this wouldn't mean the word would get out, and then I would have no visitors at all at my house. What I mean to say is, invited visitors, or rather, at least, those still clothed in skin.

Now what do you do with that information? And in my bedroom, no less. If clairvoyants see because they are clear, I must be about as dense as a fence post because I saw nothing unless they manipulated physical objects in the house. I was so glad these manipulations didn't happen in front of me because I would have probably wet my pants. I suppose being obtuse in this case was a blessing in many ways. Things would happen and I could talk myself into believing they really didn't happen, or if they did, I would come up with some kind of ridiculous explanation for it. I didn't care if it didn't make sense; it made me feel a bit safer.

My friend Jo would not allow her kids to go into my basement. She was closemouthed about it but later said the hair on the back of her neck stood straight up when she walked to the bottom of my basement stairs. I could not understand why she kept trying to get me to move my bedroom back upstairs, but she was adamant about it. Every time I saw her, she would run through the litany of reasons why she thought I should sleep upstairs. The list never included the mean-ass spook hanging out downstairs, which was her real concern. She came clean with her concerns much later, but not until she found out I knew the place was haunted. No one was talking about the elephant in the living room because they knew I had to live there alone. Kind of them, don't you think?

Sadly, Nicole did not stay long. I was still a wreck. No matter how badly I wanted to love again, I was not ready for a relationship on any level, not even close. Wanting a relationship does not mean, in any way, that you are ready for intimacy on this level. I wanted life to be normal again. Normal house, normal relationship, normal friends, but it wasn't happening for me. Nothing was going to be normal from here on out, and I should have picked up on that little tip from the get-go. Moving to Salt Lake brought many things, but normalcy (as defined by me) was not one of them.

Nicole was living upstairs now, and I was downstairs. Our relationship had crumbled into the inevitable mismatch of unmet need and undiscovered wounding only intimate relationships can reveal. I felt terrible about jumping into this level of intimacy that I now wanted out of, but that's the short of it. She moved in with all her things and her two dogs, and I realized it would never work. It's just not a very nice thing to do to someone, but my ability to see into the future was limited. I honestly thought we could be a great couple. No one else thought this, but I did. I was wrong; they were right. Anyway, I told her she was welcome to stay as long as she needed until she could find another place. Not much of a consolation, but Coley was young, resilient, and beautiful. It took her about one week before she was dating someone else. Another swift kick to my ego, I wasn't exactly the love of her life either.

When we first moved in together and it became more than clear that the house was haunted, Nicole was very at home with these spirits. I, on the other hand, even with all that had happened, still wanted to blame the occurrences on faulty wiring or poor memory. Odd that I would take this position while knowing there was no explanation for objects disappearing and reappearing in and out of the ethers. Strongly influenced by our Western culture, I suppose. If we can't explain it scientifically, it must not be so. This reasoning is such a profound roadblock to our learning here in the West. We are so limited by our insistence on learning through the mind alone as it will never be enough; it is far too finite.

The garage, which stood a few feet from the house, burned at some point in the house's history and had to be rebuilt, at least partially. One day prior to our breakup, as we stood beneath the charred rafters, Nicole's face changed, taking on a trance-like appearance with blank stare. She looked up and in a flat sort of monotone voice said, "She started this fire. She likes to play with fire." Then her inflection and tone changed as she went on to talk normally about the next event we were planning. Now the hair was standing a few millimeters higher on my arms and the back of my neck. It gave me the willies, but I didn't say anything and welcomed her change in topic. A few days later, Nicole told me, "Bo, you should be careful with candles and matches. I really think Mary started that fire." I looked at her curiously and thought, well what's she going to do, strike a match? My cocky response was soon deflated when I learned she didn't need a match.

Nicole had two dogs: Lilly, a Dalmatian who wasn't the sharpest knife in the drawer; and Abby, a beautiful black Lab who had all the brains in the family. She took the dogs to the park for a walk. I was reading in the living room by the fire. This was my first year in the house, and this was one of my first fires in the fireplace. After reading for a while, I heard Nicole come through the backdoor shouting hello as she made her way downstairs with dogs in tow. A candle was lit on the kitchen table to take care of the odor of salmon we had for supper that evening. The candle was about three inches in diameter and probably six inches high. The flame was well below the rim, four inches at least. No flame lapping above the candle's surface, so I wasn't concerned about the box of Kleenex sitting on the table two feet away.

Nicole had been home for a while when I started to smell smoke. Looking over at the fire in front of me, I got up and looked curiously at the flame and smoke, wondering why it wasn't drawing well all of a sudden. I couldn't see smoke, but I kept getting a whiff of it. I sat back down and became engrossed in the book when I was snapped back to the present by Nicole screaming, "Fire, Bo, the kitchen's on fire!"

I jumped up and ran around the corner, and there on the table was the candle, still lit and still burning well below the top of the rim on one corner of the table. On the other side of the table, the Kleenex box was going up in flames. I picked up the box and threw it in the sink, turning on the water. I looked over at Nicole who was screaming at me, "I told you to be careful with fire! You should never leave a candle burning and then walk into another room and leave it. I told you, Mary likes to play with fire!"

Nicole was in her bedroom when Abby became very agitated and kept walking over to Nicole and then walking to the base of the stairwell. They just got home from the park. Nicole could not imagine what her problem was but, out of curiosity, followed her up the stairs to the kitchen. This is when she discovered the fire. So I suppose Abby saved the day. In the back of my mind, I wondered if Nicole set the box of tissues on fire and walked down the stairs to make a point. She was a bit of a drama queen, but I couldn't imagine anyone being that crazy or taking that kind of chance. Besides, she was home quite a while before the fire started. Regardless, I was still looking for ways to dismiss the possibility of my visitors.

Weeks passed, and Nicole was in and out. The house was lonely but not empty, that's for sure. It was late afternoon when Jamie stopped by to help me with a project. I was putting together a shelf for the downstairs laundry room and needed a second hand. Since it was cocktail hour, I offered Jamie a drink and poured bourbon for the both of us. We worked on the project, and when it was completed, Jamie needed to be on her way. I walked upstairs to show her to the door. Several minutes later, I remembered my drink (which was hardly touched) still sitting on the washing machine downstairs. I went back down to the laundry room and took a sip. What the hell? I promptly spit it out, spewing what tasted like poison across the basement floor. I drink Maker's Mark; this was not Maker's. This was Maker's with a twist, and not a good twist. It tasted like chemicals. I looked at where the glass was sitting, and next to my bourbon was a bottle of 409 household cleaner. OK, now that was the last straw. Setting my kitchen on fire was one thing, but don't be messing with a Kentucky woman's bourbon, and especially not Maker's Mark, sorry bastards! I was losing my sense of humor.

The shaman classes at the University of Utah were now over. We completed the three classes offered, but there was a small core group of us who wanted to continue with Joy, and so I offered my house and living room floor for a meeting space. I didn't tell them they were coming to the Haunted Hilton. In fact, I never mentioned it at all. In addition, my house was still under construction. The upstairs bath was being ripped out, but I still had the bathroom downstairs, although you had to take the tank lid off and trip the float to get it to flush. Minor detail, I thought. Nothing we couldn't live through. No one seemed to mind the construction zone; they just stepped over things and took their place on the floor of the living room on our first night of class. They knew I was in process.

We were laughing and chatting away, taking our places circled around Joy on the living room rug. As we began to open our mesas, as was our custom at the beginning of class, the group quieted. There were seven of us. The house was silent and peaceful, for a minute. Then the microwave bell rang. Good grief, I'm thinking, the jig is up. Now I'll have to come clean.

They all looked at me in question. I said, "No worry, that's just Mary," hoping no one would ask "Mary who?" No such luck.

"Mary," they said, looking back at me questioningly.

"Yes," I said, "I think we may have spooks in here." My reply was off-the-cuff, like I had just mentioned the weather, still hoping someone would change the subject. Of course, that was not going to happen. Not in this lifetime. Instead, they all looked at me, staring silently while waiting for the details. Obviously, I was going to have to tell the whole story. I began recalling the events, one by one, of all that had happened since my arrival.

"What are you going to do?" someone asked.

"Well, I don't know. They were here first," I said.

Catherine Ann looked over at me as if I had lost my mind. "Bo, if they are trying to poison you and burn your house down, don't you think you need to do something about it?"

"Well, you may be right about that," I said. "But what can I do?"

I don't think Joy's lesson plan for the evening included house exorcism, but she was incredibly flexible, and I was about to get my first lesson in intermediate (or perhaps advanced) spook removal. Catherine Ann and her sister Romedy had previous experience. Jackie sat across from me on the living room rug and cast a nonchalant look as if to say, no problem just a normal day in the life of a shaman. Heidi was lit up and wide-eyed with excitement; she was as much a novice as I was, but probably more open to believing. Shelly, as was her custom, showed no emotion at all but quietly listened to the group voicing their collective wisdom. Shelly always appeared regal, silent, and mysterious. I was to find out later, she was probably one of the most powerful among us. I was still clinging to the hope this was an electrical short-circuiting problem, and that maybe Nicole set the fire and poisoned my bourbon. However, Nicole was not at home now, and there was no one to blame for what was about to unfold.

The conversation continued as the group began to offer their opinions, which included beliefs that these spirits were lost, stuck in our third dimension. Their final consensus was they needed to be sent "to the light" so they could get on with their evolution. Joy looked over and said with quiet stern concern, "What would you like to do? This is your house. It must be your decision."

"Well," I said, "I guess I should ask them to leave."

The words had barely slipped past my lips when Romedy and Heidi's heads snapped up in high alert.

"Is there someone here in the house with us?" Joy asked.

"No," I said, "no one."

"Well, someone is walking down the hall," she said as she stood up to look.

There was no one there, but they all heard it, the three sitting next to the hallway. Now they had my undivided attention. Joy sat back down as we tried again to center and silence ourselves to get ready for the work.

As soon as Joy sat down, she looked up now sternly and said to me, "Do you feel that?"

"Feel what?"

"The cold," she said. "Do you feel the cold?"

I looked over at her, and then suddenly, I felt it. There was a chill that settled all around me, first like being touched by the edge of a micro weather front and then suddenly enveloped by the unnatural drop in temperature. The cold swirled around me, causing me to shiver. I was sitting by the fire and said, "I bet the workers left the bathroom window open today. You know the drywall dust gets pretty thick when they are working. There must be a draft."

Joy stood up, walked to the bathroom door, and opened it. "Come here, Bo."

I was really surprised she didn't say "come on over here, Tom" (as in doubting Thomas), but she was kind and patient as was her way. I walked over to her; the window was tightly sealed. I looked at both exterior doors, also closed. Damn! There went my theory.

Obviously, my visitors were disturbed at the prospect of being asked to leave. Perhaps they were unsettled by the power of the shamanic circle formed in the living room. I don't know what caused it, but they were upset and more active than they had ever been. It was like the whole group was acting out at once. Yes, there was a group. It wasn't just Mary, it was Mary and friends, as we would find out shortly.

Joy told us we would be asking for a name. It wasn't about just pulling the name *Mary* out of a hat; the spirit had a name during its last incarnation. If you ask their name, they have to answer; and when you ask them to leave, you have to use their name. That's how it works, or so said Joy. My other friends agreed; I'm speaking of those who had done the work before. So in our circle sat three novices and four seasoned ghostbusters. Joy asked us to connect to the spirit present and then report what we felt, saw, or experienced. She used every situation as a tool for our learning. This was no different. Within minutes, we realized, it was not one ghost, I had four. True to the work of the shaman, with one foot in each world, the group unveiled some pretty remarkable findings.

Jackie met up with an elderly couple. They were lost, a bit confused, but told her they were happy to have me living in their home. Obviously quite innocuous, these two had been in the home for years and considered me to be the visitor. They embraced my presence almost like adopting a daughter. The ghost I called Mary was contacted by someone else in the group. She too was gentle and passive, oblivious to me for the most part with the exception of the times she enjoyed playing tricks on the new kid in the house. She was the one who enjoyed hiding things and playing little games like "Stopper, Stopper, Whose Got the Stopper?" It was all going smoothly under Joy's tutelage, then things changed rather quickly and without warning. The badass spook showed up from downstairs, and he was not pretty.

Suddenly there was an obvious change in Catherine Ann's face. It was so unexpected and so dramatic, it actually scared me. Catherine Ann was always playful and cheerful. She went about the work in a lighthearted manner for the most part, but there was nothing light about the look on her face at this moment. Almost as quickly as Catherine Ann's demeanor changed, her sister Romedy mirrored the emotion. What I felt coming from Catherine Ann and Romedy was not playful at all—quite the contrary. Joy was obviously acutely aware, and what seemed like all fun and games now seemed deadly serious. I immediately felt bad about asking them into this mess and started to worry something could go wrong. I sat there remembering Reagan in *The Exorcist*, waiting for the green pea soup to spew across the room. Then, suddenly, Joy broke the silence. "What do you see, Catherine Ann?"

"He's a bad act," she said. "He has no intention of leaving. He hangs out at the bottom of the steps in the basement for the most part. When I followed him into the bathroom downstairs, he looked into the mirror and the mirror shattered. He is very angry, and he does not want Bo to live here. He is the one who started the fire."

Romedy spoke up, agreeing this was not just any ordinary lost soul. I could sense the evil they could feel.

"Ask him his name," Joy said. "Ask him now." Her tone had taken on a strange, unsettling urgency that was rare. In fact, I don't think I ever heard it before or since that night, not in all our gatherings or classes. The two sisters appeared to brace themselves, and the resolve I saw on their faces was palpable.

"His name is James," Romedy said.

Joy spoke rapidly now, barking out commands, "Keep him engaged." Then to the rest of us she said, "Do not engage him. Bo, I said do not engage him." I was busted. "See the light between us?" Joy said quickly. "Focus on this light. Send the light around our circle and then see it rise up through the ceiling through a portal that is now opening there."

Within seconds we were focused on the light, the circle, and the beam of light formed from our circle now opening a gateway above our heads. Quickly she orchestrated the group into precision-guided intention. "Romedy, command him to leave now. Call him by name and command him to go to the light."

So she did, and so he did. Suddenly I was aware that the energy of the room and the house was lighter. He was gone. It was curious of me to know that I didn't notice the heaviness that surrounded me until I experienced his absence and the light left in his place.

Asking the others to leave was not nearly as dramatic. The couple Jackie connected to asked to leave in a Merkabah. I had no idea what Jackie was talking about. "A Merkabah?" I said.

Jackie smiled and explained, "The Merkabah is like a light vehicle. It is formed by a star tetrahedron, as outlined in Sacred Geometry. When the lines forming the Merkabah spin, it's like an oval globe of divine light used for transportation between the dimensions."

I don't know if I appeared "slack-jawed" at that moment, but I'm certain my mouth dropped open as I listened to yet another something I had never heard before or experienced in this lifetime. She went on to explain our loving couple thought that would be fun and requested to be transported in what I guess was a bit like a light taxi to the other world. Stepping in calmly, they smiled back in kindness as they ascended through the portal of light we held open for their journey.

Mary left next. She was the least complex and gently slipped away. I thought I would probably miss her and her shenanigans around the house. Bells ringing, lights and appliances turning on and off, and hide-and-seek games would now end. We looked around at each other. Joy giggled for a moment and then with stage voice repeated the line from *Poltergeist*, "This house is clean."

CHAPTER 16

There is a rhythm, a space reserved for dancing, a truth unheard but pulsating just below the surface of the yet unimagined. This is where we meet life. The marriage of our spirit with the unknown gives birth to love.

"JUST A LIVIN'"

MY DECISION WAS MADE TO leave Buckhorn; I had only a few weeks left when I was asked to make a house call. The patient was 101 years old, living on the side of a mountain with his youngest daughter. Their place tucked away well up into one of the many hollers that branched out from the center of Buckhorn. Mary Ann came with me as my scout, to ensure I could find the place. That was a good thing because the only part of the house you could see from the road was the tip of the roof. Our trek took us from the heart of the community down winding road to narrow lane. Suspended above us, the small cabin was tucked into the mountain, cloaked by forest and sky. Wooden stairs and a rickety hand rail, your only clue that something sat above the lane. A good flight and a half of stairs lay between you and the entrance to their small world. My patient only needed a few sutures removed, but as you might imagine, it was not an easy feat, bringing this ancient, now-fragile old gentleman down the stairs and into the clinic. So we traveled there.

I parked the car alongside the road and made my ascent to his home. I climbed, looking up to the house still hidden above me. Slowly with each step the scene unfolded, first the old house and then the old gentleman came into view. His image unveiled as I climbed higher, first the top of his hat, then his forehead. There were no lines of worry or signs of past care across his brow. A step more revealed eyes that no longer saw out across the holler and into the woods he knew as home. A few more steps and I could see the total picture. A long, gray beard covered his jaw. He was sitting in his rocking chair, no expression on his face as he gently rocked in a cadence uniquely his own. There he was, held between heaven and earth in the brittle frame that provided his soul's sanctuary. Only a shadow remained of the physical man who took his place on the earth as a mountaineer.

"Hello, Mr. Jim," I called out. "How are you today?"

The tempo of his rocking chair never changed, his vacant stare across the mountain remained undisturbed as he replied, "Just a livin'."

Over the years, I have returned to this scene, to his words. As many of us are "just a livin'," finding our repose in a gentle rocking rhythm all our own, blankly staring out across our limited worlds, unaware of all that surrounds us. It is time to wake up; it is past time. It is time to open our eyes, to question our world, to see beyond our understanding and into the next dimension of being. We become complacent. We accept as fact that which is limited beyond words. We avoid anything that challenges us, turning away from what is not in alignment with our zones of safety.

What if, for a change, we broke free from the limitations that bind us to custom and traditions? Chaos and bedlam would be better than blind mediocrity. What if, for one day or one week, we stood up from our rocking chairs, opened our eyes, and looked beyond our self-imposed creations? What would that be like?

We are not limited. There are those who would have us believe we are limited, but this is quite simply a lie. It is time for us to shake the dust off our feet and step into this present moment with new awareness. Fear is the enemy, our only enemy. "Perfect love casts out all fear." When we are in tune with our divinity, this love will spring up like the living waters described in ancient texts. I am in you and you are in me, and we are *one* with the father—paraphrased, but direct and to the point. This is the sacred trinity; why do we refuse to see it? We are deceived, believing we are helpless creatures cast out from paradise when, in fact, we are living now in paradise. We have only to awaken and take back our power; a power that was ours all along; a power that will serve not only us but each other and our world.

We are timeless, limitless creators of our reality. We are not alone, we will never be alone, and no one or nothing can separate us from each other or from our Source. We can continue to play out dramas of duality, or we can awaken and realize there is no duality. We don't need it anymore. We are invited to step out of the dramas created by our egos. "Out, out, damned spot!" Must we continue sleepwalking? Are we not just as insane as poor Lady Macbeth as she wanders the corridors asleep and driven to madness over her past? Our past is madness, and we must open the door and step beyond our limitations, beyond our past, and into our divinity. The invitation has always been there, but we have been distracted, so very distracted. We are blinded by an illusion not of our making and totally of our making.

"How long must I endure this perverse generation?" he asked. Well, Jesus, sorry, but for a very long time because, like Mary at the homeless shelter, we are still "just a 'schizophrenin' all over the place." We are fractured and fragmented beyond anything Humpty Dumpty ever endured. I guess we are waiting for "all the king's soldiers and all the king's men" to arrive and make things right again. Well, they're not coming. In fact, if they do show up, you can bet they make a mess of things. And besides, we do not need them. The power lies within us. And when we awaken from our sleepwalking, from our madness, we will finally understand, and our world will turn.

Slow to respond, we are in the special education crash course here on the planet we call home. There is no excuse for limitations now, for we are no longer limited. We continue to rock in our well-worn rut, but one millimeter to the left or right will set us on the new path. It is a simple adjustment in perspective. Yet we hold on for dear life to those traditions and old paradigms that no longer serve us. We were created to be magnificent. Is it easier to live in the shadow than to express the light that is ours to bring? Well no, it isn't, but some would have us believe in the shadow of existence. Do we have a shadow side? "You betcha!" As they say here in Utah, we do. Do we have to live from it? Well no. No, we do not. Like in the movie *Poltergeist*, we find ourselves fighting the unseen. Whether we know it or not, we are in the mix. Go to the light, Carol Anne. Leave the nice boogeyman alone.

Not so unlike Carol Anne, we are stuck in a dimension no longer meant for us, and we block the way for others who are trying to find the light. Spirit is imploring, "Run, don't walk, toward the light." This portal to the new dimension is open. They won't carry us, they won't push us through. The invitation is ours to knock, then the door will be opened. Knock and trust that what is waiting on the other side of our understanding is not so far beyond us but has been there waiting for us all along. It is our next step, our next evolution as creators.

Jesus, the great shaman that he was, lived with one foot through the portal and one foot in our limited third-dimensional world. He didn't have to walk between the worlds, and yet he did. This was his to do. He did everything possible to show us the way. "I am the way," he said. I am showing you by example; this is how it is done. You will do far more than me. That would be when you awaken, when you open your eyes, when you have the faith of a mustard seed. Oh, just a teensy weensy bit of faith, you knuckleheads!

"Say to the mountains, move from here!" St. Thomas's gospel, hidden from us for centuries, discloses the secret. Thomas records Jesus's words, "When the two become one, you will become children of Adam, and when you say, 'Mountain, move from here!' It will move." When we step out of duality, we will be a part of the family, a family we belonged to all along. This family spreads across our globe and beyond. We are not isolated here behind our walls, our borders, our cultures, or our religions. They are all facades, playgrounds of illusion. When we understand there is no longer a need for duality, "when we make the two into one," we will move mountains. The first step must be in understanding we are one, no duality. It served us well in the evolution of our soul, but it is time to lay aside childish things. We must let this old and useless paradigm go now. It is time. It no longer serves. Do you think I am dreaming? Maybe so, but I believe I am waking up from the dream. I understand and believe, "the kingdom is within."

Imagine bringing a lens into focus. First you see double blurred lines, and finally the two become one, and the image slowly transforms from blurred haze to sharp clear lines as the image takes shape before us. It was there all along, but we could not see it. The days of diploplia are nearing their end. It is our choice. We can refuse to see and remain myopic, or we can choose to see clearly the new vision with new eyes. We have held fast to our beliefs for fear of turning left or right and missing the prescribed steps into the Kingdom. I tell you it is not a step. It is a dance, and the dance is life fully lived. Only you can hear the rhythm of your ballet and no one else. We hold our beliefs so tightly and so close to us, it is no wonder we see double. Our eyes are crossed as we stare at our self-created chaos. We hold our proscribed views so closely to our face, we are in danger of blinding ourselves and missing life altogether.

I sat on the edge of the road, on my rock, and viewed my world at the age of five. My brothers used the same rock, their view similar although changed a bit by time. Within our narrow perspective, we had much the same view. Then our paths went separate ways, and the view from our rocks changed. We were exposed to different people, different regions, different cultures, and different worlds were unveiled in the same country. So we were changed by the days, years, and places that separated us one from another. They are still my brothers, are they not? At the level of the divine, we are one and will always be one. Sadly, our change comes from our focus on the third-dimension, which is the slow physical expression of life. It is concrete. We are exposed to different people and different events as we share in another's life and vision. We begin to morph and shift. We appear different from the clan although there are threads that still hold us fast to our heritage. We are weighed down, as the concrete duality we live from becomes a block around our feet dragging us into the deep, into the darkness. From this place we begin to believe we are different, our way is right. Others have wandered from the truth but, of course, we know the truth, and so the fight begins.

The fight that never ends: my clan over your clan, my religion over your religion, my way over your way, my country over your country. The story continually repeats itself in a circle of death, not life. Year after year throughout our history, we continue to follow the path of our ancestors. I say this is madness. How many Inquisitions do we have to live through before we awaken? I think one was too many, and yet they continue in large and small scale. We are incensed by the jihad, and yet how different is their holy war than the bloody massacre and torture of the innocents during the dark ages imposed by the Christians? Seems like the same song to me, just different day. I suggest the East reflects the West, and when we quit pointing our fingers out there and make our own journey within, we will have stepped onto the path that leads to peace. When we forgive ourselves, embrace our shortcomings, reveal to the light our own darkness and limitations, then there will be a great shift that will not stop at our borders but will ripple out to all the world. As this energy touches others, there will be a healing that will cover this earth in a peace it has never known.

Sadly, we are still living in the Dark Ages, but there are many who have awakened and are holding an energy, a light for those of us still stumbling in the dark. A self-imposed darkness of indifference, blind bigotry, and the endless need to be right. They call us to step into a place of nonjudgment, where the world embraces differences as a rare and priceless gift to be shared. They do not fight; they do rail against the night. They do not preach from the pulpits or roadsides. Their focus is clear as they sound their perfect note, and the tone rises up from their divinity, renewing and bringing peace to all it touches. These loving beings of light live with one foot in both worlds. Their luminosity reflects a new way as they invite us to join them on a different path.

Is our "tor-tell-ah" upside down? Maybe it is upside down. Shall we turn it over? Let's do and see what is on the other side. However, first we will have to close our eyes to this dimension and see beyond it to the new creation. First, we must release the past. We will be asked to face our greatest fear. Then we will be able to step onto the new path, the rainbow path, which holds all the color and light of our world and our universe. Only then will we be given the great vision of the condor, and we will see clearly. Our Native American brothers and sisters and other indigenous peoples across the globe and from all four directions live the medicine wheel and are very close to living this new life. In fact, some do. On the other side of the "tor-tell-ah," we will see with new eyes. The concrete-leaded heaviness of ignorance will crumble away, and there will be a lightness of being we have never known. There will be no fear because we will no longer be controlled by duality.

Does this seem daunting? I suppose it does when you approach it through the limited perspective of the third dimension. So I invite you to step out of the third dimension. Step out of your head and into the heart. This is where the beginning of the yellow brick road can be found. It does not have to make sense to be real. The magic is all around you every day. The children see it and live from this place. You have seen it in the past, you have just forgotten. We have been asleep, and now is the time to wake up from our dreaming and create the dream.

My life has been a journey. My wounding created a space, a fissure, in the hard soil of my knowing, allowing new seeds to be planted beneath the dry crusts of old paradigms that no longer served. These seeds grew, and the gentle gardeners that came along the way tended to my plantings on the days when I didn't have the energy or couldn't find my way back to the garden. Until one day, not unlike Jack in "Jack and the Beanstalk," I awakened to a magnificent vine that provided passage into a new world.

CHAPTER 17

"Atone, to unite. Atonement, the reconciliation between God and God's people." When we turned a deaf ear to creation, the music of the sacred fell silent, and we were lost in division one from another, our planet, and our God. The tone given to us is uniquely ours. When given voice, this vibration will bring us into alignment with our God. We will understand our divinity and know we are truly one with our Creator.

Over and beyond anything we can hope for or imagine, there lives in each of us the profound unfolding of the Divine. It is not to be grasped with mind but heart and the pure trusting faith of a child. For, in fact, we are the children of God, our connection lived out in the experience of each creative moment.

THE ALPHA, THE OMEGA

I HOPE YOU WILL QUESTION why I have shared these stories with you. I share them with you because in all their absurdity, humor, and tragedy, they point to an evolution, in some respects, a revolution of spirituality. Why are they worth remembering, contemplating, savoring, these living stories and reflections? Because they are real, because they are passion lived out loud in a world that at times seems mad or maddening at best.

"More than life itself." How many times have we called upon this old phrase to express how much something means to us? How deeply we love, how blindly we call upon the gods of our longing. The fears that control us keep us moving down a path that we have neither consciously chosen nor agreed upon. Yet we keep moving, taking each step as if we meant to go there.

"More than life itself." I will trade this for that. I will let go of everything to have this one "pearl of great price." I have to have this, I can't live without it or her or him. "Mine, mine, mine. Ha-ha-ha-ha, it's all mine." Please. Wake up and understand that anything you believe you must have, anything that you put out there as more precious than life, has in fact already stolen your life.

The true "pearl of great price" is just that, but few find it and few understand it. It costs everything and nothing. When this pearl is found, everything else falls away. It is not about our need, our desire, our want. We do not have to make a conscious effort to give anything up. We are focused, balanced, and in alignment with Source. We open our eyes as if we had been in a deep sleep for a very long time, and we understand we were unconscious. We see our world with new color, new understanding, new life, and new freedom. We do not find it necessary to control or judge. We do not find it necessary to let go because we come softly to this place with openness and freedom. True freedom from our fears, our judgments, and yes, even our passions. Each moment is experienced with a defining understanding, not chiseled into stone but with the grace and beauty of an energetic ballet. Particles and wave forms play through us and around us and, with our permission, bring us into a new dimension.

Did you ever wake up, open your eyes with complete disorientation, wondering "Where am I?" For those brief moments, there is no awareness of time or space. It's as if we have left our bodies and then, suddenly, we are slammed back into this dimension. We don't know what planet we are on for a minute or two. Then it all comes back, the dramas du jour. Our mind returns to the gerbil track, and we're off!

We felt, in the past, there was no choice. It, whatever it was, was happening to us without our consent, without our input. So we either wilted, imploding in on ourselves, or railed against the night in futile fury. For those of us who don't know what to do, we just freeze like a deer in the headlights until the truck coming at us suddenly mows us down and we lay startled on the highway, wondering what hit us. I suppose that is not a very pretty picture, but now I have your attention.

Many of us look beyond ourselves for the answer or solutions to our moments of confusion and pain. We wake up and wonder, "How did I get here? How in the world did I get to this place?" Well, I say, one step at a time. No one has kidnapped you. You came to this place, usually unconsciously, on your own accord. No matter how incredibly uncomfortable you may be or how battered you may be, you had a hand in the creation of your place and time. Under the trappings of the event or place or relationship, you were the master creator, in concert with your co-creators who play out the drama with you.

That may sound cruel and heartless to those of you who are experiencing or thinking about someone who is living through an illness that appears to be beyond their control. I understand. I have lost many I loved as they appear to lose their battles with death and suffering. Perhaps the cruelest was watching Lou Gehrig's disease come in and take my friend from us in a few short months. A woman full of life and joy withered away while I watched helplessly.

As a nurse, I have looked into the eyes of the suffering more than I would like to recall, but it is different when you experience the suffering from the eyes of one you are tied to in great love. "Is it her fault?" you say. No, I did not say it was her fault. I am saying it is her design. She may not be conscious of this on a physical plane, but her spirit understands and is willing. This isn't our first rodeo, friends. Well, not the first for many. Our soul is evolving over lifetimes, and we are one with God. God makes no mistakes. When we are in alignment with our core, we make decisions that can bring us great joy or great pain. We are not short of courage in this realm of being, and we will do whatever it takes to continue to push out the borders and obstacles that prevent us from expressing and creating more light. Sometimes we do this for our own soul's growth, sometimes we do it for the growth of another, and sometimes we do it for the whole world, as was the case with Jesus.

Did Jesus know what he was doing? Did he totally understand the impact his death would make while he suffered one of the cruelest forms of death that could be inflicted on another? Some theologians argue he knew his full divinity at birth, others will tell us he grew into this knowing, and still others will say even at his death he did not know fully but was still willing to die rather than turn his back on his truth or his God. We are the children of God. We are one with God, and this is no small role on the stage of creation. Jesus embodies for us the perfect mirror image of God, a soul that was focused and aligned with Divinity at every moment, fully conscious.

Our senses have been dulled over time, like a well-worn kitchen knife. What would have shocked us into action or reaction even ten years ago is now observed with a deadening silence.

I often think of the line from *Steel Magnolias* when Sally Field's character is pleading with her daughter who is in a coma: "Open your eyes, Shelby. Open your eyes… OPEN YOUR EYES!" There is no response as her daughter continues, the deep sleep enveloping her as she silently makes her passage from this world to the next.

There is a passage happening now, and we are choosing consciously or unconsciously our path. Gaia, our mother earth, is leading the way. This living organism we call home is responding to the energies surrounding and pulsing through her veins. There are those who think Gaia will shake us off like fleas as she has done many times in the past, rather than sacrifice herself for wanton disregard and greed whose end is empty and void of life. Some of us recoil in fear as we watch the changes taking place on our planet: the weather patterns, the earthquakes, the eruption of volcanoes. I invite you to see these changes as birthing pains, the great transition heralding life and the coming of more life. As we evolve into consciousness, she will no longer be forced to separate from us.

You hear the cry of fear echoed on city streets from Jerusalem to New Deli to New York: "The end is coming! The end is coming!" This is no end. This is the beginning of more than we could hope for, dream, or imagine. The end we will see is an end to unconscious living. The new world, the New Jerusalem, the new heaven, and the new earth are being created now, and we are living on the cusp of this new creation.

Many of us have sensed this new dawning. Synergistic events have brought us to the place we now stand. Awakening has been for some like the eruption of a supernova exploding into new worlds. For others, the process has been slow, gentle, and calm as if experiencing the opening of a beautiful rose. Not everyone is knocked off their horse, blinded, and left in the desert, but some may have been better served had they shared in the experience of St. Paul. Better than Shelby's end, silently slipping away into the darkness of her coma.

It's time to wake up. It's time to open our eyes and know that there is more to reality, to truth, to freedom than what we can experience with our five senses. We are the master creators of our lives, co-creators with God. We must awaken now. It is time to see clearly our power, our vision, our hope for the present, and our children's future.

We have given up our power to organized religions. We gladly defer to another to show us the way, the next step, the answer to our mysteries. We accept these moments time after time and without question. The larger the group, the larger our desire to accept their teachings so we can be rewarded with entrance into the club. We think we are safe there. They provide us with a cookbook, outlined with doctrine, defined not in the present, not by the living, ever-changing presence of the Divine within us, but by stagnant words from a different time in space and history that has very little to offer the living of this moment.

It will require great courage to stand on this precipice of knowing and embrace a free fall into a new living vision. In this space, which is no space, relationship with the all in all will be born. We are dancing in divine light. The colors are exquisite, and we are overwhelmed as the prism dividing these paths weaves them back again into one great light devoid of color. There is at once clarity and mystery. For in our living of the mystery in conscious communion with the Divine, we awaken and know that the many colors we have experienced in the end are gathered into one. Over and above, the magic of this dance leaves us standing in awe of the mystery we now live.

Never before have we stood in this place as a race, a people. Our boundaries are eroding as we understand our definition of family, identified with home and country, is far too small. This change ignites a fear welling up within many. In response, they become more rigid in their structure, creating a fragile shelter, which promises to shatter into a thousand shards of broken glass.

We are the life and breath of the Living God. We have many names for our Deity; there is no name for this force of life, the creator of all. We cannot enclose and define what is unnamable. We have tried, and for a time, there was purpose in this naming, this defining. As a people, we were not ready to shoulder the responsibility of understanding our divinity, but the time has come. We have taken the steps. We have leapfrogged over the backs of our ancestors to come to this place. Each generation from the first primate until now has laid the cornerstone for our evolution.

The time is now. We are called now to take this next step. Embracing this life found singularly and collectively, we must lay down our arms and let go of our defenses: "the lion will lie down with the lamb." We are called to this defining moment of searing trust, which burns away the chattel that was truly never ours in the first place. We must find the courage to stretch out our arms to embrace all. We are being gifted with the vision to see clearly into the eye of God by looking directly into the eye of another. The veil lifted, fear must be laid aside. We are invited to release the past as the serpent sheds its skin totally, not one scale at a time.

We are being invited to let go of everything and stand naked in the light of this new dawning. Only then will we see clearly. We will not be asked to do this once but continually, over and over in the present moment. The process is not a way to arrive at a destination; it is a living osmosis. Ever creating, ever evolving, and being born again and again until there is nothing we cannot create, experience, or savor in this current age.

If you throw a pebble in the water, you see small circles ever expanding in waves of energy, forming larger circles that continue changing the waters form far beyond the initial impact of stone meeting water. Every act, whether conscious or unconscious, mirrors this analogy. We are inflicting something on everything with each thought, deed, and prayer. We are the children of God. How could we expect anything less?

I can't tell you when I understood there was something far greater than myself, and I can't tell you the moment when I knew I was far greater than myself. What I can tell you is no matter how outlandish this may sound to you, we are one with God in ways far more profound than any of us have dreamed of or hoped for in this lifetime or in any lifetime.

We are ruled by fear. This has blinded us. We allowed ourselves to be overrun with rumors without basis in truth but only in fable. For a time, they brought comfort to our worlds, albeit small worlds. There was comfort in staying within the lines drawn by external authorities we placed on the pedestal of the "right." And in falling in line with "the right," we afforded ourselves a sense of security and salvation. This act resulted in our losing our way while our Garden of Eden was overrun by thorns of nightmarish proportion. We found ourselves in labyrinths of confusion, wandering aimlessly by night and by day, only to find we were walking in circles, our legs bloody from the barbed spikes of our own creation.

At this point in the history of our souls' evolution, we are standing on a precipice. We are entering into a new renaissance. The media and Hollywood turns a deaf ear to the wisdom of the ancients, creating spectacle and illusion instead, which is, of course, their job. The movie *2012* is the pinnacle of deception, a classic example of deflecting attention away from the door now being opened. The movie drew record-breaking crowds who feed on fear and doomsday predictions. The movie *2012* is smoke and mirrors. It keeps us twisted up in the drama creating familiar fear-based mire, pulling us down into a blinding quicksand, far more frightening than anything the producers came up with in their doomsday film.

It is, at last, time to step beyond the drama and allow ourselves to know our pure and enlightened power, which is our gift. It has been hidden by our limitations until this point in our evolution. The glass ceiling of consciousness is being broken open, and when the last shard falls, we will step into a new world, a new age. In this place, we will know our divinity and the divinity of others. We will see clearly our connection, and we will know that we are one with each other, our power infinite. A new power used to create a new world and bring about a lasting peace, rippling out like the pebble's dance on the waters.

The time is now, the new energy is here. We are arriving in a place of new beginnings. We were lost in the desert. This new energy is bringing us into the Promised Land. Awaken and understand; see the new dimension being born in and around us. We are invited to see with new eyes and hear melodies never heard before. As if looking into a holograph, our vision is multidimensional—no longer flat, no longer black and white. The time of duality is ending. Living without duality requires a new vision and a new heart. Living in the new energy requires breathing in the light. You do not need instructions. The veil is pulled back, and you will see clearly. You have but to set your intent to step into this place. As you learn to stay focused, all that distracts you will fall away. Layer upon layer will fall at your feet, and you will ascend with the masters.

"Be of good cheer." Many will try to distract you, whether knowingly or unknowingly; they will refuse to remove the mantle they hide behind. The chaos is just beginning. There will be more chaos as we move through this transition, but understand, this is the storm that will blow away all that is no longer needed. You are becoming a new life-form. So take heart. Truly, you are being born again into new life imagined by only a few. The old paradigm, the old understanding served us well, but it is time to drop our mantles. If we cling to the old, we will no longer be served but, instead, severed.

The Kingdom is among us, within us, and around us—no longer hidden. Others have experienced this place; they have lived in and from a dimension that until now was hidden from us. They stand as beacons, as flashing lighthouses, showing us the way. Until now, we were not ready. Now we are ready. This is the awakening. Many have already walked into the new dawning and are living on the edge, calling us, urging us to embrace what is ours to have, to know, and to hold. We are not left alone in the storm. Look up, look out, look within as truly there is no difference. This Trinity is the sacredness of you. You are the communion now. This is your calling, your destiny, your beginning that never has end. One with the Creator, know that you are the creator. So "be of good cheer," for when they say in their rituals, "The Lord is with you, and also with you," this is the truth at its deepest level. The Lord is with you. Yes, of course—with, within, and without. We are becoming the living Homo Spiritus.

We are living in a profound time of chaos and change. We are awakening to a new consciousness. We are in the white water of our evolution. We are riding incredible waves of energy into the new world. We can go kicking and screaming, or we can let go and allow the Divine current to take us where it may while using our intent as the rudder of this seemingly mad and crazy ride. We are not at anyone's mercy. We are the masters. We are helping to create this new existence. When we believe this, and believe it fully with our whole heart, we will move mountains. We will know with all certainty, the "tor-tell-ah" has no right side. Not really. It is simply just a tortilla, bread, the bread of life. Take, eat, my friend. Come to the table and be filled.

CPSIA information can be obtained at www.ICGtesting.com
Printed in the USA
BVOW071340120612

292434BV00002B/1/P